D0865257

Confessions of a
Long-Distance Sailor

*An account of a four-year solo
circumnavigation in a 31-foot boat*

Paul Lutus

Copyright © 2008 P. Lutus.

All rights reserved under International and Pan-American Copyright conventions. No part of this work may be reproduced in any form or by any means except with written permission of the publisher.

ISBN 978-1-4357-1027-6

CONTENTS

{ 1 }

Introduction, San Juan Islands

W hat would you have done? I didn't expect to be on the bow of my little boat, changing sails, when the big wave came and tried to wash me into the sea. I was several days' sail west of Fiji in the South Pacific, at a time of year when the sea is supposed to be calm and predictable. Several hours before, my two-way radio had come to life – "Sailing vessel Selene, this is Take Two, how do you copy?"

I recognized my friend Ursula's voice – I talked to her on the radio each day since we met in French Polynesia several months before. Ursula and her mate Bob were sailing around the world on Take Two, a fast German boat. But this wasn't

Selene underway

our normal time to chat, and Ursula sounded worried, so I picked up the microphone. "Take Two, this is Selene, you are loud and clear, what's up?" She responded, "We've just picked up a weather warning from New Zealand – there's a storm coming with 50 knot winds!"

I didn't believe it at first, and wasted time looking at weather charts that said storms never happened at this time of year, and tuning my radio to hear that, sure enough, a bad storm was coming our way. The timing couldn't have been worse – I was only twenty miles from an island I had just sailed past on the gentle trade winds, and the storm's reversed wind would try to blow me back onto the island's rocks. I realized that to escape the island, I would have to sail upwind against 50 knots – I would have to change all

4

my sails, *now*. As the sea began to pound my little boat, I pulled on my foul-weather gear and strapped on a safety harness, went out on deck and watched a dead bird float by.

I clicked my harness onto the deck safety line, and as I pulled the storm sails out of storage, I posed the question I had been asking myself since I began sailing two years before – "What am I doing out here?" Could a computer programmer really sail around the world in a 31-foot boat? I thought I had seen every cold, wet, out-of-control, salt-water-in-the-face adventure while sailing from Oregon to Hawaii and French Polynesia, but I was still a beginner – in fact, in five more minutes, the safety harness would save my life.

But I should explain a little about myself. Please don't picture a world explorer, born to adventure, native to sun and wind – no way. I sunburn so easily that if I lose my hat I begin to cower like Dracula. I have spent most of my life working indoors, fixing TV sets as a teenager, then designing electronic gadgets, eventually working on the NASA Space Shuttle, finally learning to write computer programs.

Yes: a nerd. But I have a working brain, and that has saved me. When I was young I read a lot of books, observed people around me, and came to the conclusion that most people's lives are completely boring. So I made a rule for myself – find out what most people are doing, and *do something else*. I know that sounds almost too simple to be useful, but it works for me.

So, while I was designing part of the Space Shuttle, as successful as I had any right to expect, I remembered my rule and bought some country land. When my Shuttle work was done I moved to Oregon and built a cabin on the edge of the wilderness. I grew vegetables and hiked around in the woods for a year. It was pleasant but eventually I got a little bored.

One evening I was sitting by my wood stove, reading a magazine by a kerosene lamp, when I spotted an advertisement for something called an "Apple II personal computer." It was 1977, Steve Jobs and Steve Wozniak were living in a garage, "Personal Computer" was almost a contradiction in terms, but it came to me that I could own a computer.

Now I realize you may have a hard time believing someone can get all tingly about owning a computer, so I ask that you stretch your mind a little bit. Picture the thing you care about the most – a Lamborghini, or the perfectly written real estate contract, or an exquisite watercolor, or a woman on whom nature has smiled, or whatever. Now take that feeling and multiply it ten times – yes! Cover your face and make a sound only dogs can hear! I could own a computer! Equations quickly executed, magical worlds of computer images, the perfect cold wind of logic, a computer!

Well, you've always wanted to know what nerds think, haven't you? So I bought an Apple II and it was just as exciting as I expected. I started writing programs for it, because there weren't any, and I got pretty good. Then, one day, a magazine asked me to write an article about Einstein's Theory of Relativity. Since they offered to pay me and I had almost no money left, I began writing the article.

The basics of Relativity are not hard to grasp, but there are a lot of ways to explain it, and I soon had filled several scratchpads with ideas. Then I realized I might be able to program my Apple II to be a big electronic scratchpad. Maybe I could write a program to let me experiment, put words in different ways quickly and efficiently. So I wrote a scratchpad program and used it to write the article.

The Apple Computer company, no longer in a garage, heard about my program and asked to see it. I added some things to it, made it presentable and stuffed it into a big manila envelope. As I rode my bike to the post office I thought, Who knows, maybe they'll like my program. It might be worth hundreds of dollars.

Even I didn't see what was coming. I had written what is now called a word processing program – Apple Computer named it Apple Writer, it became an international best seller, and it is why I sailed around the world.

For the next eight years I wrote new versions of Apple Writer, translated it into foreign languages, and learned a lot about computers, people, and money. Finally it seemed as if everybody was writing a word processing program, so it was time for my rule again – *do something else.*

I had been sitting in dark rooms, punching computer keys, for years. I had always wanted to learn SCUBA diving, hike around in the tropics, so I booked a flight to Hawaii. But a month later I was in – are you ready? – a traffic jam on Maui. I wanted to climb Mount Haleakala, the island's biggest mountain, but first I had to get to it. I gazed along the row of cars stretching away in the distance. Occasionally I moved about a car length. Then another tourist banged his car into mine. I gave up and went back to Lahaina, the tourist ghetto on the West side of the island.

I spent the day walking around Lahaina, and eventually made my way down to the marina. As I walked along the row of boats, I saw a sailboat was about to depart, and the skipper asked if I would kindly cast off for him. I figured out he wanted me to untie his ropes from shore. The skipper motored away from the dock, then turned and began gliding out of the marina. He waved to someone on another boat, then, outside the breakwater, he turned off his engine and put up a sail. The boat heeled over and began to move, and in a few minutes all I could see was a pretty sail surrounded by blue water.

I understand now, from the moment I touched that sailboat's dock lines, I was doomed to sail. First I realized to actually see the Hawaiian islands I needed a boat. Then, slowly, the idea of sailing away from everything began to play itself over and over in my mind. I started meeting sailors, visiting boats, asking questions. Can you live on a boat? How long can you be away from shore? Are there pirates? How much does (ahem) a boat like this cost? And why doesn't the boat just fall over when the wind fills the sail?

I read books about sailing. Most of the respected ocean sailors think you should buy an old-fashioned heavy boat, with a keel that extends from the front to the back, and a rudder attached to the aft end. And, after wandering San Francisco's marinas, that's what I bought – a

The novice sets out

heavy, clunky, old-fashioned boat that looked as though it would stand the sea's abuse. It wasn't very expensive, because that kind of boat isn't popular any more (most sailboat owners don't sail across the ocean). I started adding equipment I thought I would need – a radar, two-way radios, a satellite navigation receiver. Soon I had the most high-tech old-fashioned boat around.

I knew I had to do something about the boat's name. The former owner had named it "Pagan Princess." Since then I have seen about a thousand boat names, and "Pagan Princess" is still near the top of the dreadful list. I renamed it "Selene," which is the Greek goddess of the moon. The former owner heard about the name change and said, "It's bad luck to change a boat's name." I said "It's bad luck to have a boat named 'Pagan Princess.'"

A little digression. You only get to name your boat once, so you should give it some thought. A lot of men name their boat after the woman who tolerates the boat's existence – this is dangerous, because the boat may outlast the relationship, then you have to start over. But most people try to show some personal cleverness or make a statement. While I sailed I kept lists of boat names – most pretentious (example: "Born Free," a boat probably owned by a bank), banal (please, no more "Sea Breeze"), hard to spell out on the radio ("Thalassa Experience III"), and just clever (a tie between "MicroShip" and "AllSummer's Disease").

Selene is a "double-ender," meaning it resembles a big canoe – the hull comes to a point at the back as well as the front. It's an old-fashioned design and it *looks* old-fashioned. The keel is long and not very deep. The rudder is attached to the aft end of the boat, with a post rising up outside the hull. A big stick called a tiller attaches to the post.

At first I wondered whether I was being too conservative in my choice of boat. But in the years since then I've banged a lot of coral reefs and rocks near shore, and out at sea I've collided with big things that went bump in the night. If I had bought a modern, lightweight racing boat I would have sunk somewhere by now. Also, Selene is the heaviest, therefore the slowest, boat in the fleet – it always arrives last. On the other hand, when the weather gets terrible I just take down the sails, go inside and read a book until it's over.

It's not easy to get seasick on a heavy boat. But that might just be me – I don't get seasick very easily. I did get seasick once, before I started sailing on my own – Apple Computer had chartered a fishing boat for a day, and I was in town so I went along. The boat made its way under the Golden Gate Bridge, and then things got bumpy. At first I was afraid I was going to die. Then I was afraid I wasn't going to die. They say motorboats are the worst, because of the exhaust fumes. Also they don't weigh very much, so they bounce like corks. But I never got seasick again.

After I equipped Selene the way I wanted, I decided to sail to the San Juan Islands in Washington State – this was to be my shakedown cruise before sailing to Hawaii. First I sailed from San Francisco and tied up in Brookings, Oregon, a short ride from my house. Then I worked on the boat for several months, installing more equipment and making overnight test sails off the coast. I waited until June to sail up to Washington, because the weather is supposedly better then.

A word about weather along the Oregon coast. At the time I am writing this I have seen weather all over the world, and the weather in Oregon is consistently the worst. One day, in the Red Sea, the weather was almost as bad as an average day in Oregon. For two days in the Caribbean, between the Virgin Islands and Panama, it was just as bad. But on the Oregon Coast it goes on for weeks.

Most of the shelters along the coast are river outlets. Over time these outlets develop piles of debris called "bars" at their entrances, and they must be dredged regularly to keep them passable. When the wind comes from the West and the waves are high (as they usually are), the waves break on the river bars. This makes these entrances deadly.

On the first of June I sailed for Cape Flattery, the point between Washington State and Canada that leads to the San Juan Islands. But I should have sailed earlier, no matter what the monthly weather summaries said – the wind blew at 40 miles per hour, directly from the North, all day, every day, and the waves were huge. I had to motor all the way between Brookings and Cape Flattery, a distance of 370 miles. It took 15 days, an average speed of one knot. A person walking on a beach of hard sand can make four knots, a thought that crossed my mind more than once as I bashed and banged through the water. I tried to stop as often as possible, usually to refuel as well as sleep.

I ran low on fuel near one small town, and ducked in just before dark. I got a good night's sleep, and the next morning I got my fuel and was all ready to go – I asked the Coast Guard station about the bar conditions. They told me the bar was dangerous, so dangerous that they would be obliged to physically prevent me from leaving if necessary. And why? Because the wind had shifted around to the West during the night. I realized if I was outside the bar with a West wind I would be sailing happily along on a beam reach (meaning a nice sail, with the wind blowing from the side). But I had to wait three days. Finally the bar was safe again. Why? Because the wind had shifted back to North. I motored the rest of the way.

The San Juan islands were beautiful. I learned a lot about sailing in a relatively safe and sheltered area. I sailed up to Canada and saw snowcapped peaks in August. And I discovered that a certain number of sailors are complete morons.

One day I anchored in a big, big bay (this is a form of literature called an "anchor story." This anchor story is simple. Later on they get as complicated as relativity). I dropped my anchor out in the middle of the bay, well away from everything, and took a nap. After a while I woke to the sound of country & western music. I came out of my cabin to discover another boat had anchored directly in front of me, about two boat lengths away, over my anchor. I couldn't leave, because my anchor was beneath the other boat. I had to listen to country & western music all day and half the night. It was two miles to shore in any direction, all perfect anchoring. Why were they here?

The next place I anchored was called "Echo Bay," on a beautiful outlying island. This time I decided to make it impossible for another boat to anchor near me. I used my navigation chart to locate a pass, between two rocks, that led to a small

At anchor, Echo Bay, Sucia Island

anchorage off to one side of the bay. Anyone that followed me in there would have to be very experienced or a complete idiot.

During the afternoon the tide came up and covered the rocks I had passed between. About 3 PM I was working in the cabin when I heard someone motoring nearby – very nearby. I came out of the cabin and saw a boat headed directly for one of the submerged rocks!

I waved my arms and yelled "Submerged rock! Turn to port!" The skipper yelled back "Okay – which way is port?" But he managed to miss the rock. Later he told me he thought he was in the clear since I had anchored so far off to the side. He had no chart.

Most of the time people left me alone, which was just as well, since I was making plenty of my own mistakes, learning how to sail and anchor a 16 thousand pound boat alone. I was willing to do completely embarrassing things, but not while drifting sideways into someone's expensive yacht.

If I had to tell the truth about my summer in Washington, I would say I began to depend on Selene – for a sense of purpose and for consistency as well. If I was lazy about anchoring on a certain day, the wind would blow, something would break, I would pay for laziness right away. Another day, if I stayed alert to the details, things would go well, I would have a nice time and begin to think myself embedded in nature, in the wind. At the time I thought how charming those lessons were, even though they were really just coincidences. Yes: I had a lot to learn.

Soon it was September, time to sail the boat back to Oregon and prepare for the Hawaii passage. I was looking forward to sailing down the coast – I had fought those fierce winds all the way up, burning an ocean of diesel fuel. Now I would sail back on wind power, downwind, really fast.

I rounded Cape Flattery on a sunny afternoon with brisk winds, I put out my largest sails and began to move. Within twelve hours the wind died and fog rolled in. I had to motor back to Brookings.

During the winter I installed more equipment and filled the lockers with things I thought would be useful. I installed a wind generator and solar panels, so I could charge the boat's batteries without having to run the engine. I went out for more test sails.

One day I decided to visit a bay a short distance up the coast called "Hunter's Cove." It was supposed to be okay for anchoring. How did I know this? There was a little anchor drawn on the chart.

There was no wind so I had to motor, and by the time I got there it was after dark, not a good time to enter an unfamiliar bay. But this wasn't a reason to change my plan, after all, I had just come back from a long journey to Washington State and Canada. I was a hotshot sailor.

But, just to be safe, I turned off the engine so I could listen for breaking waves, and scanned the bay with binoculars, looking for rocks and white water. Things seemed calm in the bay, there was no wind, so I got the boat ready – I untied the anchor so I could go forward later and just drop it off the bow. I motored into the bay, using the radar to find my way among the rocks.

I watched the depth sounder too – I wanted to stay in water depths of 20 feet or more, because waves might break in shallower water. I saw the depth I wanted and began turning the boat around to face the waves. Just then a huge wave entered the bay, broke, and came careening down on my boat! It sounded like a freight train – as it collided with my boat it almost drowned out my plea "But I'm in *twenty feet!*"

Because I was turning around, the wave hit the boat beam-on, the worst orientation. The boat rolled down so the spreaders on the mast nearly touched the water, the anchor fell off the bow, and everything movable flew across the cabin. Water poured through the hatch.

The wave pushed the boat a considerable distance toward shore, which meant shallower water and more breaking waves. I hit the throttle, hoping to round up into the breaking seas and get out of there. But the engine speed wouldn't rise above an idle – something was wrong with my engine! I dove into the cabin and pulled the engine covers off. As I examined the engine two more waves hit the boat, pushing it closer to shore. The water depth was now 12 feet. I finally realized the electric fuel pump had quit and wasn't delivering any fuel. I started hitting it with a wrench as another wave broke aboard. My engine came to life!

I jumped back into the cockpit and tried to point up into the waves again. The boat turned and took the next wave on the nose, a much less violent experience. But then the boat just stopped! It was then I realized the anchor had fallen off the bow. That was why I hadn't been thrown onto the rocks, but it also meant I couldn't just motor away – I would have to raise the anchor first.

I put on my safety harness and went to the bow. Between each of the breaking waves – which completely covered me – I was able to reel in the anchor chain a bit. Finally the anchor cleared the bottom – I ran aft and started motoring.

When I reached safety, clear of the bay, I stopped and listened. I *still* couldn't hear the breaking waves, and the sea seemed calm in the deeper water outside the bay. I learned my lesson – after that night I didn't try to anchor along the coast any more. Instead I would get well away from land, make my tests, take sextant sights in the evening, let the boat drift around while I slept until daylight, then sail some more. It was safer than going near the shore.

Sometimes when I was at home I would jump out of bed and try to figure out where I was – I would look out the windows, see houses and trees and begin to panic. I would try to find the tiller, turn away from the land. Then I would wake up, standing there, and it would come to me that I wasn't on the boat. This made me realize I was a lot more afraid of sailing than I admitted, and the fears I was hiding came to the surface after dark.

I would sit in the dark and ask myself what I thought I was doing. Could I turn myself into a sailor? What did I want to do with my boat?

But I knew, I knew. If I sailed far enough, if I didn't crash my boat against some rocks, I would put my anchor out in some foreign land. I would climb a hill and meet a goatherd. We would sit under a tree, drink wine and eat goat's cheese. He wouldn't have heard about Chernobyl or disposable diapers, and I wouldn't tell him.

He would tell me his story and I would tell him mine. We would look at the hills, the sky. And I would walk down the hill with the fine touch of a natural person, someone who belongs to the earth, to the sea. Someone beyond the reach of the evening news.

And that would be enough, the fear would go away. I could lie down again and sleep.

Finally it was May – time to leave for Hawaii. I had conducted every test I could think of, and packed lots of interesting treats for the passage.

{ 2 }

Oregon to Hawaii

May 5 – Day Three

As departure day came near I worked to build my confidence – in my mind I would jump on board, throw off the shore lines and sail out of sight of land. But I mustn't have talked my inner self into it – as the days went by I found myself becoming numb. I just couldn't feel anything.

As my friend Mary drove me to the marina, she looked at me as if to say, "What are you feeling right now?" I tried to reassure her by telling jokes – "My inner child just ran away" – but I didn't know what I felt. I think now it was a mixture of mortal fear that I would finally sail out of sight of land, exhilaration for the same reason, and a sense that I would suffer complete humiliation if I couldn't sail off as planned.

I almost crashed my boat by pushing the throttle the wrong way as I tried to back away from the dock, a mistake I corrected before driving the boat up on shore. I think that might have been a clue to my state of mind. My friends have been so nice lately, my town brighter, more inviting than usual.

But I managed to pull away from the space between the boats, built some speed and took the tiller in hand. Did you know you can't steer a boat that isn't moving? Just like a life.

Then I glided past the end of the dock, leaned out and kissed Mary as I went past. It was an act of sheer arrogance, leaning away from a heavy, moving boat to kiss someone. But I was showing off for myself – I needed to know I could control my boat.

The only bit of land between Brookings and Hawaii is the Point St. George lighthouse, 14 miles from Brookings – after that, 2300 miles of open water. The wind was so light and variable that I took five hours making my way to the lighthouse. I could have used the engine but I was feeling pure – it would have seemed craven to motor the first day. Past the lighthouse the wind shifted to Northwest, my sails filled and I was able to take off.

Later in the day I found myself gazing back toward land, first looking at the lighthouse and coast, then in the evening I picked out shore lights with the binoculars and tried to make out what they were.

By dark I was in the shipping lanes about 30 miles off the coast. I had to dodge several freighters – one got so close I could hear his engines and smell his exhaust. After dinner I scanned the ships and clouds with my binoculars. Watching the big vessels in the moonlight was my first chance to relax and feel confident about being on the sea.

The next day I checked my position and found I had made 103 miles in the first 24 hours. That's a respectable distance for a small sailboat that isn't racing. Later on Day Two the wind picked up to 20 knots, gusts of 30. I double-reefed the main and rolled up most of the jib.

Today the gale got stronger (30 knots with gusts of 40) so I crawled forward and pulled the mainsail down completely. I rode out the wind with just a small bit of jib unfurled. I needed to charge my batteries, but the wind was too strong for the wind generator, and I didn't

Selene's dark, all-teak interior

want to put out the solar panels for fear that a wave would knock them off the boat, so I charged them with the engine. Several waves broke across the boat during the day.

Now the wind seems to be moderating. I have put the mainsail back up and started the wind generator. The weather advisory charts say this area is always rough, no matter the season.

May 7 – Day 5

I'm able to write today because the wind has slacked off to below 25 knots for the first time in two days, and the sun has made an appearance.

Yesterday the wind blew steadily at 30 knots from the Southwest, a hard wind to sail against, and waves broke over the boat regularly. It's quite an experience when a wave hits the boat – usually it's because the boat happens to be where a wave is breaking on the open sea, a "whitecap." It sounds as if someone hit the hull with a wrecking ball, followed by water, water everywhere.

The cabin is a salt water rainstorm – I think the overhead skylight lets in more water than light, and some of the closed portholes squirt water inside when a wave hits them. I wanted to print a weather chart from the radio, but just then a wave came along, the printer took a splash of salt water and died. Now I have no way to make weather charts.

For the first couple of days I was in a state of physical ruin. I was cold and wet, all my spare clothing was wet, and the inside of my sleeping bag was wet. Apart from the dripping skylight, the worst part was lying in my bunk at night listening to my boat creaking and groaning, thinking it might break. Then I began to come down with something respiratory, so I started taking vitamins and extra vitamin C. Gradually I'm getting used to the conditions, also I'm so tired I've stopped listening to boat noises with quite so much attention.

I have many electric toys on this boat. I want to sleep without crashing into a freighter, so I run my radar all night. If a ship comes near, the radar beeps me. I have some navigation receivers that tell me where I am. I have a ham radio setup that I use to talk to my house. And I keep a light burning on my mast all night. All these things take electricity, which comes from batteries. Every day I have to figure out a way to put as much electricity in my batteries as I take out. I can use a windmill that makes electricity when the wind blows – unless the wind is too strong, then it breaks. I can put my solar panels out – if the sun is shining and waves aren't splashing my boat's topsides. Or in desperation I can start the engine and it will charge them.

My LORAN navigation receiver stopped working this morning. The LORAN system relies on shore stations and has a range of about 500 miles. I have started using my other navigation receiver, called "satnav" (satellite navigation), but I am going to try the LORAN again from time to time (it's useful to have two ways to know where you are, especially if they agree with each other).

The wind is blowing abeam at about 15 - 20 knots right now. I put up the staysail (the small third sail) for the first time on this crossing. This sail seems to have balanced things so the wind vane keeps a steady course. The wind vane is a mechanical gadget that uses wind power to steer the boat – mine isn't very good, it only works when the wind is strong.

I have made more than 100 miles each day so far, in spite of the conditions. But I didn't expect the wind to blow this hard, or from this direction – I expected to be running downwind before force 4 (11-16 knot) winds in a wing-and-wing configuration (a sail out on each side). But that may happen as I get farther away from the mainland and into the trade winds. I'm still only 280 miles from San Francisco.

On day three I went out and raised my flag for the first time. I didn't particularly want to go for a walk on deck in gale conditions for such a seemingly unimportant job, but I was in international waters with no flag showing. This morning I noticed the wind has shredded it.

I plan to sail from Brookings to a point in the middle of the ocean at 25 N, 135 W, then continue to Hilo on the Big Island of Hawaii. This should keep me away from the Pacific High and is only a little longer than a straight line.

The "Pacific High" is an area of high pressure in the Eastern Pacific between the West Coast and Hawaii. Wind circulates clockwise around the high, so one sails South of the high going to Hawaii and North of it coming back. There's no wind at all in

Printing a weather chart while underway

the center of the high, so straight-line sailing is out. But, just to make things interesting, sometimes the high moves out of its normal position.

May 8 – Day 6

The weather is gradually improving, but the winds aren't. They had been steady abeam at about 8 knots, but now they're blowing directly from where I want to go. So I'm sailing Southeastward, to move away from the area of the Pacific High.

I was able to fix my weather chart printer – I realized if I took the unit apart and sprayed the circuit boards with alcohol (which I normally use to start my kerosene stove), it might wash away the salt water. It worked. So I am making weather charts and can see what's going on – a storm headed for the Oregon coast has pushed the Pacific High down this way. I am practically in the middle of it. I hope it moves back to its old neighborhood soon.

Now I know why they call this "blue water sailing." The water is as blue as I've ever seen, like the water at Crater Lake in Oregon. It's hard to believe the deep blue color, especially the side of the boat away from the sun at midday.

I was able to have a conversation with Mary by way of the ham radio message system. Its signals are coming in well now. It will be interesting to see whether they hold up all the way to Hawaii.

The relatively calm weather made me overconfident – I filled one of my wine glasses for dinner, put it down and looked away for a moment. A tiny wave came along and upset it. It fell off the table and broke – glass and wine everywhere. The sea punishes arrogance so quickly.

The radar is proving itself on this crossing. On a couple of occasions a ship came within a mile of me, and the radar alarm woke me up to deal with it. I probably wouldn't sleep very well without it.

The Pacific High has come to where I am, so the wind is light and my mileages are going down – but the weather is pleasant. I'm waiting for the classical trade winds to begin.

May 9 – Day 7

Today is the third day with contrary winds, although in trade it's sunny and clear. The wind is blowing almost directly from where I want to go, so I have to tack to sail as close as I can to the direction I want to go. The trick is to see which tack, port or starboard, takes me where I want to go most efficiently.

When the boat doesn't point directly where I want to go, only some of the boat's speed takes me toward Hawaii, but more than I would have thought at first. I punched some calculator buttons and discovered if I point the boat 45 degrees away from Hawaii, I still get there with more than 2/3 of the boat's forward speed.

I didn't believe this result at first and checked it again, but it's true. And when I am 30 degrees off course, my boat still sails toward Hawaii with 86 percent efficiency. When I discovered this I realized there's no reason to struggle to point exactly toward Hawaii, it just wastes my energy and the boat's.

I changed tacks this morning – I decided I had gone Southeast far enough. If the Pacific High ever goes back to its normal position for the month of May, I'll be ready.

I think tomorrow I'll stop doing math and try doing my laundry. Supposedly you can wash clothes in cold salt water if you use dish soap. I've heard you have to rinse in fresh water, though. I have to decide whether to do the laundry, or just store it and use the fresh water to wash myself. That might be a tough choice.

May 10 – Day 8

The wind started getting stronger, particularly after midnight last night. I was up even more than usual, steering away from a freighter, changing sails, tacking to see which tack was best, and generally not sleeping. The seas are very steep and short, and the wind has held all day at 18-22 knots, unfortunately directly from where I want to go. It's uncomfortable trying to make any headway against these seas. A low pressure system has stalled off the California Coast, and until it moves I will be running against strong headwinds and seas. The wind is blowing opposite the normal direction for May.

I tried to wash myself with salt water, which I heated on the stove (with a special kettle I use only for salt water) and added that to a bucket of sea water to get the right temperature. It wasn't as bad as I expected. Of course, I won't know whether it really has worked until I try to sweat and can't because of all the salt in my pores.

I realized I haven't had a complete night's sleep since setting out. My personal indicator for enough sleep is vivid dreams before waking. It's supposed to be very unhealthy to miss out on REM (rapid eye movement) sleep, the sleep accompanied by dreams. Maybe the wind will back off tonight and I won't have to adjust sails or dodge freighters. The daily weather report said the low pressure system to my Northwest was "weakening." That may be true, but it's also moving in my direction.

I sail differently at night. I slow down so as not to be thrown around so much, even though it makes the passage longer. In daylight I have more energy to cope with the rough motions of a fast sail. But last night a sudden increase in wind after midnight wiped out my careful planning, so I had to get up, get dressed, and change sails. The wind increase also threw off my power generating plans – it got too strong to use the wind generator. I had watched a movie (I have a tiny TV and some videotapes), thinking I could use the windmill to recharge later. I had to use my high-power deck lights to change sails, so I ended up running down both batteries almost completely by this morning.

The wind is starting to get to me – it's been blowing this way for three days now, with short, choppy seas. If I decided to take a break and heave to for a while, I'd end up going backwards – drifting with the wind and the ocean current the wind makes. I am ready for any change for the better – a change in the wind's direction, a lull in the wind for the sake of sleep, anything (except another gale).

May 11 – Day 9

Although the low to my Northwest is weakening, it's been moving toward me over the last three days. As a result, tight pinch day 4 is starting out with 25 knot winds. I've stopped the wind generator to save it from itself, even though I could use the power. The solar panels are working, so the batteries will still get charged, although more slowly. I am making about three knots, well heeled over and close to the wind.

Last night I realized I was going to have to get some deep, uninterrupted sleep. So I reduced sail, brought the speed down to about two knots to make the ride more comfortable, tied down all the noisy gadgets and slept. With these heavy seas, a small change in speed makes a big difference in comfort – I got some good sleep.

I can't believe this low has remained stationary so long. If only the high will do as well when it comes back.

May 12 – Day 10

Today I got my wish – the low pressure system finally made its move. The day started in the normal way, wind too strong and from the wrong direction. The seas kept getting rougher and the wind stronger. I saw a wall of clouds approach from the West. Then, about 3 PM, the big show began. The seas became high and completely confused, with big waves from all points of the compass. The cloud wall passed over and rain began.

As the wall came up the wind gradually weakened and turned clockwise, then dropped away almost completely, but the seas stayed high. And it turned out the cloud wall had a well-defined back as well as a front – behind the wall, a warm wind was blowing at about 12 knots from the West, where before it had been a colder 30 knots from Southwest. About 6 PM the sea calmed and the clouds moved off to the East.

As the sun set I adjusted my sails, and I thought how much like a conversation it had been – I couldn't shake the feeling the sea and sky were talking to me. I don't mean I heard the theme from the Twilight Zone, but everything was there for me – all I had to do was pay attention. I realized I knew exactly what the wall meant – it might as well have been words. And when I pulled my lines and moved my sails, I answered.

May 13 – Day 11

Another high has settled in, and I'm so close to its center that I don't have any wind to speak of – just a slight variable Northwesterly. I have stopped using the wind vane (there being no wind to vane it) and now the electronic autopilot is having trouble holding course because the boat is moving so slowly. Occasionally the autopilot beeps me, thinking it can't possibly be attached to the boat any more. Then a breath of wind comes along and makes it happy.

It's cloudy, with moments of sunlight. The sea is grayish blue and almost flat. It's so quiet that sailing seems almost make-believe. If you tug a line or push the tiller, it doesn't have the usual effect, so you begin to feel as though you aren't really sailing, but rehearsing it all in a dream.

During the night I got up to check the sails, and afterward I sat watching green phosphorescent particles coming off the hull. Then I realized I had company – dolphins were surfacing and diving all around the boat. I couldn't see them clearly, mostly I heard them calling and saw their splashes.

I'm having some interesting dreams. I'll dream I'm on a lake, with land all around, and if I don't watch out I'll run my boat aground. I wake up so often at night that these dreams stay in my waking thoughts. Then, after doing whatever task got me up, I sit in the cockpit and let it come to me where I am – far, far from any shore. But in my dreams I surround myself with land. Last night I was on Lake Victoria in Africa – I was about to run the boat onto a beach and say "Dr. Livingston, I presume?"

Sometimes I see a long-winged bird that soars just over the waves, hunting for fish. I have some bird books and have eliminated Magnificent Frigatebird and a few others. I still haven't decided what it is. I see fewer as I move away from land, but I see at least one a day. It is brown with a light-colored bill, has long wings with a curve in them, a very efficient glider. Maybe the descriptions in my books are leading me astray – they describe most of the likely ocean birds simply as "black."

I haven't seen any other vessels in three days – I'm tempted to shut down the radar at night to save power. But if the wind picks up and the sun comes out there will be more electricity than I can use.

I have some entertaining ways to use power on this boat. Apart from the indulgence of movies, I listen to short-wave radio, mostly the B.B.C. (the British Broadcasting Company), and some AM radio stations from the West Coast. I have 5 multiband radios, tucked away here and there. Some have special purposes, like the ham radio, or the direction-finder set. Others I just brought along to have "a backup radio." The most-used radio is one I bought at Radio Shack – it gets the most use because it is very easy on electricity. If I didn't care about power I would use the ham radio receiver, because it is easiest to use, and it has the boat's biggest antenna all to itself.

You want to have at least one good radio on a boat. It should receive short-wave, and it should run on its own batteries if need be. Here's why: (1) You can receive time signals to adjust your clocks, so your sextant positions are accurate. (2) As you get close to your destination, you can use it for radio direction-finding. (3) It's nice to hear a human voice once in a while.

May 14 – Day 12

Things are very slow right now, because there's (again) a low off the coast of Oregon that's pushing the Pacific High right over me. I've been printing the weather charts and watching the barometer. I am only a couple of millibars from the center of this high. Until the low near Oregon moves, the high is likely to stay in the wrong place. But I am still making 2-3 knots in these light winds.

At night I reduce sail even though it slows me down, because a big cloudburst might come along while I sleep and rip my fully extended sails. I plan to continue toward my waypoint, then as the winds pick up I'll turn toward the islands.

May 16 – Day 14

Well, the wind finally came back – directly from my destination. I tacked back and forth all afternoon, doing some interesting wind calculations, but not making much progress. Then I chose the right tack for overnight – my guess was the wind would veer to the Northwest. That turned out to be right. Now I am on a close reach at 3.5 knots – but directly toward my waypoint. My laptop computer (which I also use to write these notes) tells me I should make the waypoint about the 18th if I can keep up speed. It also tells me I'll get to Hilo on the Big Island June second at this speed. Most of all I'm hoping for trade winds – rumors persist that they happen out here.

During the night I had vivid dreams – of cities, crime, desperate lives. I think sailing brought that out, because of the contrast between ocean and city life. It also means I'm sleeping soundly again.

Today is my birthday. Not a bad location for a birthday party. No cake, though.

The temperature continues to rise. I think it's going to be hot today – the sun is in a cloudless sky. I know I'll tug and pull the solar panels around the deck, keeping them from being shaded by the sails. Then I'll watch a movie, indulge myself on my birthday. I'll make it an afternoon matinee – that way the solar panels can recharge the batteries after I've run the TV and before nightfall.

I think I'm about to see a change in the wind. I am close to the latitude where trade winds begin, also the high that's been hanging over me should move North soon (as a low near Oregon dissipates, making room for it), and simple probability says I ought to have some wind from behind, at least some of the time.

May 17 – Day 15

In the afternoon the wind began to swing around behind the boat, and by sunset I was making 4 1/2 to 5 knots. If this wind stays, the second half of this journey will be a lot shorter than the first. I'm having a rougher ride *The wing-and-wing configuration* with many dramatic rolls, and even in the cabin there's no doubt the boat is moving through the water.

Sometime today I'll reach my halfway point – both Hilo and Brookings will be 1130 nautical miles away. Also I'll pass North of the waypoint I've been aiming for until now. Since I have enough wind I'm turning toward Hilo.

Last night I decided to start the Honda generator, another way to charge my batteries. But the starting rope broke, so I tried to fix it today.

Wrestling that little generator around the cockpit was really a spectacle. The boat would roll severely every 20 seconds, throwing tools and parts all over.

Sleeping last night wasn't easy. I put the special retainer line in place that keeps me from falling out of the berth, but the rolling motion kept up all night. Maybe I'll get used to it.

May 18 – Day 16

In the afternoon the wind built to about 25 - 30 knots. I was sitting, marveling at the high knot meter readings when the whisker pole broke (the whisker pole holds the jib out for downwind sailing). I spent some hours repairing it – it's

Broken Whisker Pole

working again but about three feet shorter when fully extended. It's probably just as well that it's shorter.

Today the knot meter momentarily displayed a speed of 6 knots – it's been a long time since I've seen that speed. Last night I averaged 4.9 knots, and that seems to be closer to the average. I have to adjust to the new boat motion, but these are the winds I was waiting for. I notice I can go faster when the winds decrease below 25 knots, because the wave heights go down along with the wind and the boat isn't constantly banging into waves. The wind is slowly moving from about 60 degrees starboard of aft, to dead aft.

I have passed the midpoint – now I am closer to Hawaii than the mainland. Almost immediately I started to imagine what it will be like in Hawaii this summer. I guess the midpoint was a psychological barrier, before which I would only think about the passage itself. Now I am free to think about Hawaii.

May 19 – Day 17

I am thinking again that I could go faster if the wind would subside. The surface is too rough to take advantage of the wind, and slows the boat down more than the wind speeds it up. Of course I could put up every inch of sail and tie myself down somewhere as the racers do, but I want to get to

Hilo with my boat in one piece. Selene went an average speed of 6.1 knots overnight. It was a rough ride, but I didn't realize it was that fast – that's half a knot under the boat's maximum design speed.

May 20 – Day 18

The wind is decreasing but the surface isn't calming down. Today I have scattered showers and plenty of wind speed and direction changes. The rough surface makes me think there's some wind hiding out there, waiting for me to put up a ridiculous amount of sail before making a surprise visit. So I want to act cautiously until I see a day's worth of this new wind. During the night the wind varied between 25 knots and nothing, and the surface stayed rough.

I have decided the mystery bird (that patrols the sea just over the waves) is a "Flesh-Footed Shearwater" *(puffinus carneipes)*. The picture in my bird book is a good likeness, and it is an open ocean bird. It's described as "sooty black" in the text but the photograph shows more of a brown coloring such as I have seen, so I think it's the best guess for now.

Another bird has appeared. This one was easier to identify – "Red-billed Tropicbird" *(phaethon aethereus)*. It has a long distinctive tail. Of the two I saw, one tried to land on the boat. It aimed for the windmill, but reconsidered at the last moment. The whirling blades must have

Red-Billed Tropicbird in a near-miss

caught its eye – and just as well, they would have torn it to pieces. A pretty visitor, more than 900 miles from land.

May 21 – Day 19

The day began with scattered rain showers, but then settled down with very smooth conditions and winds in the 10 - 12 knot range. It was a beautiful run – I put up every inch of cloth and just sat back. The ride was smooth and stable. As soon as I saw how smooth it was going to be, I took a nap. Sometimes it's easier to sleep in the daytime and attend to the boat at night.

In the afternoon, rain clouds developed again. Rain clouds have radial winds, winds moving out from the cloud in all directions. If the cloud is behind the boat (remember the wind mostly blows from behind now), the wind picks up – sometimes over 20 knots – and I have to reduce sail. If the cloud is in front, the wind decreases, sometimes to nothing. If the cloud is to the left or right, it changes the direction of the wind, sometimes radically. I have to pay close attention and use much less sail, so as not to be caught off guard.

In the evening I played with radios. I put up a separate short-wave antenna for the Radio Shack receiver by hiding some wire along the edges of the cabin interior. I use the Radio Shack radio a lot because it takes less power, but until now it didn't have a proper antenna. Then I tried tuning in some AM stations.

To my surprise I picked up several Hawaiian stations (I'm about 700 miles out). So I tried direction-finding on them. Radio direction-finding relies on the fact that the antenna in AM radios is very directional – if you point the long axis of the radio (and the antenna) at the station, it fades out. Of course, the station could be off either end of the radio, so there's some possibility for confusion. But I found my boat's long axis was perfectly aligned with the Hawaiian stations. So I have another way to guide my boat – with a radio.

My ham radio link is working better than expected. Before I started this sail, I spent some time installing and testing ham radios and computers in both the boat and my house in Oregon. I wanted to be able to write a message here, transmit it by radio, and print it on paper in Oregon. At the Oregon end, because a normal person (not a radio nerd) has to be able to use the system, there's a simple "message screen" on display. A person just sits down at the computer and types a message, then presses a key that saves it. The next time I make contact I collect the messages.

I feel as though I've adjusted to being on this boat, out on the ocean. I am getting more sleep (mostly because of better sailing conditions), and I feel much better than I did at first. In some ways I'll be sorry when it's over, but I am looking forward to visiting Hawaii.

May 22 – Day 20

I haven't talked much about food. As I planned this passage I packed a lot of canned goods, and then bought some fresh fruit just before departing. Granny Smith apples keep well – I could have packed more of those. I wanted some kind of cheese, so I bought a bunch of the travel kind that are dipped in wax and wrapped in red paper. They seem to hold up well. I also bought some Monterey Jack cheese that had been packed in a regional center rather than the store itself. These packages, which you can identify by their fancy plastic wrapping sealed by automatic equipment, keep well, but not as long as the wax-enclosed kind. I bought four blocks of Monterey Jack, and by the time I got to the fourth (about a week and a half) I had to trim off an outside layer of green.

I brought along some freeze-dried dinners. They are great, although fairly expensive. Other dinner staples: cans of Boston baked beans, chicken stew, fruit cocktail for an occasional treat, applesauce, mixed vegetables. Cans of nuts for snacks while on watch. Jars of dill pickles. Crackers of various kinds.

This sounds like a diet for someone who can't cook, but the idea is to have food you can eat even if the stove breaks down. Or a snack that you can eat without taking time away from an emergency.

But I brought along some wine, too, in case things went better than expected. I thought it would be pleasant to have a glass of wine in the afternoon, when things had settled down. But as often as not, in the evening the wind would pick up, it would get dark, and I would have to work to bring the boat under control. The tasks of late afternoon and evening would seem all the more irritating if I also had to come back from wine bliss. So I have given up on wine for the time being – maybe it'll be more enjoyable when I'm anchored somewhere.

Here's a typical day on sailing vessel Selene: Wake up about 7:30, turn off the masthead light and radar (I haven't seen another vessel in 16 days but I run the radar anyway), go on deck and check the sail trim. Watch the sea for about an hour. Go down to the galley to start making breakfast – first step, boil some water in the teakettle. I use this for cocoa and oatmeal. Turn on the satnav for the first of two daily fixes.

About 10 AM, I print weather maps on the computer printer. Then I decide how to charge my batteries. If the sun is out I put the solar panels where the sun can get at them, and remind myself to move them later. If the wind is blowing more than 15 knots, I start the wind generator. But if there's isn't enough sun or wind, I charge batteries with either the Honda generator or the main engine for about an hour.

Then I do this – I write a while. My notebook, by the way, is a computer, a small "laptop" machine with a cover that doubles as a display screen.

By now the satnav receiver has a new fix. I enter the fix in my logbook and calculate how far I traveled since the last fix, what average speed and heading that was, and write that down also.

Then I go watch the sea some more, adjust the sails, stay alert for rainstorms that might change the wind speed and direction, change tacks from time to time. Look at the sea some more. Read. Play music, usually in the form of compact disks, but I have a concert flute and a recorder (a medieval flute) and some sheet music.

Mid-afternoon. If the sun is out and the wind is brisk, chances are the batteries are completely charged and can't absorb any more electrical power from the solar panels and the windmill (this doesn't happen very often). What to do with all that extra throw-away electricity? Watch a movie! Otherwise make a snack out of pickles, cheese, nuts, crackers, etc. Read. Refill the kerosene lamps. Read some more. Watch the sea go by.

Evening. Turn on the masthead light. Light the kerosene lamps. Turn on the satnav. Make some dinner. Listen to the news on the B.B.C.

Late Evening. Knowing I am about to run the masthead light, radar, and autopilot all night, I decide whether the wind generator can supply the necessary power. If not, run the engine again for about an hour.

Later Evening. Turn on the radar. Check heading and sail trim one more time. Get into sack and read some more. Sleep.

Even later, after the tiniest bit of sleep: Get up, light a light, find my glasses, open the hatch, and discover why the sails sound as if they're being beaten up by juvenile delinquents. Repeat as necessary to guarantee no REM sleep.

May 24 – Day 22

I wonder if I'll be as anxious about ending this voyage as I was about starting it? I remember being absolutely petrified, about to say good-bye to my friends, the shore, life as I knew it, and cast off lines for a spell that could have lasted a month or more. I didn't want Mary to leave the boat, because when she did I would have to start. No more preparations, actually leave.

I remember lying in my bunk those first few nights of bad weather, listening to random creaks and groans, thinking "That's breaking. It's *breaking*. I'll die out here and my friends will tell unkind stories."

Now I feel as if the shore life is the fragile construction, more likely than this boat to have been assembled by incompetents. I'm starting to like this life. The return to shore will be another difficult adjustment.

Now I think I can explain being out in a little boat on a big ocean. Well, I can try. At about the halfway point, over a thousand miles from San Francisco and an equal distance from Hawaii, I was watching the afternoon sun move behind some clouds. Sunbeams were making their way through holes in the clouds, making islands of light on the water. I thought to myself how this would make a good picture for a fundamentalist, who would argue that God was up there, pulling puppet strings of light.

Then I thought to myself – as I tend to when faced with a ridiculous example of natural beauty – okay, again you've decided how not to think about this, but don't go too far. Don't be so careful and skeptical that you leave yourself with no sense of wonder at all. You can enjoy this without falling into superstition, you know. It's been done.

So I stopped thinking about what it didn't mean, and just watched the show. Then it came to me that I might be the only person seeing it – I don't mean in the sense of a rainbow, everybody having a slightly different angle of view – but nobody within, say, 500 miles of the place. I realized this cloud bank, this scene, was mine – I was the only witness. I wouldn't be able to ring up a friend later and say "Did you see the nice sunset?"

This orange mixture of sunlight and clouds was not part of normal human experience – it didn't pass through panes of tinted glass, or throw shadows across floors. No apple vendors or tax accountants would look up and see it – just this one guy, on a boat. Watching a sunset that only I could see gave me a peculiar sense of responsibility. If I didn't see it and enjoy it, no one would. Only the dolphins and the birds.

May 25 – Day 23

The wind has slacked off a lot, and my speed is going down. Surprisingly, the wind now picks up during the night. I have gotten accustomed to letting the full mainsail fly during the day, and setting one reef (reducing size) in the last of daylight.

The weather chart says it all. Now there are two highs, one to the Northwest, one to the Northeast. I am between their wind patterns, but not getting the advantage of either. Right now there's not enough wind to keep the Genoa properly inflated. Nevertheless, I'm doing four knots – almost twice as fast as during the headwind phase of this voyage.

There were two more flying fish on deck this morning. They're getting bigger. I wish I could hear them flapping their wings or something so I could save them, throw them back into the sea.

I have started cleaning up the boat in preparation for arrival. The galley was very grungy, so I started there. Imagine the humiliation of having a customs inspector come on your boat and kill himself on a banana peel.

Today is sunny and very pretty, and the wind is mild. I could have slept until noon. Days like these discourage me from wanting to get anywhere.

Maybe sailing is one of those ready-made roles-in-miniature, giving you a feeling of clear, simple purpose in an otherwise cryptic world. Just put out sail, take in sail, look through the sextant, immerse yourself in the minutiae of going somewhere slowly and deliberately, while secretly hoping you'll never arrive.

May 26 – Day 24

Yesterday, about 130 miles out, I tried to see the big island through binoculars. The biggest peak is very high – over 13,000 feet. I calculated the big island should be just above the horizon – but maybe I looked too soon, considering how cloudy and hazy it was.

The sailing is still slow. If the wind would just pipe up I would be in Hilo before dark tonight, if not I will have to decide whether I want to enter the bay after dark. There's some moonlight right now, but there's also a reef near the entrance, and you can't see the reef at night, moonlight or not.

I have been making subtle adjustments to the approach of land. I put my wallet back in my pocket. I gathered all the boat papers and put them in my day pack. I am flying the "Q" flag for customs (I haven't figured out whether I count as a foreign vessel, or just an American sailboat that

Hawaii at last

happens to have crossed the ocean). I tried putting on shoes, just as an experiment.

In spite of the times I was becalmed and felt as though I *had* to get moving again, it's ending too soon. I only read 1 1/2 books. My pickle jar is still half-full.

10 AM: The morning clouds are lifting and I can make out the Big Island, 30 miles off. This is a bittersweet moment – there's something solid in front of my boat, not just a particularly high wave. I have to stop and deal with it – I can't just sail past.

I found this island, out in the ocean, mostly using satellites and radio signals, but also by looking at stars with my sextant, the old-fashioned way. I might want to say I got here against hard seas and confusion – there's some truth in that – but a greater truth is the sea was kind to me.

4 PM: I can see people in long racing canoes, paddles striking the water. I hear the sounds of the land. Maybe I don't want to sail past after all.

{ 3 }

Hawaii to Marquesas

I am starting this journal chapter while tied up in Hilo, before departing for the Marquesas, so at least the beginning will be coherent. When I am underway no night's sleep is completely uninterrupted, so that the perfect word or phrase is taken from me by force, as I wrestle with a sail that is a lot more awake than I am.

I spent last summer sailing from one gorgeous island to another, starting with the Big Island and making my way to Kauai, which turned out to be my favorite. I began to dive each day, exploring the island reefs. At first I thought I would use my SCUBA tanks, but refilling them was too much trouble, so I began to free-dive (with fins and mask but no tanks). Free-diving turned out to be a good idea – I dove a lot more by not needing a tank for every dive.

The reefs in Hawaii are beautiful, and the fish are interesting. I saw several octopi – they are supposed to be intelligent and they are certainly shy. Also *The west coast of Kauai* some white-tipped reef sharks – not particularly dangerous unless cornered. I started staying down longer and longer on a breath – by the end of summer I could stay down three minutes.

Also I bought a wind surfing board, one designed for Hawaiian wind conditions – when the wind stops, the board sinks. I found some excellent wind surfing beaches, both on Maui and Kauai, where the wind blows steadily all day, and if you are good you can lift off the bigger waves and fly through the air.

In the fall I sailed my boat to a marina in Honolulu for winter storage and flew back to Oregon.

I returned about February 10. I had intended to stay in Oregon somewhat longer, but I wanted to paint the hull of my boat and the Honolulu boat yard I wanted to use would be closing for two weeks at just the perfect time.

When I arrived at the marina, everything that could have been wrong with my boat, short of sinking, was. The cockpit was full of water, the water level in the bilge nearly covered the cabin sole, and the batteries were flat. At first I couldn't get into the boat because the padlock had rusted shut from non-use. All this for $250 a month, frequent phone calls, and reassurances that they were looking after my boat. You can't imagine the indifference to boats and boaters in Hawaii – you have to see it firsthand.

I had left the flexible solar panel connected, thinking it would keep up with the bilge pump and charge the battery. Then while I was in Oregon I imagined the sun beating down, keeping the batteries happy. But no – once the bilge pump started, the solar panel lost the struggle for the batteries.

I took my boat to the yard and they hauled me out. I replaced some of the valves that pass through the hull, that seal my boat from the outside world. One of the original valves simply wouldn't close any more. The handle had fallen off another. I might use these valves to save the boat if

In the boatyard, Hawaii

a hose burst, so they have to work. And one can only replace them when the boat is out of the water.

I also cleaned and painted the boat's bottom, something I hadn't done before. I have a feeling I will be doing that regularly. This boat sails noticeably better with a clean hull.

I had a great sail recently. I wanted to sail from the Southwest corner of Molokai to Lahaina on the West side of Maui. It was blowing hard (30 knots) and I needed to go upwind, so I wasn't expecting smooth sailing.

But, since I had just painted the boat's bottom and was willing to trim sail a lot, I had a chance.

If you've been paying attention until now, you know you can't sail directly into the wind. When you want to go in the direction the wind is coming from, you have to sail off the wind about 45 degrees one side or the other, and switch sides occasionally. When you switch it's called "tacking." So I started out by sailing across the channel between Molokai and Lanai, then tacked back. This moved me several miles. I quickly realized it was going to be one of those days when the boat would sail itself – I just tied the tiller with a line and the boat sailed itself at just the right wind angle. Then I spent some time trimming sail for best efficiency.

When I got to Molokai again, I thought I might just make it past the East side of Lanai on the next tack, which would get me on my way to Maui. So I just tied the tiller again and let the boat sail itself. I spent my time whale watching.

You may not believe this, but during the next six hours the boat sailed itself across to Lanai, past a place reassuringly named Shipwreck Point (with a rusted freighter aground, lest anyone miss the point), and across the channel to Maui. At about sunset my boat had followed the wind to

Anchored at Tunnels Reef, Kauai, Hawaii

within one mile of my destination – and I hadn't touched the tiller all day. It was a great sail, not to mention that I saw several whales doing various whale-type things.

I am collecting more anchor stories, without honestly wanting to. In the 90 days since leaving the boatyard I've collected three. The first took place in Haleolono, on the South side of Molokai. Haleolono is one of my favorite anchorages. It's small but well protected, there is no town nearby, and there are some nice beach and backwoods walks. When I arrived I was alone in the bay, so I took the center and put out plenty of anchor chain.

But a three-day weekend was coming up and boats from Honolulu started appearing. Soon they packed the bay. On Saturday afternoon one of the last arrivals was a 20-foot sloop with three people on board.

I had a funny feeling about this particular boat, so I watched it. Then I noticed the Coast Guard Auxiliary flag on its mast. That's it, I thought, this guy will turn out to be the least competent sailor in the bay. This cynical observation came to me because of my experiences with the Civil Air Patrol in my time as a pilot. Supposedly paragons of virtue around airports, in my experience they tend to be the worst pilots, getting themselves killed in greater numbers than their vanilla counterparts and generally making life miserable for everybody, while occasionally going out to search for a downed plane. But I digress.

This guy motored around my boat a couple of times, even though there was no room to anchor near me. On the third time around I watched him, anchor in hand, pass across my anchor rode looking to windward. Without looking aft, he dropped the hook – right on top of my rode, and about 50 feet in front of me. Things deteriorated quickly after that. Within three minutes he had wrapped his line around my chain, around my boat, around his keel, and around his propeller. I watched it, I have thought it over since, and I still struggle to believe it, but there it is.

Now that he had no anchor and no motor, he began to drift toward my boat helplessly, and I pushed him off so we didn't crash. When he drifted aft and the amazing tangle of line grew taut, he began to realize his predicament. I saw it was time to put down the binoculars and do something.

First I rowed over in my dinghy, thinking I would raise his line and untangle it. At that point I didn't realize how bad things were. Failing at this, I put on my free-diving outfit and dove on his boat. The boat's skipper floated alongside wearing a snorkel and mask, and he poked with a boathook at eight turns of line around his prop. But he wouldn't go below the surface of the water! Meanwhile another crew member tugged and pulled on the line, apparently thinking about the rocky breakwater 200 feet aft, thus making it impossible to untangle it.

So I made a couple of suggestions to the crew, then unraveled the line in repeated dives on his boat, my boat, and my anchor. I thought to myself, this guy is way behind the situation – he hasn't acquired the water skills he needs to rescue himself from his own lack of anchoring skill. His boat's continued existence depends on the good will of those around him. I had seen examples of such utter dependency in automobile drivers before, but this was my first example on the water.

The setting for the second anchor story is a bay on Maui called Honolua, a pretty marine preserve on the Northwest part of the island. It's a small bay that can safely hold about three boats. I wanted to spend some time there, write letters and dive on the coral reefs, and when I arrived I found it empty. Perfect, I thought, no interruptions, nice solitary dives.

After I had been there a day, a big kona (South) wind started blowing, and I realized I was in a rather good place to ride out a storm, so I put out another anchor and decided to stay longer. I heard radio reports of awful wind and wave conditions at Lahaina, where I normally anchor.

On the second day of the storm I was napping in the afternoon when I heard someone trying to hail me. I came out on deck to see a boat directly astern, banging on the reef. The boat had no anchor and no motor.

Without thinking about what I was getting myself into, I tossed him a line and began to haul him off the reef. I had securely anchored my boat, using a full-chain rode to a 35 pound CQR (a kind of anchor – pronounced "secure") and a chain-and-rope rode to a 25 pound CQR, both buried in sand. I had gone down and inspected both anchors so I knew they were firmly set. Because the wind was gusting to 25 knots, I used a sheet winch to haul him off the reef. The skipper implored me to pull him off faster. I struggled to move him. Finally he reported he couldn't hear his boat smacking the reef any more. As he said this, his boat surged forward and crashed into my aft pulpit, mangling my windmill mount and satnav antenna.

Now I had hauled him off the reef and his boat had crashed into mine. If I drew him any more forward his bow would get intimate with my engine compartment. If I slacked off he would go back on the reef. On top of everything else the wind was getting stronger. So in a moment of acute insensibility I loaded my third anchor into my dinghy, motored over and attached it to his boat, then stretched it out over the bay. Once the hook was in place the skipper started hauling it in, bringing his boat near mine and smashing me a couple more times.

Once he was clear of my boat so no more collisions were likely, I suggested we take a break and plan our next move. It turns out he had an anchor but he managed to drop it over the side without first attaching it to his boat. So we dove for the anchor and made up a rode for it out of scraps of line he had on hand. But he didn't like that anchor. He wanted to keep mine for a while.

For the next three days I towed his boat around the bay with my dinghy and outboard, setting and moving various anchors, took him ashore through the breaking surf and back to his boat (his dinghy sank during his last sail), all in trying to get my anchor back so I could leave. When I finally got back to Lahaina it turned out he has collided with every boat he managed to approach, and his boat is a gallery of scars from previous collisions. The skipper is well-known, not to say notorious. Repairs to my boat take about a week.

The third anchor story is all mine. One day I stopped at Molokini Crater, a crescent-shaped bay on the way from Maui to the big island. It's one of my favorite stopping places and it breaks up an otherwise long passage. This particular afternoon the wind was strong and the waves were somewhat bigger than usual, and the crater was a lee shore (meaning the wind would blow you toward it). After I arrived and set my hook, I decided I was too close to the reef. So I started my usual single-handed procedure for changing position: go aft, start the engine, go forward, raise the anchor, go aft, motor to new position, go forward, drop the anchor, and so forth.

So I raised the anchor, secured it, and ran aft to motor away. I couldn't waste any time – as soon as the anchor came off the bottom, the wind started moving the boat toward the reef. I jumped into the cockpit, hit the throttle and grabbed the tiller in one motion. Then I glanced aft and realized the dinghy wasn't trailing behind as usual: after I raised the anchor the boat and the dinghy drifted together. So naturally the dinghy line got sucked into the prop. The line tightened and the motor stalled. Now I have no motor. So I sprint forward and drop the anchor again. Don't forget the boat is being blown ashore all this time – by the time the anchor takes hold, the hull is nearly touching the reef.

So now I have an emergency on my hands. The bottom of the boat is inches from the reef, the wind is trying to blow the boat onto shore, and the waves are breaking all around. I grab a diving mask and jump over the side, and for the next five minutes I use my pocket knife to cut the dinghy line away from the prop. On the third of these dives I stay down a long time, tugging and cutting the line and watching the hull come nearer and nearer the coral, so when I am ready to surface I am desperate for a breath of air. I reach over my head to bring myself up and manage to stab the dinghy with the knife, deflating one of its sections. But I have the welfare of a bigger boat to worry about. I pull my wet self aboard and start motoring against heavy seas and wind, dragging the anchor across the bottom. It takes about 20 minutes to move 500 feet.

The boat smacked the reef once during this episode, making a scar in the rudder, and I had to patch the dinghy, but there was no serious harm. I spent a few days wondering whether.I had fallen out of grace with the sea. I finally decided if I had, my boat would have shifted and squashed me against the reef, and the sea was merely reminding me of the small margin between a normal anchoring experience and disaster.

Notice how sympathetically I treat myself in this story of stupidity. I don't get to describe some stranger as a loser in the great genetic sweepstakes as I dive on his boat – it's my boat, it's my dumb predicament. But I handled the situation – no one could have helped me, no one was there.

Today is March 22. I plan to depart tomorrow for the Marquesas. Local sailors say it's not easy to get there from here. One must sail as close to the wind as possible for a long time. Maybe I'll get lucky and a storm will come through, giving a wind direction other than from the East. Otherwise I might have to accept the will of the sea and change course for Tahiti.

I have plenty of new books and I've provisioned the boat well (i.e., many kinds of cookies). My attitude toward this departure is different from my last. I was frankly petrified to go out from the mainland last May. I had so many rough-weather days during my winter practice sails off the Oregon coast that I was able to imagine a month of that kind of sailing. But my fears turned out to be exaggerated then, and the month of April is supposed to be mellow between here and points South.

I still have to go through the adjustment to solo sailing, after a week of frequent visits with other sailors here in Radio Bay. A woman traveling on another boat has raised my morale a bit – we visit and take walks (her boyfriend won't take time away from lacquering the wood on his showplace boat). Her acceptance makes me think I might only have to sail solo on the water.

March 25 – Day 3

On Day 1 I made one last trip to the post office, but a letter from Mary still hadn't arrived. It was a collection of things – a letter from a relative being remailed, some news stories, some bank forms. Now they'll have to mail it to the Marquesas or Tahiti, assuming it isn't lost altogether. Six days seems a reasonable amount of time to move a first-class letter from Oregon to Hawaii.

I raised anchor about 9:30 AM and crossed the Hilo breakwater at

10:15. Winds were very light near the island. Since I want to conserve fuel I motored only until there was enough wind to start moving on sail power.

The first two days were difficult – getting accustomed to being underway and a rough beat to weather. Most squalls seem to wait until the predawn hours, then spring up and oblige me to strike the windmill and reduce sail.

At night I've been running the radar, which is quite a power user, and using the windmill to power it. But the windmill is very noisy and becoming more so, as its mounting wears out under the stress of the boat motion mixed with its own gyroscopic forces. I am tempted to do without the radar in order to shut down the windmill. And I haven't seen any other vessels out here.

My original destination is looking more unlikely. The wind is East Southeast, which has me on a course of about 150 degrees true, too far to the Southeast to make the Marquesas. But I am going to sail as close to the wind as I can for a while longer in case the wind changes direction. I figure if I get due North of Tahiti without any change in the wind I will take that as a sign, bear off a little and pick up speed for Tahiti.

I am impressed by the boat's performance this close to the wind. When the seas aren't too rough, the boat moves at 4.5 knots while 50 degrees off the wind. Of course, that's after three days of sail adjustment.

I am using the wind vane to steer, so in principle the boat doesn't require any electrical power to carry on. I just wish the heavy seas didn't head me off so much – when the surface is smooth the headings tend to be more consistent and more Easterly as well.

March 26 – Day 4

There are plenty of squalls at night and in the early hours of daylight. They mess up the wind direction, so I have to work to keep moving the right way. Today – in the last 4 hours – I've seen 35 knots and 3 knots. But right now it's blowing about 15 - 20 knots and I've tuned the boat for that. I am doing about 5 knots while beating just 50 degrees off the wind. That's remarkable for this boat. The surface is somewhat smoother than it's been, that helps.

I also stopped using the wind vane – it wasn't very efficient, and the boat seemed to wander unnecessarily. I now am "automatically" guiding the boat with a piece of line tied around the tiller. I've learned that a well-balanced sailboat boat guides itself on a close reach, turning as the wind turns. All I have to do is adjust the course from time to time.

I now know about the wind vane that it doesn't work upwind and it doesn't work downwind unless the wind is very strong. I noticed I gained another half knot when I removed it, because of the energy taken by its searching motions and the extra paddle in the water. Maybe it will work abeam. I haven't sailed abeam enough to test it.

There's still no wind change that would favor the Marquesas. But the sailing has been getting better, so I am content to just beat as far East as I can, then when I get to the equator I'll decide whether to continue.

I made a sunshade for the cockpit out of a little tarp. It is a relief to sit beneath it when the sun is high.

The boat collects a lot of water during rough weather and seas. I discovered the beam scuppers are leaking. I must remember to take them apart and seal them when conditions allow. One of these leaks carries water right into a little electronic storage cabinet – everything I put there has to be in a plastic bag.

March 27 – Day 5

Yesterday afternoon and today I've devoted my time mostly to technical problems. I couldn't get the ham radio to tune its antenna consistently, so I began tracing the problem. I thought it would turn out to be an intermittent connection, but I finally realized it was a bad piece of coaxial cable. Of all things, a piece of wire doing different things at different times.

Cruising feels normal again. I can write on this computer without having to grip it with one hand and type with the other. When I am underway I begin to dwell in a fantasy in which I meet life's grand purpose by simply moving the boat through the water. Not too fast or too slow, and with small worry about getting any particular place. So I guess the secret role of the boat's electronic gear and its problems is to keep me from lapsing into a terrifyingly natural state.

The squalls have abated for now. The wind is from 80 degrees at about 17 knots. It seems to be moving from East to Northeast, slowly. That would be a favorable change – it would get me some of the Easting I've been trying for. But I can't go fast today because the water is rough.

Each evening I use the Big Dipper to locate Polaris, the North Pole star, to see how close to the horizon it has gotten. I expect I'll stop seeing it well before I get to the equator, lost in the clouds near the horizon.

The piece of line I have tied around the tiller is doing a perfectly good job "steering" the boat. I just set it for the wind angle I want and the boat follows the wind around at the chosen angle. If the wind swings South, I want to keep sailing while I hope for a change, and if it swings North, I want to follow that change too, and go as far East as I can. So the boat can follow the wind better than I can tell it to, and the boat guides itself better than any of my electronic tillers.

March 28 – Day 6

When I woke up this morning I noticed the radar had quit working. I saw this happen in Hawaii last summer, so I bought a replacement magnetron tube for it. The repair center suggested that as the most likely problem. I stowed the old magnetron after marking it as flaky.

The radar has been working perfectly for five days, all night long, every night. I thought I had fixed it for good.

This failure has some implications. I have been sleeping soundly, thinking the radar's alarm would alert me to an approaching vessel. I certainly can't fix it out here. So I have to accept a greater level of risk. Naturally I accept risk in sailing alone, but I don't want to increase the risk level. For this part of the journey the risk posed by sleeping is small – there just aren't any boats out here. But I will eventually have to replace the radar – since it takes five days to reveal its flaw, it would be cheaper to start over than to attempt a repair.

Rising temperatures seem to be making the radar worse – it has been getting significantly hotter over the past few days. Fortunately there have been fewer clouds as well. In the Inter tropical Convergence Zone near the equator the winds are light to nonexistent, there's plenty of moisture in the air, and it's really hot. So I'll have to be on the lookout for thunderstorms when I get down that way.

I decided to find the old magnetron and erase the nasty things I wrote on it when I thought it caused the radar problem. When I finally located it, I realized why my hand bearing compass, mounted on the midships bulkhead, had been giving bad readings. The magnetron was in a cabinet about two feet away – close enough for its powerful magnet to influence the compass. At night I look at the hand bearing compass to verify my heading without going on deck, and it had been obviously wrong for some time. I had completely forgotten about the magnetron stored nearby.

I am feeling somewhat more resilient about equipment failures. Before I start a voyage I am a total perfectionist – I have to finish all my shopping and repair lists before I'm happy. But as I get underway the true nature of sailing makes itself known to me – only through a shameful design oversight is anything still in one piece at the end of a voyage.

Before I start a passage, I think I can perfect the boat by simply locating some special piece of stainless hardware. Toward the end I am happy if I haven't fallen off and become shark food. But it's not an unpleasant change – after a week I begin to accept the torn and broken reality of sailing.

The trend toward Northeast wind is continuing, and the sea state is improving, although not as quickly as the wind. I am averaging about 4 1/2 knots, and my heading is gradually swinging to the East. If things continued to improve I might make the Marquesas after all.

I contacted Nancy Griffith and her shore station in Kealakekua Bay on the Big Island last night. Nancy is captain of "Edna," a big boat she uses for her island trading business. She had been underway when I visited there last month so I missed her. We talked mostly about computers – Nancy has been thinking about getting one to keep track of things in her cargo business. It was nice to hear her voice. I think I'll tune in again.

The ham rig is now back to normal. I was able to send a message home yesterday, saying among other droll things that no one should panic if they don't hear my messages – any number of things, now known to include bad wire, could stop the ham radio sea link in its tracks.

I have been using the radio more, listening to the B.B.C., thinking about making some amateur radio contacts. Also I have been watching movies. Last night I watched "The Wild One" with Marlon Brando. As I watched, I thought how terrifying a schoolyard killer or an airliner blown to bits over Scotland would have seemed to those who saw this film in the early '50's.

During my last long sail, a service called AFRTS (Armed Forces Radio and Television Service) was broadcasting domestic U.S. news feeds and other typical AM-radio fare on the short-wave bands. I would use it to keep up with American domestic news. But they have come up with some other way to transmit to overseas military bases, possibly using satellites. I'll miss that service. I will probably also discover that the B.B.C. and others provide better coverage of U.S. events.

March 29 – Day 7

The wind has backed around to 40 degrees and 17-20 knots, which is taking me more East than I expected a few days ago. I am now making calculations to see whether I can intercept the classical sailing course for the Marquesas. I am due North of Tahiti today. If I had given up hope on making the Marquesas I could bear off for Tahiti now, but I am going to try for my original destination. This plan requires that the wind not become Easterly again.

I found some rather big flying fish on deck this morning. I suppose I could try fishing, but if I caught something I would be honor-bound to eat it. Also I haven't worked out where on the boat I would clean it. Some sailors I met in Hilo said they just use a light nylon parachute cord with the tackle attached, instead of a rod and reel. That increased my enthusiasm for trying it, since I wouldn't have to dismantle the boat to gain access to the fishing rod. The lures and hooks happen to be within easy reach.

The radar gave a full night of service. I have a new theory about the radar failure that doesn't fault the radar itself – during the night the battery voltage falls too low, the radar gets into a peculiar state that shuts off the transmitter, the battery then recovers somewhat. Then I wake up to find the radar flaky, and an apparently good battery. This theory will be shot down if I let the windmill run all night and get a failure anyway.

I have a roller furler on this boat – this means I can roll up the jib without having to go out on deck to unhank the sail. Also I can change the jib's effective size. There are some ways to make a jib that rolls up without wrinkling, none of which apply to mine. I think most sailors would agree the convenience of changing the size of the jib just by pulling a line outweighs the problems caused by the wrinkles. I may modify this sail when I get to a sail shop – because the jib wrinkles it makes noise and luffs sooner than if it was smooth. With a smooth jib I would sail more efficiently and point closer to the wind.

I am running a single-reefed main, full staysail, and the jib. The jib makes the biggest difference to boat speed and performance because it gets the wind at a somewhat higher velocity than the other sails, and wire-mounted foresails are just more efficient than the others. People have been known to use only a foresail with good results, but in these rough conditions I think the boat balances better with the full set. Also when the wind increases I can strike the jib and run on just the staysail and main for a while.

Today I am at 12 degrees North, 149 degrees West. Ideally, if the winds had favored me up to now, I would be about 200 miles East of here, on the normal route to the Marquesas. The current can't be very strong here – the satnav positions give a true speed that differs only slightly from the average knot meter reading.

It just occurred to me that this passage would be unbearable in anything but a full-keel, heavy boat like this one. It's bad enough listening to the bashing the bow is taking, and having one rail in the water about a quarter of the time. I can hardly imagine what it would feel like in a fast, lightweight boat with a fin keel. No wonder cruising writers discourage use of this route, those that bother to mention it at all.

I haven't seen a bad squall for a few days now. As I mentioned earlier, there is an outward-moving radial wind pattern around all but the smallest clouds, even those with no rain, so if the cloud is to windward the wind picks up, if to leeward the wind slacks off. In an area with many squalls it can be tricky deciding which course to take, to avoid too much or too little wind, to use the wind pattern to advantage.

March 30 – Day 8

The winds are still from about 40 degrees, so I am going as far East as I can. I have decided that maintaining a speed of four knots isn't absolutely necessary for the time being, since I can go farther East if I allow the speed to drop. My overnight average was 3.7 knots, not bad considering I was only about 45 degrees off the wind.

I have set up a waypoint for myself at 6 degrees North, 140 degrees West. One writer suggests that the equatorial counter current (a band of ocean current that runs to the East instead of West) be used to get to 140 West before going South toward the Marquesas. I noticed that the Southern edge of the counter current is at about 6 degrees North – I figure if I make the waypoint I will make the Marquesas for sure. And, assuming the wind continues to cooperate, I'll make my waypoint in about 6 days.

The vane fell off the windmill last night. The windmill has been giving signs of wanting to fly apart nearly since I installed it. It vibrates a lot while running, and most of the shaking ends up wearing out the mount and attachments like the vane. My quick fix was to attach a line to the handle (which hasn't yet fallen off) and tie the line so the windmill faces the wind. Since the boat itself is weathervaning into the wind, this works as well as the windmill's own vane. Better, actually, if you count how much less noise the thing makes when I lash it down – now it can't rotate every time the boat rolls and shake the entire vessel with wasted gyroscopic energy.

I depend on the windmill to keep the batteries up to snuff during the night while the radar and masthead light are on. Again, the radar worked okay and the windmill was on all night. But it hasn't been particularly hot either. I'd like to know why the radar flakes out.

Somebody needs to design a real sailboat windmill. This one is an example of that time-honored American practice of selling a product that no one has tested in real conditions, and letting the customers discover what to change.

I had to take down my sunshade. The wind began tearing it apart, and it was a lot of trouble to get past, for example to go forward I nearly had to crawl on hands and knees. I think I'll have a piece of canvas made to size that can be removed easily.

It's not nearly as hot as it was a few days ago. There are some high clouds, the wind is about 17-20 knots again, nice conditions.

I am trying to identify a new bird, which might be a Laysan Albatross or a Red-Footed Booby. I have to watch for it with the binoculars some more, give it a good long look and compare it with the pictures in my bird book. I have also seen more Red-Billed Tropicbirds, a very pretty, mostly white bird.

I am a creature of habit. When I was in Hawaii I wanted that to go on forever, sailing from island to island, making friends, diving on beautiful reefs. Starting this sail was difficult, although not as difficult as leaving the mainland. I was miserable for about 48 hours, felt close to seasick each evening as darkness fell. I guess I will call it the usual transition malaise. Now I like being out here. Even though it's an upwind beat, I will probably not want it to end. I will read some books, make ham radio contacts, watch birds for days, maybe even put a fishing line in the water.

March 31 – Day 9

I bathed in salt water yesterday, using one of those plastic bags that lets the sun heat the water, with a shower spigot attached. I used salt water soap and even washed my hair – the whole thing worked. It felt great. I read that salt water was suitable for anything except your hair, but the special soap worked even for that. I used the cockpit as a bathtub (it sort of looks like a tub anyway) and hung the water bag on a line overhead.

The wind continues to back around, now coming from 25 degrees. This means the boat's heading is almost East, although because of leeway (the boat's sideways drift) the actual course is still somewhat Southeast. I'm doing all I can to take advantage of this wind while it lasts, pointing as close to the wind as I can, trading speed for direction of travel.

I am seeing more kinds of birds. Sometimes they hover over the boat, as if they are trying to guess what it is. But after watching them for a while, I realized they are also taking a ride on the air near the sails, like the dolphins that sometimes ride along on the bow. The dolphins take advantage of the mass of water pushed in front of the boat to increase their own speed, the birds glide on the air wave pushed up by the sails. Sometimes they seem to be trying to land on the mast, but they always come to their senses at the last moment.

Amateur radio has its moments. Yesterday I talked to someone sitting in a car in Salt Lake City. He was as surprised as I was.

This boat sure takes in water when the topsides get wet. I pump about 5 gallons of water out of the bilge every day, just from leaks through the scupper on the leeward side, the anchor rode lockers forward, the leaky portholes, and the hatch under the dinghy, which gives a squirt every time a wave breaks from windward on the bow.

Someday I am going to own a boat in which the builders have taken modest precautions against the possibility that the ocean might crawl up the sides of the boat from time to time. The only watertight hatch on this boat is the one I installed in Lahaina just a few weeks ago. After a rainstorm I realized nothing I could do to the cabin top hatch would ever stop it from leaking, so I bought a European-designed hatch that has a huge window in it. It's the same size as the original hatch, it just lets in more light and no water.

April 1 – Day 10

What a night! Thunder and lightning, wind varying from none to 30 knots, big waves from every direction, the works. I may get a repeat performance this afternoon and evening, but I hope not. Right now I'm headed East using the autopilot to steer with winds abeam. I'm making over 5 knots, highest speed in many days. I am using the autopilot because the wind is varying too much in direction to use my trusty line-on-the-tiller method.

I have started checking in to one of the amateur radio maritime nets. I give my position and some other important facts each day at a prearranged time. I decided since I was talking to hams every day I might as well try this also. It also gives me a chance to hear where other boats are sailing.

It is very wet, and there's no sunlight for the solar panels. I almost broke down this morning and started the engine, during a spell of no wind.

I'm glad I didn't – later I noticed every line on deck was trailing out the scuppers. One of them would surely have fouled the prop. So I went forward and cleaned up the mess, coiling and hanging every line.

It's exciting, watching the lightning after dark, counting off the seconds for the thunder, noticing whether any of the flashes is to windward, thinking how much electronic gear would get wiped out in a stroke.

April 3 – Day 12

There are some landmarks on this cruise, most of them just abstract curiosities. I passed the halfway point last night – now Hilo is farther away than Nuku Hiva (both about 1000 miles). There's 140 degrees West longitude, the point at which I officially can make it to the Marquesas, even though I am reasonably sure already – that happens about two days from now.

There are the equatorial counter current's North and South limits – At 8 degrees I think I may already be inside the borders of the current and getting a small additional Eastward push. There's the day when the sun is directly above, after which it will be to the North of the boat – about four days away, at 5 degrees North latitude (early April position). There are the dreaded doldrums, areas of no wind and occasional thunderstorms, where I may have to motor across, a privilege not extended to old-time sailors, who sometimes waited weeks for some wind to come along. There's the equator itself. All these are new experiences for me.

I still haven't decided how far East to go, before curving back West to Nuku Hiva. If the winds near the Marquesas are Southeast, I will be glad I went East a good long way, so as not to be sailing too close to the wind at the end of the crossing. If they are Easterly, that extra distance will be wasted.

I am still sailing with the tiller tied down. I have experimented with the electronic tiller from time to time, but decided I got the best results with the simplest method. If the wind changes direction, I still want to sail, so I might as well follow the wind rather than the compass. So far the desired compass course and the wind course have been very close.

Once I get reasonably past 140 West longitude I will either use the electronic tiller or the wind vane to get a sailing angle more abeam (wind from the side), for the equator crossing. I have been moving East at a relatively high latitude because the winds are strong and more Northerly than they supposedly are at the equator. I need to be sailing closer to a beam reach when I meet lighter winds, just to keep moving.

I finally saved an innocent flying fish. Late last night I was sitting out on deck with the boat lights turned off, looking at the stars, when I heard a fish-like racket in the starboard gunwale. I used the flashlight to find a flying fish that had just jumped on board and couldn't get back in the water. I grabbed his wing and tossed him back. I always wanted to do that.

April 4 – Day 13

Last night was very tough. I must have slept a total of two hours between squalls trying to blow me down, the staysail clew mount giving way, and assorted annoyances. I now have the staysail tied to its boom with a piece of line – inelegant, but I'm sailing.

The radar has been working all night, every night. I've been using what's left of the windmill to keep the batteries charged, and the association between high battery voltage and radar reliability is getting circumstantially reinforced.

Yesterday I put a fishing line in the water. Within an hour a fish had hooked itself, a story that would be more noteworthy if I had succeeded in getting it on board. Since then, no nibbles. The one that got away was just big enough to eat, too.

Today's weather chart shows me in the middle of a band of clouds, some of them squalls. But the charts are nearly 24 hours old when they are transmitted – right now the barometer is creeping up and it's almost clear. I hope I get to sail in the clear for a while, the squalls impede progress by requiring either sail reduction or all-night watches. Also the surface is rough near the squalls.

It's hot and humid. This would be easier to take if I could open ports or hatches, but occasionally the boat collides head-on with a wave, throwing water over the top of the cabin. I am happy to say the new European-style hatch hasn't leaked a drop.

I've decided (again) to sail as close to the wind as possible. If the winds lighten up near the equator I'll have to bear off to keep moving, so there may be no slack in this plan – I'll get to Nuku Hiva only by sailing a close reach all the way.

I want sleep. I want REM sleep. Lack of sleep magnifies the significance of every little crisis, and there are plenty of those.

April 5 – Day 14

Yesterday afternoon I was able to fall off the wind and increase speed because the wind had become even more Northerly than usual, such that for a spell I was actually moving away from the Marquesas. However, during the night a high pressure system moved into position to the Northeast and the wind shifted around to 110 degrees at 15 knots. My course is now South, more or less. I hope this isn't the last of the Northeast wind, or my well-laid plans will be dashed.

A classic of sailing – one day things look rosy, wind favorable, waypoints falling one by one, why not fall off the wind and pick up speed, no need to pinch the wind so hard any more, next day can't move an inch to the East, need to desperately.

I don't have the satnav position yet this morning, but I think I am on three of my landmarks today – the South limit of the equatorial counter current (near 5 degrees North latitude), 140 West longitude (I hope), and the sun directly overhead.

The wind isn't that strong but the swell is now astern, so the boat is moving briskly. Too bad it isn't moving Southeast.

But this course will take me so close to the Marquesas that I'll tack my way in if I have to. It's just a question of elegance, the 2000 mile curved passage that lands me neatly on target, a giant version of my afternoon sail between Molokai and Maui.

April 6 – Day 15

The wind change I saw yesterday may have been an abrupt and permanent shift to the Southern hemisphere's Southeast trade wind pattern. Looking at the log entries and calculating for true wind I see that the wind changed from 50 degrees to 105 degrees magnetic, two nights ago. And it hasn't changed since.

It doesn't say anywhere that the shift from one trade wind to the other has to happen right at the equator. Anyway, notwithstanding the disadvantages of this new wind, the fact that it happened all at once may mean there's no band of doldrums to have to motor through.

And to think I started out looking at the daily weather charts for clues to wind direction. Having spent weeks in winds not marked on the charts, I now realize the chart makers simply draw wind lines around the isobars, clockwise around highs, counterclockwise around lows (in the Northern hemisphere). They have no way to discover what the wind direction is, only what the simplified meteorological model suggests it should be.

They should tell people the charted wind velocities are no more than educated guesses based on pressure differentials and a handful of observations, and the wind directions are fairy tales. Today, for example, the chart calls for an 80 degree wind, when it's 110 degrees – but then it also called for 80 degrees a few days ago, when it was 30 degrees. I guess in an age of diesel-powered boats, the wind direction isn't a weather forecaster's top priority.

But the charts are useful for locating bands of squalls and thunderstorms. That information seems accurate. Of course they just transfer those markings from the satellite cloud-cover image. For this they need no insight into the workings of nature.

Today I am out of the band of clouds on the chart, so I'm hoping for clear weather and no cloud-induced wind changes. The wind usually drops off in the early afternoon (the opposite of the pattern I am used to), then picks up again in the evening and blows steadily all night. If I'm headed for doldrums, the afternoon wind pause will deepen. I've been watching this pattern very carefully.

I haven't been able to contact the radio link to my house for several days now. Conditions on the 20 meter amateur radio band haven't been very good – I hope that's the only problem. I have been checking into the maritime radio network each evening – it's a pleasant ritual. I get to hear where the other boats are (there are 12 in transit, mostly from Mexico), what weather they're having, that sort of thing.

I've been working on my tendency to pick a problem, preferably one about which nothing can be done, and worry about it constantly. The close reach, for example. I keep thinking, I could have let the boat sail Northeast, that last day of Northern-hemisphere trades when the wind actually blew from the North for a while. I could figure out a different sail plan and pinch up higher than I am. That sort of thing. It's the tinkerer in me – I can't seem to leave things alone.

In computer software development, tinkering is the essence of the experience, although it explains why nothing ever gets done on time. I like having my own personal software development projects with no customers and no deadlines. Then I'll tinker to a kind of saturation point, when it occurs to me that even I won't be able to detect any improvement from the tinkering.

So I am trying to curb the tendency (even though, if you think about it, that's tinkering too) by giving myself permission to enjoy the ride nature's giving me, indulge myself in a book, talk on the radio a lot when the solar panels are making extra power, generally enjoy the place I am in.

After that one fish bit my hook during the first hour it was in the water, no more bites. Maybe fish are psychic. Maybe I should change lures – naah. Apart from the fact that's another tinker, I probably wouldn't be in the mood for fish if I caught one.

April 7 – Day 16

Yesterday and today the wind has backed (turned counterclockwise) enough that I don't feel a sense of impending doom, as in being blown completely away from the Marquesas. I am using this new wind direction to make some more Easting, so I have some leeway, this time quite literally. Before it became an English idiom, "having leeway" meant having some maneuvering room on the windward side of a land mass or obstacle, such that you could sail past without going aground.

I did some laundry today – it had started to pile up. I washed the clothes in the sink using Joy and salt water, rinsed once in salt and then in fresh. Now it is all hung to dry on some lines strung about on the stern. I wanted to dry them the best way (wind and sunlight) but I didn't want them sprayed by breaking waves, so my makeshift lines are well aft. The wind is a bit stronger than I wanted, but noon is approaching and the wind has been slacking off in the early afternoon for several days now. Once I've collected my laundry the wind can blow hard again. I don't want to litter the Pacific with my T-shirts.

The wave heights seem to have decreased over the last few days, so I am getting a higher boat speed for a given amount of wind. The sailing has been improving since a few days ago, when I watched enormous thunderheads rising into the late afternoon sky, like huge inflatable buildings in a dream city skyline. I enjoyed the sight, but knew it would be a rough night. It was.

Now I see scattered clouds in the afternoon and plenty of stars at night. I know there's another band of squalls near the Marquesas, so I'm glad for this interlude of calm sailing.

April 8 – Day 17

Today I am within a degree of the equator, and sometime late tonight I cross over into the Southern hemisphere. The wind has been changing direction, but I still am making some Easterly progress every day. I think I can start aiming for the Marquesas at about 7 degrees South, instead of riding close to the wind with the tiller tied down as I have been doing.

The wind blows hardest at dawn, and softest about 3 PM. I have been shaking out a second reef on the mainsail for daytime, and putting it back in for night – ordinarily I can furl and unfurl the jib to control the overall size of the sail plan, but winds that vary between 8 and 25 knots require more than that.

I am thinking about my plan for this year – the Southern hemisphere's cyclone season is ending (apropos, I just heard a report of a storm near Fiji), and it begins again in November. So I have to (1) tour all the islands and tie up in New Zealand in November, to stay and visit through the cyclone season, or (2) move somewhat more quickly and get past Australia before November. There are several alternatives like anchoring in the South Pacific for the next cyclone season, a somewhat more risky plan.

I am also trying to decide whether to travel by way of South Africa or the Mediterranean. One cruising book I have with me makes the Med sound wonderful – I hadn't seriously considered it until I read that chapter. All I have to do I slip through the Red Sea without being kidnapped by terrorists. That sounds easy from the perspective of the Pacific Ocean near the equator, when I haven't seen any vessels since Hilo. I wonder how I'll feel as I pass through the Suez Canal?

Dolphins playing on my bow

Some dolphins came to play yesterday evening. They swam around the boat and jumped in the air – an unbelievable dolphin show.

I've been looking for the star Polaris in the evening, but there's usually clouds near the horizon. I saw it last at 4 degrees North.

April 9 – Day 18

I'm now in the Southern hemisphere. I am East of 139 degrees West longitude so I've started to use the electronic tiller to set a more direct course for the Marquesas. Now that I'm not pinching the wind so tightly the speed is going up – 5 1/2 knots at the moment. I feel bad about giving up the boat's natural steering, it was very effective over about 1500 miles of ocean.

The weather has been pleasant – the wave heights are decreasing, no squalls in days, mostly sunny weather and consistent winds. My sleep is regular, thoughts clear.

I sat and watched the crescent moon last night and thought about vision. Supposedly our eyes are never better than when we are about ten years old. I read about an experiment conducted by an astronomer who knew this – he compared the ability of young and old people to make out the crescent of the planet Venus, a very difficult object to see with the naked eye. To prepare his subjects he had them look through a telescope at Venus, then look with the naked eye, then report what they saw.

His telescope was made for astronomy, not for baseball games, so there were no extra lenses or prisms to make things appear right side up. As a result the telescope reversed the image of Venus, made it appear upside down. Most of the young observers politely pointed this out, but most of the older observers didn't – they incorrectly believed they saw the same orientation in the sky as the eyepiece.

Because Venus is so difficult to see, the experiment demonstrated that the visual acuity of the young is even greater than had been supposed. It also demonstrated that people don't want to admit that they can't see what they can't see.

When I was ten years old I picked apricots for spending money, then bought a small astronomical telescope. It had a three-inch mirror mounted in a cardboard tube. It was a very modest telescope, but I was a very proud owner.

I spent hours looking at the moon's craters, Saturn's rings, Jupiter, star clusters. That telescope, and my time spent gazing through it, was one of the wedges driven between me and all the things I should have been doing. I was becoming a misfit – I could absorb enough in a day to pass the school's examinations, and was too arrogant and insubordinate to play along with the slow pace of the classroom.

They punished me for things that seem even more ridiculous now. Reading ahead, for example. I was supposed to control my reading pace, apparently to match that of the slowest reader in the class. Notwithstanding the benevolent educational theory behind this practice, I wonder how much benefit that slow reader derived from my whispers and baleful stares.

I also wanted to write before that was on the curriculum. Denied pencil and paper, I scratched words into my desk. That was the first time I was taken to the principal, although he would see me regularly in years to come.

I was tugged resisting past a flagpole and manicured lawn into a large building from which I expected never to return.

I whined loudly as I was pulled into position before a big desk and a bigger male stranger (until then I didn't know there were men in schools). This giant male human tried to soften his delivery as he explained that I mustn't scratch marks into my desk, even though generations of misfits had already recorded their frustration there. I sadly missed most of his speech, being in a state of such terror that I wished only to hide somewhere dark. But I did grasp that I mustn't think for myself.

It was with episodes like this that my personal investment in discovery and the public education system were separated forever. My native curiosity was thwarted far too often in those paste-scented chambers, but never more eloquently than by the teacher who said, "Young man, don't be so smart!"

What kind of person would I have become, had mischievous intelligence been cultivated, directed, by an educational system less completely aligned with the interests of the state? It was certainly true that I was of no use whatever to the state (except in the sense that a robbery victim is useful to a robber), but what other discoveries might I have made? What other things uncovered?

After I exhausted the telescope's possibilities, I developed a passion for electronics. At the height of this stage I would collect my neighbors' broken television sets and turn them into powerful amateur radio transmitters. Over time my designs improved until it was possible for the police to summon their patrol cars while I was on the air.

I remember one particular Saturday morning, at a time when my economic and social prospects were as close to zero as the science of numbers allows, sitting in a chilly garage before anyone else had risen, turning knobs on a homemade radio receiver, listening to voices from across the ocean.

At that moment, normal boys my age were gathering in baseball fields, or lost in contemplation of a particular girl, or discussing the insides of automobile engines. I might as well have come from another planet, surrounded by vacuum tubes glowing orange in my dark room. When I finish my transmitter, I thought, my signal will reach across mountains and valleys. People will tune in my dots and dashes. My voice will shake the wheat in Kansas.

I was a weird kid. After I took an I.Q. test in fifth grade, impressions of me among my friends became evenly divided between those who didn't know about the I.Q. test and those who did. For those who didn't I was a stupid nerd, ha ha. For those who did I was an egghead, ha ha.

The annual school spelling bee provided an opportunity for what they now call cognitive dissonance among the former group. Some of my teachers regularly described my dropout status to bring a straying soul into line. These teachers lived in fear that I would again become the school's top speller, an occasion I contemplated with relish.

An educational system like this bears bitter fruit. It taught me that obedience equals stupidity, since I couldn't simultaneously obey and learn anything interesting. And the method is self-defeating for the society that permits it – potentially creative people end up either obedient empty shells or lifelong rebels.

My jib is starting to shred. I should never have used this particular sail on what I knew would be a long upwind haul, it's too light for these strong winds. I will repair it in Papeete – it should hold together until then.

After several days of looking back at the bright red flies at the end of the fishing line and seeing no fish, I decided to haul out the line and look more closely. It turns out the flies and hook shafts were there, but both hooks were broken off at the curve! Some big fish have apparently gotten away. I immediately felt stupid for not having investigated earlier.

ROCKET SCIENTIST TOWS BROKEN HOOK 500 MILES
I was busy reading and eating cookies, he says.
Film at 11.

I have added a bungee cord to the line to absorb the shock of a fish taking the hook. Maybe that will prevent the hook from breaking, and secure the fish next time.

April 10 – Day 19

Well, again something enormous ripped a brand new hook off the end of my line. The loop at the end of the stainless steel leader was still closed, meaning the hook's own loop broke. Apparently the bungee cord couldn't absorb enough shock. I've put on some larger hooks. These big, mysterious fish should make a tasty meal, assuming I bring one in.

The wind is now aft of the beam, for the first time on this crossing. I have dropped the staysail and am running a billowing genoa and a reefed main. I don't need to move East any more – I can relax my sails and sail a more Southerly course. About 7 degrees South I will turn directly to my destination.

These long passages make me optimistic about relationships. At this distance from land I look forward to meeting new people, forming friendships, lasting associations. I suppose it would be more convincing if I showed such optimism on land.

I may be more enamored of the principle than the thing. After all, notwithstanding all my chatter about the fulfillment potential of a relationship, most of my choices reduce my suitability (or availability) for one. I guess I would rather have the unfettered principle than about half the relationships I've experienced.

My life was simpler once. When I panhandled and slept on rooftops, anyone who got involved with me had no obvious ulterior motive. Now the myth of the male provider and the gingerbread cottage permeates all my relations.

My candor makes things worse. I come from a family in which secrets and outright lies did enormous harm, so when I decided what kind of person I would be, I placed frankness high on the list. So when someone asks me what I do for a living, I tell them. Maybe in the interest of cultivating less burdened relationships I'll become a hypocrite and throw out one of my cherished standards – I'll learn to lie. Or maybe the IRS will figure a way to clean me out, and I can resume panhandling and sleeping on rooftops.

April 11 – Day 20

Late last night the wind died, then the squalls began. The wind velocity varied between none and 30 knots. All night long I started and stopped the engine, broke out and struck sails, and was generally miserable. Now I'm way behind on sleep. I am in a relatively normal area right now, but there are cloud buildups fore and aft. I hope I get to approach the Marquesas in a state other than exhaustion – the chance of meeting another boat is greater, and there are outlying islands and reefs.

I am 192 miles from Nuku Hiva now, so if I can keep the speed up I expect landfall within 48 hours. O please let it be a nice couple of days...

There is an incredible number of things that broke on this crossing. I need to rebuild the windmill vane. I need to find and seal some topside leaks (something you have to be out in snotty weather to test). The autopilot just ripped out one of its mountings – fortunately I have two. But I have to think up something new for that mounting. The genoa needs extensive repair, which may have to wait until Tahiti.

Even though it nearly self-destructed on the way, the genoa was useful on this trip. Most of the time I had to roll it up too far for it to work efficiently, which is why it began to tear, but when the beam and aft winds started a couple of days ago it really began to move this boat. Now I'm averaging over five knots and I saw a reading over six knots when the surface was calmer.

I am now well East of the Marquesas and tonight I am going to start pointing directly, using my satellite navigator full-time as I come close to land.

April 12 – Day 21

It was another snotty night – a succession of big blows, torrential downpours, and calms, meaning I had to be up the entire night adding or reducing sail or starting the engine. Right now it's overcast, the wind is very light, and the sea is high and confused. It's not great weather for an arrival.

I expect to anchor at Nuku Hiva either late tonight or early tomorrow. I will probably have to stay up again to make the landing safely. There's nothing worse than trying to sleep while careening toward a land mass.

April 13 – Day 22

I crossed into Tahiohae Bay at 5:30 AM, so the enroute time was 20 days, 20 hours and change. Quicker than I expected. I am getting ready to go ashore and visit Customs.

I am sure when I've had some sleep the list of repairs won't seem so intimidating. I've added the mainsail top track slide to the list. It must have torn out during one of the squalls.

It's pretty here...

{ 4 }

Marquesas to Tuamotus and Tahiti

April 23 – Day 2

T his is the second day underway from the Marquesas to the Tuamotus. It's a different kind of sailing than I am accustomed to: beam reach, six knots plus change in the daylight hours, five knots after dark. It's also going to be short: four or five days.

The Marquesas was a tough place. I (and most yacht people I met) spent most of our time visiting each other's boats so as not to be eaten alive by insects on shore. People collected rainwater because it was safer than the water in town. Several people contracted Dengue fever from the mosquitoes. As time passed we found fewer and fewer reasons to go ashore.

My shopping list is long. There was virtually nothing in the Marquesas: no food, no supplies, restaurants only sometimes. But friendly people and a fruit that looks like a grapefruit and tastes like an orange.

My Heart inverter (a gadget that makes house current on a boat) got destroyed one windy day. I left the windmill running while visiting another boat, and while I was off the boat a big thunderstorm hit, with gusts of 50 knots. Many boats were damaged. Anyway, my theory is the windmill started delivering a lot of current and tripped a circuit breaker, isolating the inverter and the windmill in the same circuit, separate from the batteries. This allowed the windmill to deliver a very high voltage, which overloaded the inverter. I hope I can find some parts for it in Papeete.

Meanwhile I have to run the Honda generator to show a movie. As I expected, my little theater is making Selene popular in the anchorages.

One of the jobs I took on in the Marquesas was to change the whisker pole's storage location from the starboard walkway to the mast. I realized I was spraying the fittings for the fourth or fifth time with lubricant to unseize them, and I have yet to use the pole this year. I decided salt water was splashing it too often on the walkway.

I came up with an elegant mounting that involved drilling a few more holes in the mast. Then, the next time I tried to turn on the running light, it wouldn't light. I tried the anchor light. It wouldn't either. It almost goes without saying that the third light on the mast, the strobe, was also dead.

I worked an entire day and climbed the mast about six times, first thinking I had broken some wires in the mast, then being completely mystified, then realizing someone had installed the masthead light incorrectly, so that if the running light burns out,  *Selene from above* the other lights won't light either, like old-fashioned Christmas tree lights. All that was wrong was a burned-out bulb, which chose to burn out immediately after I worked on the mast, making me think I caused the problem. I never looked down on my boat so often in so short a time.

In compensation, at one point I looked down from the mast just in time to see a big manta ray cruise by – about a five-foot wingspan, completely black, swimming just below the surface. Quite a sight from forty feet up.

From time to time I think about sailing, whether overall I am enjoying it. It certainly has its moments – last night there was a nearly full moon shining on what can only be called a kind sea. Small waves, light wind, satisfactory speed and smooth boat motions. A classical, but rare, picture of sailing.

After the Marquesas visit I know why some people try to sail forever and never arrive anywhere – who pretend they have a destination in paradise, when in truth the sail is itself the destination.

April 25 – Day 4

The wind has declined somewhat. Yesterday around sunset it nearly died. The jib started flapping and wrapped around the mast steps – ripped my sewing to shreds. I hope there's a sail loft in Papeete.

On that subject I have noticed the wind frequently declines around sunset (if blowing from the East) and I have a theory about it. When the sun is on the horizon, my boat is between a cooling air mass to the East (where the sun has just set) and a still-warm air mass to the West. The air mass to the East starts cooling and contracting just like a little low-pressure region. This effect reduces the wind velocity for about an hour around sunset, then the wind builds up again.

Naturally I expect a reverse effect at dawn, and in fact I remember while sailing from Hawaii being regularly awakened by a sudden increase in wind as the sun made its appearance.

The radar quit again. I think it responds to both low voltage and high temperature. The company that made it should be ashamed of themselves. I resisted the temptation to drill some holes in the case for ventilation, realizing that would also let moisture into the works. The cure might be worse than the disease.

I have been talking to other boats on this route every day. We compare notes about wind and weather. Some are people I met in the Marquesas and are headed where I am.

This sail has been beautiful. The weather has been mild and consistent, very few clouds, easy seas. I'm not pumping gallons of water out of the bilge every morning. The smooth conditions probably explain why I am not in a grand funk about my shredded jib, which, by the way, sails much better than it looks.

I expect to reach Manihi Atoll sometime late tonight, not a good arrival time. I will either heave to (stay in place on the sea) or anchor outside the reef until morning. I've been told the water there is clear and the diving is great.

I have been thinking lately about the rapid entropy of sailboats, the rate at which everything decays. For me that offers a bigger contrast than most sailors, because I write computer programs. Computer programs get better with time (up to a point, anyway) and don't decay at all because the machine regenerates them electronically. Once you write a worthwhile bit of code you can set it aside and it will always be there, just as you left it. You can use endless copies of it in different programs. Each copy will work perfectly, assuming the original did.

So programming attracts me intellectually because a program is like a good joke: it keeps working, so I keep using it. It attracts me emotionally because it tells a tale of immortality: little functional elements that do the same thing forever. Many years after their purpose has come to seem silly, they spring to life with the same spare tenacity, making the same inquiries, cranking out the same responses.

I want to adjust to the sailboat reality, but not give in entirely. I favor it because I live in a body that is more like a sailboat than a computer. I disfavor it because it confronts the idealism of the well-crafted program.

I don't want to give up the passion of the all-night programming session, so I won't paint my entire world with sailboat pragmatism. I don't want to suffer unnecessary agonies either, so I won't apply a meticulous, infinitely patient work style to this boat. A perfect example is my sewing the jib for six hours in Nuku Hiva. It was a great job of hand-stitching, but it all ripped out in five minutes yesterday when the wind changed. I should have looked at the jib in all its raggedness and resolved to do something about it later – much later.

May 14 – Rangiroa Atoll

For the last two weeks I've been having great adventures among the Tuamotus, and meeting new people.

At Manihi Atoll I met a Canadian family that built their own boat out of wood from their own land – they sail with no fancy equipment. They have a sounding line to measure depth, and they reduce their sextant sights with pencil and paper. They are also very likable people.

But first things first. I entered Manihi Atoll early in the day, after looking at the pass through binoculars for a while.

A digression. The best time to enter an atoll is about noontime (so you can see the coral clearly), at high tide (maximum depth) and slack water (so you aren't being sucked onto the rocks by a strong current). On a given day you try to choose a time when at least some of these conditions exist. But I was tired – I didn't want to wait until noontime, or find out when slack water was. I wanted to have breakfast and take a nap.

The first part of the pass was well marked and deep – 70 feet. But the far

Typical scene inside a coral lagoon

side opened out very wide, no markings, very shallow, incoming current very fast (because I didn't wait for slack water). So I had to choose to go to port or starboard around a marked obstacle in the middle of the pass – on the port side the water was broken up into ripples and mini-whitecaps, on starboard the water was smooth. I thought, "If this was a river the smooth part would be the deep water." So I decided it was deeper on the starboard. Wrong. Before I knew what was happening I was in four feet of water. A coral head scraped some paint off the port side of my keel.

Fortunately I bought a boat with a full keel and keel-hung rudder, so I only scratched my bottom paint. So I list safe grounding on coral among my boat's advantages. There are some things I dislike about it, such as its tendency to let water in too many places – but it tolerates stupidity rather well.

Also my conversations with other boat owners make me realize I didn't spend very much for it. I have been aboard a number of boats that were bargain-priced at a quarter million. I have also seen some boats that had no business being sailed across the ocean.

One such boat is anchored here in Rangiroa – because the atoll surrounds the anchorage, the waves are tiny. But the boat, a Cal 40, rolled fiercely and perpetually. It is simply too light for its size, and it has a nearly round bottom to achieve high downwind speeds – so it rolls in the slightest swell. It was awful being on it in this protected anchorage, so I found it difficult to imagine sailing it across the ocean.

So my experiences in the Tuamotus are reassuring me about my choice of boat. One author thinks a full-keel boat like this is essential for operations near coral reefs.

Rangiroa is my third atoll, after Manihi and Ahe. The local people at Ahe were friendly – they held several feasts while I was there. Some of the boat people and I played music on various instruments, and the local people played also. The atoll closely resembled the mental picture most people have of a tropical paradise. I spent a day walking from motu to motu, wading through tide pools, drinking out of coconuts and pretending to be an island explorer.

But Rangiroa is the best. The water is much clearer here, and there are fish everywhere. I joined another boat and we decided to cross over to the less-traveled South side. We spent three days diving with Hawaiian reef spears (a kind of pole with a rubber sling attached) spearing big, slow fish called "groupers" and having fish dinners in the evenings. Since I can hold my breath for a long time I ended up being the hotshot fisherman.

I also decided to practice old-style sailing. Since I was inside an atoll I raised anchor, sailed to the South side, and reanchored without using the engine at all. I have always wanted to do that

Playing music at Ahe Atoll, author at center

– I tried it a couple of times in Hawaii but the wind would die at some point and I would have to motor. So I made the entire round trip without engine power. I felt like a real sailor. I am sure this arrogance will evaporate, but it was a momentary sense of achievement.

I am somewhat tough on myself, so when something goes right like this, I come up with a justification for humility. In this case it's easy – having a motor on a sailboat is an incredible luxury. People have been sailing at the mercy of the wind for millennia, and many still do. But then I did it single-handed. On the other hand, Joshua Slocum sailed all the way around the world single-handed, without a motor or any electronic gadgets to help him. Oh well.

Tomorrow I leave for Papeete. I have a long list of repairs and purchases, including rebuilding the genoa and buying a new outboard motor. My outboard sounds like a robot complaining about taxes.

May 16 – Enroute to Papeete – My Birthday

This is the second consecutive year I've had my birthday while underway. Last year at this time I was on my way to Hawaii, feeling rather blissful in my first trade wind sail.

Somebody ought to collect boat stories and print them in a scholarly journal. I keep hearing new ones, the majority having as their theme the corrosive effect boats have on relationships. It seems that boats eat relationships faster than salt water eats boats.

Here's an example of such a story. I am using this example not because I think it's true, but because it's typical – it doesn't describe actual events as much as reveal the attitudes of the people who tell the story. Even if it's true, this story gets retold for reasons other than truth.

It goes like this: A man and a woman plan a voyage. They go out for practice sails and everything is peachy keen. The big day arrives and they set sail for parts unknown. But just when they are nearly out of sight of land, the woman goes into some sort of trance, jumps overboard and starts swimming toward the disappearing land mass.

She is plucked out of the sea and the departure is aborted. After lengthy conversations and debriefing, they decide it was all a fluke brought on by anxiety, and everything is all right. They set out again, and she jumps overboard again.

This story has a big serving of one of the major themes of sailing stories – how women aren't cut out for a life at sea, how women can't confront their anxiety about it, etc.

The sea story that makes women look foolish is just one element of sailboat politics. The most important element is that most boat owners are men – and not just any men, but very often men who want to be captain of something, anything. If women's increasing status makes you anxious, you can always buy a sailboat and set sail for the 19th century.

Based on my conversations with sailing women, I think it is generally true that women can't think of anything they would rather do than sail the South Pacific, and they are already accustomed to dealing with male behavior, so they sign on with a boat owned by a man. But some of these women are unprepared for the combination of close quarters, isolation, and the streak of arrogance that commanding a vessel brings out in men. It's sort of like taking your favorite radio into a closet and turning the volume all the way up.

For balance I have to report that I meet many women who are out here because they want men to order them about – who knew exactly what they were signing up for.

There's an advertisement in the boat magazines for a sailing school run by women, for women. They say "No yelling!" I hear they are doing well. If no yelling is taken as a sign of a well-run boat, I would flunk. I sail alone and I yell at myself regularly. Someone who yells at himself can't be expected to resist yelling at someone else.

As I visit anchorages I envy those with companionship. I confessed that to a woman visitor, who quickly told me I was the subject of great jealousy among the men I know – I was sailing solo, I could do as I pleased, no crew disagreements. Apparently many sailors regard solo sailing as the only true form. I hadn't thought of that.

I have made some friends among the boats, which after all are moving toward the same destinations at roughly the same speed. Part of the reason is that I fix broken things – in some instances very important things like satnavs and radios. Another reason is I don't engage in threatening behavior, like focus my attention solely on women. And I make good conversation.

I just realized I have visited about 20 boats and I'm the only solo sailor. Of course, I could make a similar remark about the town I come from – apart from me almost none of my friends voluntarily lives alone.

Since it's my birthday I'm thinking about larger time scales. What will happen to me? Will I have better relationships in the future than the past? Or have I become a sugar daddy forever, doomed to endless frustration at the hands of people who just want money? Is this sailing adventure just one part of a future in which I am no longer a solo voyager? Or will I stay a single hander in life as well as sailing?

Who knows? Who cares?

Ah. I can just make out Tahiti on the horizon. I should be ashore tonight. I think I'll announce it's my birthday and shame someone into taking me out.

{ 5 }

Tahiti to Darwin

June 20 – Day 2, Bora Bora to Tonga

This is the second day out from Bora Bora. I spent about a month in French Polynesia, equally divided between Papeete, Moorea and Bora Bora. Papeete was awful, but I needed to get supplies and mail so I had no choice about the time spent there.

I have an amazing anchor story that happened to me in Papeete. After you read it you won't believe it happened, but it did – honest.

To moor in Papeete you drop an anchor some distance out, then back up toward shore and throw out a couple of lines – they call this "Tahiti Style." It's not easy to accomplish while single-handed, and when the boats are packed together it's a work of art.

Tahitian landscape

When I arrived in Papeete it was a windy afternoon – I decided to wait for morning to try the Tahiti-style mooring, so I just dropped my anchor in the middle of the bay and rowed the dinghy ashore. The next morning there was no wind at all, so I got ready. I neatly coiled two shore lines, placed them strategically in the cockpit, and tied the dinghy alongside so it would be available but not tangle in the propeller. The boats were close together so I couldn't afford to be sloppy. I planned my every move.

I chose a place for the anchor, dropped it, and swung around so my stern was toward shore. I gently motored into position and put the throttle in neutral. Now the hard part: I had to get two lines ashore before I drifted sideways and hit another boat. So I got in the dinghy and rowed one of the lines ashore, tied up the dinghy, jumped ashore and tied the line. Then I went back to the dinghy, untied it, and rowed out to the boat for the next line.

Now I had an audience, since one rarely tries to do all this stuff alone. I took the second line and rowed ashore. About ten feet from shore, the line grew tight. So I was either too far from shore or I just didn't choose a long enough line. But maybe, thought I, the line is just tangled or hung up on something. I'll give another pull and break it loose. So I gave another tug on the oars.

What happened next defies belief, and a Hollywood special effects team would have charged a lot to make it happen. What I didn't realize is the line was wrapped around the throttle lever, and when I tugged on the oars the line pulled the throttle into the full-reverse position. My boat's engine came to life in a blast of noise and black smoke, suddenly and purposefully heading toward shore. I couldn't believe my eyes. My sixteen thousand pound, unoccupied sailboat was backing up, full throttle, toward a pile of rocks. This gives "solo sailing" a whole new meaning.

I was sitting in a rowing dinghy, about 100 feet away, trying to absorb what was happening. Before I could get the dinghy turned around and row back, the boat raced toward certain destruction on the rocks – and then stopped, drawn up short by the anchor. Unable to destroy itself against the pilings, the boat consoled itself by chewing up the lines. It took about an hour of diving to unravel the tangle of lines, which the propeller had efficiently twisted into a ball during about 15 seconds at full throttle.

I don't know whether I am becoming a better sailor with experience, but my anchor stories are certainly becoming more baroque. Ah, for the good old days when the anchor would hang under some coral, requiring an extra 30 seconds of effort to pull free and sail off into the sunset.

Theft was a big problem in French Polynesia. Anything that wasn't bolted to the sidewalk was stolen. I hardly got to ride my bike because something would be stolen from it at the slightest opportunity. By the time I left it was mostly replacement parts. It still can't be ridden because the seat was stolen on Bora Bora.

Chain is commonly used on dinghies to discourage theft. The chain joins the dinghy, the motor, and a solid part of the dock. One thief was so angered by this method that he destroyed someone's motor and dinghy with a blunt instrument.

Moorea and Bora Bora were beautiful, as expected, but the constant thefts and the risk of mosquito-borne Dengue Fever meant fewer explorations of the land than I would have liked.

I got a chance to use my hotshot Hawaii-style wind surfing board when the wind blew hard at Bora Bora. It was a fast ride in a pretty place.

My tiny 1 1/2 horsepower Evinrude outboard died shortly before I got to Tahiti, so I replaced it with a 4 horsepower Mariner. I noticed nearly everyone had a Mariner in spite of stores filled with other brands, so I took this as a sign. It's a good engine. I can plane my 8-foot inflatable with it (meaning ride *on* instead of *in* the water), but only if I am alone in the dinghy and I hold my tongue right.

I couldn't get replacement parts on Papeete, and there are some things I need, like a new anchor windlass. Tahiti is the last South Pacific island you can sail back to Hawaii from, so I realized I was at a crucial turning point: if I sailed West I was committed to go at least as far as Australia. I decided I could raise my anchor by hand for a while – I decided to sail.

But yesterday, the first day out from Bora Bora, I discovered things were worse than I had realized. I tried to get an afternoon fix only to find out my satnav is dead. I am practicing sextant sights with a sense of purpose – it's now my only navigation method,  *Taking a sextant sight while underway* and the water between here and Tonga is chock full of islands and reefs that I have to avoid. Fiji is the closest island with a large city and possible marine supplies, and Fiji is a long way off.

Even though shopping in Tahiti was frustrating, I found some useful products that I doubt even exist in the stores at home. One is a cheese from New Zealand that they wrap in foil, so it has a good long shelf life without refrigeration. Another is whole milk in powder form. At home only skim milk comes this way. But there weren't any big cans of chicken soup, one of my staples.

I am sailing in the company of another boat that I met in the Tuamotus. The boat is "Take Two," and the crew is Bob, an American man who lives in Germany, and his wife Ursula, whom he met in Germany. Bob writes computer software and Ursula teaches high school mathematics. Bob and Ursula plan to sail around South Africa and I am thinking about the Mediterranean route, so we'll have to split up sometime in August. We talk on the radio every day while sailing, and have shared some anchorages. We are about 30 miles apart right now, too far for the short-range VHF marine radio but an easy contact on our middle band "HF" radios.

Today the relative wind is varying from 30 to 60 degrees aft of the port beam. I have the jib poled out on the port side, main to starboard, and staysail tightly sheeted on center to reduce the rolling motion for which downwind sailing is notorious.

June 21 – Day 3

The wind is shifting to Southerly, so it's almost a beam reach. My average speed is close to 6 knots. Normally I compare two satnav readings to find out what my true speed is, but the errors in the sextant readings are greater than for the satnav, making it hard to find my exact speed and course.

But my confidence in my sextant skills is increasing. I took four sun sights yesterday and computed all combinations of them as a test – the greatest difference between any two was only ten miles. Then in the evening I took some star sights and these also seemed consistent. So, although I won't know where I am with the precision of the satnav, at least I can get to Tonga safely.

I make sextant sights in a rather high-tech way. Rather than use a wristwatch to note the time of the observations (not easy when you're working alone), I attach a push-button to my computer. When I want to mark the time of an observation I press the button and the computer records the time. Later I list the times and the star angles and feed them into a sextant program I wrote. The program does all the calculations and tells me where I am.

If only I had been willing to buy a proper sextant. My plastic sextant goes out of adjustment too easily for accurate observations. Now that I'm entirely dependent on the sextant I naturally daydream about a fancy metal one that "real sailors" own.

I am glad to be underway again. I find my attitude toward sailing to an island and getting there is being changed by experience. If this trend continues I may just sail and avoid getting anywhere.

June 23 – Day 5

The day before yesterday I killed the batteries by running the radar all night. There wasn't enough wind for the windmill to make up the power used by the radar, and by morning the batteries were in a very sad state. I couldn't start the engine to recharge them – they were too flat for that. So I ran the Honda generator until I could use the batteries to start the main engine. After adding distilled water to the poor batteries, I decided I'll have to give up using the power-hungry radar as an all-night watchman. Instead I will have to wake up at intervals during the night and take a look around, just like a normal solo sailor. Or maybe I'll take to sleeping in the daytime, since the risk of a collision is less then. And I think it's time to shop for better batteries, after which I may be able to resume my decadent ways.

I'm feeling confident that I can use even this plastic sextant to find my way across the ocean. I have been taking two sun sights during daylight and some star sights in the evening. The positions have become so consistent that I actually think I know where I am. This is a tale that can only be told by a modern sailor, who used satellite fixes *before* the old-fashioned method.

I'm glad I took the time to write my sextant computer program. It's quite accurate, and has some features like listing the navigation stars that are visible at a particular time and place. When I get to Suva I think I'll try to acquire a better sextant. I am more likely to find a good sextant than a replacement satnav, but I'll buy both if I can. And some better batteries. As you can see, I am imagining Suva will be a shopper's paradise, just as I did with Papeete. This particular learning curve is taking a long time.

This crossing has been very enjoyable so far. The wind has been favorable, speeds high, and I get to talk to my friends every day. We are comparing positions as we go. "Take Two" is a modern, lightweight German-built racing boat with a longer waterline than mine, but they haven't been able to catch up – mostly because their boat becomes too uncomfortable during high speeds and rough conditions. So to avoid seasickness they reduce their speed.

June 24 – Day 6

The wind has really picked up. There's a high pressure cell to the Southwest that's greatly increasing the wind force. It started yesterday and by nightfall the electronic tiller mount had broken twice (because of big waves). I just fixed it and sailed on. But about 10 PM it broke again so I changed over to the wind vane. The wind vane on this boat doesn't track very well, when it works at all – I had to slow down to 4 1/2 knots so it wouldn't wander excessively. I fixed the tiller mount again this morning, but this time I used better hardware. I think it'll hold up now.

I was afraid I wasn't going to get a position today – it was cloudy at dawn. But eventually there were some breaks, the sun peeked through and I took some sights. I was near Palmerston Island and I wanted to be sure I didn't bang into it. Even though it was very rough and the sun was only partly visible, the sights agreed with each other reasonably well. I'm starting to believe the sextant positions.

I felt discouraged yesterday but today my confidence is back. Not being able to steer the boat in a straight line sort of takes it out of me. Also I haven't been getting regular sleep for a couple of days now.

Two days ago I was worried about discharging my batteries by running the radar all night. Now, because of the high wind, my windmill is putting out too much power. I have to remember to turn the radar on to keep the batteries from overcharging. Pretty ridiculous.

June 27 – Day 9

Yesterday I wanted to give up and go home. It happened after I broke the whisker pole. I hadn't had a decent night's sleep in three days, very rough weather and gusty winds, satnav broken and weather overcast so I couldn't get a fix with the sextant, two sails need repair, then the whisker pole collapsed. It was one of those days.

Repairing the whisker pole in the cabin

Now where I go and what I do depend on what I can buy in Fiji. If I can't find a satnav or a whisker pole it's going to be hard to go on. Torres Strait, North of Australia, is a difficult place to navigate when you know exactly where you are, but if there should be overcast weather and no satnav I will probably end up crashing into something.

Also during this crossing I've realized that I can't use the radar on nights when the wind isn't blowing hard. Better batteries would help alleviate that problem.

My growing shopping list is a lot to expect from a South Pacific outpost, especially after my experience in Papeete. But this time it decides whether I go on. An alternative is to sail to New Zealand, where I can certainly find boat parts. But I want to stay with the present plan and timetable to avoid the bad part of the year in the Indian Ocean. If I sail to New Zealand and then continue from there, it will add a year to the voyage time.

Meanwhile I've been thinking how pleasant it'll be to visit the Indian Ocean and the Mediterranean. So when I've had some sleep and the sun comes out I still am enthusiastic about this voyage.

I cross the International Date Line sometime tomorrow. My friends on "Take Two" and I plan a long-distance party to celebrate the crossing. "Take Two" has suffered some damage during this passage. The wind has been high and the sea rough – waves have knocked them down several times. During one knockdown some stanchions were bent and their stove came out of its mountings. They report their ride is uncomfortable and noisy. Ursula was seasick for the first three days.

July 28 – Notes on Fiji

I have been in Fiji since July 12. I like this place – the people are friendly and interesting, the outlying islands are very pretty. And it's likely I can get most of the equipment I need.

The two main ethnic groups are Indian and Fijian. The Indians own the shops and hold most of the middle-level bureaucratic posts in the government, while the Fijians hold the lower-paying jobs in Suva and are almost the only occupants of the outer islands. In a recent coup, a group of native Fijians wrestled the top governmental post, and basic control, from the Indians. Because the coup happened in Fiji, there were no casualties – just some roadblocks and days of confusion. The Indians tell me they were in panic at first and many left the country, but that stage is over and some emigrants are returning.

My friend Ursula in Fiji

I would have liked to visit the outer islands for a longer time, but the task of re-equipping my boat is taking all my attention. Some essential items are coming from the States after considerable confusion about whether they could be gotten at all.

But before I realized I would have to baby-sit my order full-time, I visited Astrolabe Reef, also called Kadavu. I had been given some medicine to deliver to the village of Vambia on Ono island. A doctor on board another yacht had visited the village, examined two little girls afflicted with scabies, and acquired the remedy when he was back in Suva. He asked me to deliver the medicine.

On the day of my visit I heard by radio that my equipment order had come unraveled, so I was, to say the least, preoccupied with getting back to Suva. But I had promised to deliver the medicine, and I was only two hour's sail away from the village.

Vambia is a very pretty village, even in the context of Fiji, where ordinary things seem unreasonably beautiful. Nearly everyone has a garden. In the center of the village is a large courtyard of grass, surrounded by gardens. According to custom I was presented to the village chief, and I presented an offering of Yaqona, the root used to make Kava, a remotely intoxicating ceremonial drink.

The chief of Vambia is a woman. At great risk of categorical stereotyping, I immediately jumped to the conclusion that a connection existed between the beauty and orderliness of the village and the sex of the chief. For that I deserve to be flayed within an inch of my future income potential by a group of outraged feminists, if any could be located.

In 1979 a violent hurricane struck Fiji – the death toll for this one village was 23, all but one of whom were killed when the church, in which they had taken refuge, collapsed on them. When I heard this I thought to myself how prosaic that the most dangerous place in the village was the church, as true during a hurricane as any other time.

But this thought only reveals my urban cynicism, my colorfast polyester incapacity to see the value of religion in traditional cultures. In any case, even I was impressed by the aftermath of the tragedy – with the help of a clever architect the village built a new church, hurricane-proof and structurally beautiful as well. A roughly cylindrical inner chamber is surrounded by radial supports of cinder block, which give the structure the overall aspect of a crouching marine animal.

As I gazed with wonder on this excellent building, I thought to myself: If there was a hurricane, if coconuts and pieces of roofing tin were flying through the air at 100 miles per hour, would I take shelter in the church? Once inside, would I hold my nose? Plug my ears? Grab a hymnal and try to appear inconspicuous?

I then met Skelly, the man whose daughters were to receive the medicine. When I saw the advanced stage of scabies from which they suffered, all doubt about the need for the visit evaporated. Then Skelly invited me to lunch in his house. During my visit I played my recorder (a medieval flute) to the delight of what seemed two-thirds of those under eighteen, who gathered around the house in curiosity.

For lunch we had fish spiced with curry, a kind of unleavened cake like a Spanish tortilla, and cassava, a somewhat bread like fruit. Naturally, surrounded by an environment indistinguishable from paradise and pleasant, hospitable people, all I could think about was that I had to go back to the "big city" and try again to order things I need to safely sail to Australia. So I said my good-byes and departed in the afternoon for Suva.

August 22 – Day 8 of the passage from Fiji to Darwin

After delays and foulups too numerous and baroque to mention, the equipment I ordered arrived on August 14, just one day shy of the day I had decided would be absolutely too long to be in Suva. Bob and Ursula had waited also, because they had some items arriving with my order. So we spent that day getting the equipment away from customs and installing it.

After I ordered my equipment I thought I would have a normal visit in Fiji, sail around, visit interesting places. Well, apart from having to re-order out-of-stock things and generally baby-sit the order through to Suva, I really couldn't safely travel around without an anchor windlass, one of the broken items. After the windlass broke down I started using my lightweight anchor, since I had to raise it by hand. As it turned out, this wasn't such a great idea.

One afternoon I met Take Two on the East side of an island in the Kandavu group, South of Suva. They had anchored there because the wind was blowing from the Southwest, an abnormal direction. I didn't like the place. I worried that the wind would change to normal Easterly trades again, putting us on a lee shore. So I anchored well out from shore, in 50 feet of water, and I used the light hook. The rest of the boats were in 20 feet of water, close to shore. Oh well, said I. They all have extra hands on board, electric anchor windlasses, all that stuff. If the wind changes I have to raise the hook and motor off by myself. But I'm just preparing for a remote possibility.

In the next four hours – after dark, naturally – the wind changed from 12 knots Southwest to 30 knots Southeast. One by one, the boats raised their hooks and left. But I couldn't leave – there was no way I could raise my hook by hand, out of 50 feet of water, in a 30 knot wind, alone. In an emergency I would have to cut the line and motor off.

Then I started getting paranoid. I watched the anchor rode bouncing around, thinking how quickly I would be on the rocks if the rope parted, say, by rubbing on some coral. I knew I wouldn't be able to sleep unless I dropped the heavy hook – even though the water was 50 feet deep, even though I would have to raise it by hand later. So I dropped the heavy hook and a lot of chain, and went to sleep.

An hour later the boat turned sideways for a moment as (yes, you guessed it) the rope rode chafed through on a coral head. Then the second hook caught and stopped the boat. The next morning I had to dive to retrieve the light anchor, re-splice its rode, then raise the all-chain anchor to depart.

That's why I spent most of my time in Suva: my boat wasn't safe until the equipment arrived, and the equipment didn't arrive until it was time to leave. Ideally I would carry a spare of every critical item on board, if that was possible on a 31-foot boat.

But the real shock came when I ordered five items from the catalog of a large West-coast marine supply house and they didn't have *any* of them in stock. Not one. Finally I expressed my order this way: "please send any satnav, any manual anchor windlass ..." and so forth. Their slick, brightly colored catalog was a fairy tale.

I bought the sextant from a small shop in Suva, after the disaster described above made me realize mail-order and mail-delivery are separate events, not necessarily causally related. This is a real sextant, made out of metal, with a little telescope mounted on it. When you take a sight of the sun, you can make out sunspots. During my first few days on this passage I tested it on morning and afternoon sun sights. Then I compared the result with the satnav – one calm day there was less than one nautical mile of difference.

I ordered the Heart Inverter because the Honda generator finally and quite literally dissolved in salt water, leaving me with no way to run power tools and my little vacuum cleaner. Vacuum cleaner, you say – isn't that just a little trendy, sailing around the world with a vacuum cleaner? All I can say is, try to pick little pieces of glass out of the tiny cracks in the cabin floor, so they won't later magically migrate into the soles of your feet. I always seem to miss a handful of slivers even with a vacuum cleaner, and they always find me later.

A word to the wise: avoid glass, any glass, on a sailboat. On an ocean voyage the sturdiest glass containers end up being plucked out of elbows and knees.

I guess that's enough about equipment. After five days of nice sailing Ursula called on the radio to say that a gale was headed my way. What? A gale, in August in the South Pacific, near the equator? I looked at the regional weather chart: zero chance of gales in this area, at this time of year. So I thought maybe the meteorologists were being cautious, maybe they meant a gale was possible, not probable. But I made some preparations anyway.

The predicted wind velocity was 50 knots. In the Beaufort scale of wind velocities, that's Force 10 or "Storm." "Storm" is listed above "Gale" and "Strong Gale." During the next 24 hours the highest velocity I was willing to sit in the cockpit and observe on my wind meter was 45 knots, but I assure you, gentle reader, it was a storm. The rain moved horizontally through the air and hurt you when it hit. Dead birds floated in the water. The tops of waves blew off and flew through the air. The sea and air moaned out loud.

The cabin was a carnival of dislodged books, clothing, tools, all moving, all wet. And I realized I had to go upwind, to avoid an island that was about 20 miles to leeward. So I went out on deck to double-reef the main and put up my storm jib, a tiny sail for high winds.

A wave nearly swept me overboard as I installed the storm jib. The storm jib rides on the staysail wire, located nearly on the bow, a very unstable place in rough conditions. I wore a safety harness, which is attached to lines that run the full length of the deck on both sides. In storm conditions you try to do your work with one hand while holding onto the boat with the other, while also looking out for waves. I was playing with one of the copper hanks on the jib, trying to work it free and attach it. I had tested the hanks in the safety of the cabin, using a plier on those that had gotten stiff, but I managed to miss this one. But I think I can – *wham!*

The breaking sea pulled my hand from the shroud with an authority that had to be experienced to be believed. For an instant I saw the harness and the deck line stretched tight, as a wall of water tried to push me off the opposite side of the boat. It was sort of like falling and hitting a frothy sea, except the water came to me.

Later, in the cabin, I asked myself some questions. Was I being foolhardy going out on deck at the height of the storm? But I had to put the storm jib in service to move upwind, or, to be more precise in these conditions, not to go downwind. My highest priority was to stay clear of the island behind me, so I had to go on deck as soon as the wind became too much for the existing sails. I wore my safety harness in the prescribed way (attached to the upwind side of the boat). Of course, I wasn't planning a full-on harness test just then.

The next day the wind blew at 30 knots from the same direction (the direction I wanted to go). The following day saw lighter winds, same direction. Today the wind is finally turning to the South, and I am again moving West. The three days of contrary winds quite literally make this passage three days longer, since I hardly moved West at all.

I have just heard that the sea swept a man off his yacht during the storm. He had a wife and children aboard, but they were unable to rescue him. His wife is guiding their boat back to Fiji by means of radio instructions. I have been thinking about that incident – was he wearing a harness? Did he teach his family how to turn the boat around to recover him? It seems the answer is no to both.

August 30 – Day 16 of the passage from Fiji to Darwin

Today I am sailing near 13 deg South, 150 deg East, between Australia and Papua New Guinea. In about three days I will pass through Torres Strait, an interesting, shallow, confined passage first negotiated by Captain Bligh of HMS Bounty. I mean the first European, you know, the only important people, to hear Europeans tell it.

This passage began with no wind, and I had to motor for the first 12 hours. Then a storm, about which enough has been said already. Now classic trade winds have taken over, about 15-20 knots. I have my sails rigged wing-and-wing, mainsail on the port side, jib poled out on starboard. I have arranged my staysail, the small third sail on a cutter rig, to close the gap between the other two sails.

There have been almost no equipment problems on this passage. One problem that came up concerned the little electric motor that moves the tiller on the autopilot. One night the autopilot started beeping an alarm – on investigation it turned out the tiny brushes inside the little electric motor were almost completely worn away, so that they only sometimes touched the armature. As a temporary measure I twisted their mounts to get a last little bit of service time. For a while after the repair I thought the motor would fail again right away, there being only a microscopic amount of brush metal left. But I'm still on course four days later.

Apart from adding replacement electric motors to my shopping list for Darwin, I have been thinking about how this big boat is being guided across the ocean by a little electric motor, not very technically sophisticated, not very costly. When I am sleeping, a black box is sensing the earth's magnetic field and moving the tiller back and forth, by way of this little motor.

Of course, a well-designed wind-vane steering system is more philosophically appealing – I could have a complete electrical failure and the boat would still make its way to port. All I would have to do is adjust the vane for changes in the wind. It's totally organic, as they say in California – the wind pushes a vane back and forth, and an ingenious scheme of rods and levers amplifies this small natural force to steer the entire boat, so that the vane stays in the position chosen by the operator, and the boat keeps the same angle to the wind. I actually have a wind vane on this boat, but in describing its operation the words "ingenious scheme" must sadly be left out. The company that built it offered a refund to anyone not satisfied with its operation. By the time people began demanding payment, the company had gone out of business.

When I first sailed this boat, I marveled at the wind vane's ability to hold the boat at exactly 50 degrees off the wind, a desirable point of sail called a close reach. What I didn't realize at the time was I could have gotten the same result by simply tying the tiller down with a piece of line – this boat, most boats, are very efficient at guiding themselves on a close reach. My wind vane wasn't really doing anything, the one thing it does well. But there are much better wind vanes than this one, and someday I am going to have one.

Now that I have compared the simple, elegant wind vane with my electronic contrivance whose little motor might fail any time, I think it only fair to point out that Bob and Ursula on Take Two have switched from their decent wind vane to an autopilot like mine. During this voyage I had been steadily gaining on them, about ten miles per day, even though their boat is unquestionably faster (because it weighs less and has a fin keel and spade rudder). Then they decided to try out their new electronic toy, freshly acquired in Fiji, and I am no longer gaining on them. The drawback to a wind vane is that when the wind changes direction, the boat does too. Now that their boat is moving in a straight line, their effective speed has gone up, and I can't close the gap between us.

This is classic trade wind sailing. If the temperature was much higher, squalls would be a constant risk, and as a single hander I would have to run under reduced sail, so as not to be caught unprepared by a sudden wind increase brought on by a squall. But temperatures are moderate, the wind blows at a constant speed all day, slightly stronger at night, so I can run plenty of sail.

I have decided to break one of the rules offered me by an old salt I met in Brookings, as I prepared for the Hawaii passage. "Never let out the last reef," he said. I usually obey this rule, since it would be very difficult to drag down the full mainsail and set the first reef if the wind was to suddenly come up. But there have been no significant wind changes or gusts for about 10 days now. So I am running all the canvas I have in an eight to twelve knot relative wind.

The approaching land masses of Australia and New Guinea are beginning to block some of the open-ocean swell, so the surface is becoming smoother over time.

Take Two and I are planning to stop overnight in Torres Strait and have a dinner before continuing to Darwin. In our daily radio contacts we have been debating whether to risk stopping in Sri Lanka during the Indian

Ocean crossing. It is located perfectly to break the passage into manageable parts, but there is a civil war going on.

September 7 – Day 23 – Gulf of Carpentaria

Torres Strait was quite an experience, neither ocean sailing nor port – something in-between. The water was very shallow. One could, at least in principle, drop anchor at any time. Reefs and obstacles were everywhere, some "marked" with a ship gone aground.

Bob and Ursula on Take Two contacted another German boat, "African Queen," on the radio, then we met them face to face in Torres Strait. We decided to try catching some fish, then get together for dinner. So I put out about 100 feet of rather heavy nylon fishing line and a plastic squid on a stainless steel leader with a little lead weight. I had previously used a shorter line, but Ursula told me she uses a longer line to keep the lure out of the boat's wake, making it easier for fish to see. Anyway, after I took this advice I barely got the line in the water when a big fish took hold. Ursula caught one about the same size, so there was plenty of fish for dinner.

We anchored near Twin Island, a bad anchorage, poorly

A big fish that didn't get away

sheltered from the wind and with a rocky bottom. The wind was strong, and had been so for several days. After dinner I suggested that everybody pile into Bob's dinghy and come to my boat to watch a movie. This idea caught on fast.

Now get this. After the movie, we were all standing in the cockpit getting our bearings when we realized "African Queen" was gone! I broke out the spotlight and we managed to locate her, about 1/4 mile downwind from where she had started. Fortunately there was shallow water for a great distance, so the anchor had caught firmly on something after a long drift. Since it was now blowing 30 knots and the current was running better than a knot, Bob wisely declined to try to dinghy over to African Queen – if the motor should fail or a wave swamp the dinghy, it would mean the loss of all on board.

So I decided to raise my anchor and deliver African Queen's crew to their boat, then deliver Take Two's crew to their boat. The first part of this plan went well, and African Queen's crew recovered her. Then I discovered I couldn't motor against the wind, something I should have foreseen. So I unrolled a small bit of jib and tacked back to the anchorage. It took a long time, but everybody got back to their boats.

African Queen then radioed they couldn't keep their anchor set. They explained they were using a Danforth, an anchor that doesn't work at all in rock. I persuaded them to throw out their small CQR, a hook that until then they had regarded with contempt. It caught and held them well – so well they broke their anchor windlass trying to raise it the next morning.

As we approached Torres Strait we heard from yet another German boat, sailing in the Gulf of Carpentaria, that a suspicious boat approached and closely followed them about nightfall. A freighter then appeared and the boat took off. So we all interpreted this as a thwarted attempt at piracy, and decided to sail as a group. Naturally I am the slowest boat, but no one wants to get too far away because I have a shotgun. Yesterday I tried to add some speed by going wing-and-wing using the new, big whisker pole. The whisker pole held up and I saw over six knots for about 30 exhilarating seconds, then the whisker pole mount broke. The mount is a stainless steel ring on the mast, which should be no problem to replace in port, but meanwhile I can't go very fast. I now have a list of about eight items to buy in Darwin, including another autopilot.

The first time I limped into port after only three weeks at sea with a scarcely seaworthy boat, I believed that would be a rare event. The fact is every time I come into a port after more than a week underway, I have a list of purchases essential to leaving again. I guess that's a reality of cruising, and I may even be adjusting to it.

On the personal side, on these long passages I review the events of my life. Lately I've been thinking about times I have missed an opportunity to get to know a woman. I started this train of thought with the recent past, but soon I was reviewing events from 25 years ago.

Some of these missed opportunities arose from a lack of self-confidence – but, no, that doesn't put it strongly enough. Let me try again. I come from a family that was not only non-functional by conventional measures, but when the children went out into the world, some second-order effects took hold as well. The most important was a sense that we were guilty of some black deed, and eventually the thought police would discover this, take us outside, and shoot us.

So my brothers and sisters and I staggered into the real world with one priority: avoid being found out. We believed we could live among real people and enjoy some of the fruits of life in the West, while hiding our basic unworthiness, our black secret. We knew we could do it because our parents had done it.

What this meant for me personally was that if someone took notice of me, they would have to be explicit indeed to overcome my belief that I was unworthy of notice. I'm not saying I am now beyond this kind of self-doubt, but when I look back I see amazing situations in which a woman signals me to draw near, I am as oblivious as it is possible to be while still breathing, and she naturally feels rejected, or at best disregarded.

An example. I lived in a house in San Francisco with several other people, during the so-called Summer of Love. One evening a woman who lived in the house sat down with me over a cup of tea and explained that she was feeling very frustrated sexually, and thought it would be in her interest to strike up with a younger man. She was about 35, I was 22. I listened sympathetically, and offered suggestions. Oh, I was the perfect sympathetic friend, but for the life of me – why didn't I realize she was discreetly inviting me to get involved?

An earlier example. When I was 18 I fixed television sets for a living. I still lived in the neighborhood of my high school, renting a room from a family that took me in after my parents threw me out.

From time to time a young woman visited me in this household. She was the daughter of a teacher who had given me an I.Q. test several years before, with results that surprised the rest of the teachers. She may have been motivated more by fascination than anything else: here's this dropout with a high I.Q. – an overly bright, complete misfit. She and I would sit in the dark kitchen and talk about things. She was very pretty, I mean I would think so now, not just as an eighteen-year-old. And very smart.

My God, my God. I can hear my monotone even now, describing the inner workings of television sets. In retrospect I can't think of a more discouraging experience for a young woman. I could have suggested a date. I could have placed my hand on her shoulder and told her that I appreciated her visits, that her willingness to sit with me made me feel like a real person. I could have turned on the kitchen light and fixed her a cup of tea. Of course, to do any of these things I would have had to risk rejection, and (to hear me tell it at the time) rejection would have killed me.

In the "natural order of things," women are required to say "no" a whole lot, and if they are lucky a person they would choose chooses them, making any overt appeal unnecessary. I'm not saying I approve of this, I think it stinks – but I can see the reasoning. But it encourages the very behavior in men that it implicitly criticizes – we have to be outspoken to a silly degree to discover where we stand. A man who won't act aggressively toward women, no matter how appealing in principle, is doomed. I hate to say it, but I think it's true.

We are about four days from Darwin. Everybody is getting excited at the prospect of being in port after so long a passage. There's a lot of talk about restaurants and bookstores and repairs.

September 12 – Darwin

On my arrival yesterday the Australians radioed me to drop my anchor offshore and wait for Immigration to come aboard. I don't really mind these delays, and besides I find it difficult coming ashore suddenly after 27 days at sea.

The immigration official was efficient, competent, poised – and a woman. I am not happy with the confession I am about to make, but I feel I must include it – to cast it out would be false. This young woman briskly fulfilled her responsi-bilities, making the

Ursula & Wallaby, near Darwin, Australia

relevant enquiries, placing items of intelligence in her forms – while I drank in her khaki uniform and practical shoes, and let her voice wash over me. I've always been a sucker for a woman in uniform.

In the same moment I loved her and hated myself. I've spent my life encouraging women to enter professions, ridiculing those who stay home, barefoot and pregnant. And yet here I was, confronted by a government official whose sole and genuine wish was to meet her responsibilities for Australian Immigration – and all I could think to do was slip downwind from her and breathe more deeply than usual, which I did. She was a no-

nonsense professional, and she smelled great.

But I revealed nothing of my anguish, gave no sign or word. I can take shelter in this small achievement: I behaved respectfully. I didn't lean toward her, didn't touch her shiny dark hair. In that moment I became a foot soldier, moving through a landscape of desire, under orders to resist the sight of nature's perfect form.

I sat with my hands folded, responding to her enquiries, while something awakened and twisted inside me, something born at sea. Chemical messengers screamed in my ears, nearly drowning out reason. And as she rose to leave, I shook her hand, said "It's been a pleasure meeting you." It was an absurd understatement, but the words of a gentleman. Also a lie, for this woman has shown me something – the sea has made me part animal, and left me on a strange shore.

{ 6 }

Darwin to Sri Lanka

In Darwin, I decided to haul and paint my boat, as it had collected a few scars since Hawaii. This took about four days, after which I joined Bob and Ursula and other friends in an enclosed marina with a lock. And why do they have a marina with a lock in Darwin? Because the tidal range is about 21 feet, that's why. Before I got into the protected area I set anchor in 22 feet of water and rowed my hard dinghy ashore. I had some idea that there were tides here, so I carried an extra-long painter and the dinghy anchor. I threw the anchor out to hold the dinghy off the dock so it wouldn't get trapped underneath in a rising tide, then I climbed about two feet to the dock.

Anthill near Darwin

When I got back I momentarily thought someone had grabbed my dinghy, but who takes a silly little rowing dinghy? Then I got to the edge of the dock – and saw the tide had gone out. Way out. My dinghy was a little oblong dot far, far below. Another dinghy was hanging in the air, its line too short for the tide. I climbed down the ladder and cast off, thinking how lucky that I brought long lines.

Then I began to worry about the big boat. If the tide changed that much, maybe I didn't have any more water under my boat. I rushed on board – and found just one foot of water beneath my keel. This takes some getting used to after Tahiti's six inch tides.

I was able to find a seat post for my mountain bike – I hadn't had the use of it since Bora Bora. The bike turned out to be very useful in Darwin, since a key boat-shopping area was too far to walk in the heat. Also I replaced one of my two computers, the Toshiba 1100. It turned out to be so out-of-date they couldn't repair its memory. The new machine is nice, much faster, a better display.

Bob, Ursula and I visited Kakadu National Park for two days. We saw lots of crocodiles and some spectacular views. We swam in a pond regarded by local people as safe – "just one croc." After we left the pond, I was told someone dove straight into the croc's domain – and the croc made a sudden, threatening appearance, discouraging any repetition of this behavior.

Some things about Australia come to mind again and again. The dry, wild landscape East of Darwin. Anthills twenty feet high. A pack of dingoes working over a road-killed animal in the sunset. A bird that woke me up in the bush by singing a complete melody, as if it knew something about human music. And a group of aboriginal women walking along a road in Darwin, adrift in the twentieth century, each wearing light pastel-colored dresses – yellow, robin's egg blue, light green – they looked like refugees from a war they lost, and perhaps that is literally true. It was a very confusing moment for me. I thought they looked terrible in those particular colors, as if they were advertising how out-of-place they were – but since white men destroyed Aboriginal culture, how can we deny their effort to live in ours?

As I pedaled past on my bike, I recalled some of the facts about Aboriginals' lives in modern Australia. Even if dressed in perfect colors they would be denied access to their ancestral lands, they would still drink themselves to incoherence, and they would still die young. Modern European culture is something that is inflicted on them. So the impossibility of their dress reflected the impossibility of their lives. Which meant

Outback Australia. Note the croc at bottom center

the colors were, in their own way, perfect – because you couldn't see them pass by and still believe Aboriginals are happy and content.

Anyway, after about three weeks of restaurants, movies, and repairs, on October First Take Two, African Queen and I decided it was time to go. We had heard more disturbing radio reports from boats sailing near the Indonesian coast – accounts of being shadowed by mysterious craft, possibly pirates. We decided to continue sailing as a group, within sight of one another.

There wasn't much wind early in the day so I motored for a while. Then in the afternoon there was enough wind for a close haul. I put up all my canvas – full main, full genoa, in a 12 knot breeze. I noticed I was doing four knots only 40 degrees off the wind. That's good performance for my boat, and I was thinking it's because I tightened the rigging, especially the headstay. Just then the headstay broke – *bam!*

So I had to bid my friends farewell and turn around – I was only half a day out from Darwin. It took six days to acquire and install the replacement rigging. I decided to replace the entire rig, a good decision as it turned out – the backstay was frayed and close to giving way.

These things delayed my departure to October 6, yesterday. There's almost no wind out here – I've been motoring much of the time. Take Two is about 500 miles farther West, and there's no wind there either. They have used up most of their fuel, so when the wind quits they drift and wait.

The regional weather charts show a stretch of about 600 miles in which the wind is either light or from the West (caused by the land mass of Australia), after which normal trade winds start up. The trick is to get past this dead zone before running out of fuel or supplies. At the moment I am making 2.5 knots in a 5 knot breeze from 60 degrees off the port side. Yesterday I was making 3.5 knots out of a 10 knot wind only 35 degrees off the bow – the new rig has greatly improved this boat's upwind ability. I hope this remains true when I get to the Red Sea, supposedly a long upwind haul against much stronger winds.

Yesterday evening the radar flaked out. Fortunately I was able to bring it to life by disassembling it and trying my usual makeshift repairs. If the radar quits for good, I intend to continue, but I will have to sleep in the cockpit and wake myself every 30 minutes or so. A terrible prospect.

So this is the beginning of a more difficult kind of passage, one in which sailing cleverness, constant attention to the wind, and careful fuel management will decide the outcome.

October 10 – Day 5

Today I met the pirates I've been hearing about. No shots were fired, no knives were drawn, but they meant to board Selene, and I stopped them.

About 10 AM I saw an odd-looking sailboat about three miles in front of mine. I was sailing close to the wind, as I have been doing so far this crossing. I watched this boat just to be sure we didn't smack each other. After a few minutes I saw we were on a collision path, so I changed course to clear them – then they changed course also, dead on. They were sailing downwind, so they could match any course change I made, so I decided to bear on and see what they were up to. I also loaded my shotgun.

The boat's sails were my first clue that it wasn't a European sailboat – they were large bolts of printed silk, cut to match the dimensions of a wooden mast and boom. When there was about 1/2 mile left to go, they stopped their boat in the water and launched a dinghy. Well, I thought, this is classical, except things like this usually happen at night.

I decided on a strategy – I would make sure they saw my gun, then if they approached within touching distance of my boat I would fire a warning shot, then if they tried to board I would shoot them. I have heard enough pirate stories to know if they got on board, my chance of staying alive wasn't very good.

One person rowed the dinghy the short distance between my boat and theirs. I took up a position on the rail with shotgun in hand, trying to be conspicuous. He wasn't going very fast in his rowing dinghy, but I wasn't going very fast either, maybe 3 1/2 to 4 knots. Just as he reached out to grab my boat and be towed along, he saw the gun and stopped. As he came alongside he smiled and made a sign that I should let him and his friends on board for a drink. I looked beyond him to the sailboat and could see at least four more men on board. I shook my head and waved him away with the gun.

He rowed back to his vessel, and after they had secured the dinghy they tried to sail toward me for a while. I found this particularly scary, since they knew I was armed and they were trying to catch me anyway – therefore, I thought, they are also armed and plan to shoot it out. But I was sailing close to the wind and they couldn't match my speed or course, and they soon broke off the pursuit.

The critical moment in this episode was when the man in the dinghy reached out to my boat to pull himself along, and I came to the rail and stopped him. We looked across the barrel of my shotgun for a moment, and he realized I'd use it if I had to.

I didn't have time to think during this episode – afterward some things occurred to me. One is that I could have been in the cabin reading, as I do for hours at a time, and at least one person would have been on board before I knew. Another is a description I read of typical pirates in these waters – part-time fishermen who raid passing boats.

I personally think there is no way I could have kept them off my boat without the shotgun, and the appearance of the gun was pivotally discouraging. Today I think anyone who sails these waters without a gun – and a willingness to use it – is a fool.

(Later: Ursula visited a freighter at Cocos Keeling and told the captain the pirate story. She asked whether he thought they were pirates or just fishermen. The captain said, "Anyone who approaches you on the high seas is your enemy.")

Today Take Two is about 600 miles away, in an area normally filled with trade winds, but they are still sometimes becalmed. So I am taking this to heart – I have to resist my tendency to fire up the diesel anytime the speed falls below two knots. On the plus side I am seeing performance in this boat I never thought possible – most of it arises from the new, very tight rigging. I can sail just 35 degrees off the wind if the surface isn't too rough, so I am going to patiently sail in lighter winds to save fuel.

I'm also going to watch more carefully for boats.

October 15 – Day 9

Yesterday there was plenty of wind of the kindest sort – nearly abeam, 13 knots, very smooth, four to five knots boat speed. Today there's almost no wind again. Now, at 118 degrees East, I expected to have reached constant wind. But there are some good signs. What wind there is seems more Southerly, a favorable change.

I have about half my diesel left. I can motor continuously about 3 more days, or more if the wind blows part of the time, after which I will have to drift and wait for wind. My strategy has been to motor as far West as possible before rationing the fuel, because the strong winds are West of here. Now I have to begin to take greater care with the remaining fuel, since I could sail into a calm anywhere in the 1300 miles left to go.

It is very hot here. Light seas, light wind. I see dolphins most evenings playing around my boat. They gather around the bow and, if I take a position there, they swim past and look me over between dives and broaches. In my opinion the combination of an Indian Ocean sunset accompanied by a performance of the dolphin follies easily wipes a storm off the sailing account books.

A few days ago, during one of the calms, I dove on my boat and cleaned the propeller (since I have been motoring a lot, I wanted it clean). So I have gotten off the boat while underway, supposedly a no-no for a single hander. I naturally took down all the sails and tied the tiller to one side to keep the boat from sailing away. I spent half my time scrubbing my prop and the other half looking for Jaws.

I still talk to Take Two twice a day. In the morning chat I try out my German on them, usually with hilarious results. Rule number 1: you can't just translate English into German word for word, unless you want to hear giggles on the radio. I have a couple of German travel books and a dictionary, but I haven't learned German grammar.

I am playing catch-up again. Now I'm catching up to recover the time lost in the return trip to Darwin. The cruising guides say the best time to leave Cocos Keeling is at the end of October, which I will just make. So I expect to spend just a short time there, about five days, then make another long crossing to Sri Lanka. Take Two and I plan to spend a longer time in Sri Lanka, probably a month, the civil war notwithstanding. Some boats in Sri Lanka tell us things seem normal unless you read a newspaper.

My shopping is becoming more prescient. On this passage I have enough cookies and sodas, probably for the first time. Staples have never been a problem. I have always had the mental twist required to load three shopping carts with identical cans of chicken soup. But I find it harder to make stacks of potato chips, cookies, sodas, you know, goodies. Things that a sailor's diet mustn't have too much of, or too little.

Sleep has been difficult on this crossing, because of frequent changes in the wind. I have taken to setting an alarm that goes off every two hours, and most of those alerts have been useful. Either the boat has stopped dead in the water, or has decided to sail back to Darwin without consulting the captain, or the radar has flaked out from the heat and needs a 30-minute rest. Once I get to normal trade winds (if such a thing exists out here) I expect to recover my usual disposition. Meanwhile I feel sort of beset, under an abnormal amount of stress. Also my voice is nearly gone – it's hard even to talk on the radio.

October 20 – Day 14

I found the wind. As I began this sail I was in the wind shadow of the continent of Australia, but that's all over. In the last 24 hours I averaged seven knots (!) with some help from a favorable current – that's 168 miles!

Now I understand the reports I was getting from Take Two about a week ago (when they were here). It was discouraging at the time – I was making about two knots, mostly motoring, and they were about 100 miles farther away each day.

Bob and Ursula have been telling me about Cocos Keeling (where they are anchored now) – it sounds like a fun place, a coral lagoon with a couple of small towns, nice diving. I will only be able to stay a few days before starting for Sri Lanka (still making up for the six extra days in Darwin).

Stingrays on patrol

After the first ten days I began to like this crossing, in spite of the light-to-no winds and the pirate encounter. I have a good collection of books, having replenished my supply in Darwin by trading and buying. I bought enough treats, there's no way I'll run out of cookies this time.

Soon there won't be any electronic gear on the boat that I haven't replaced at least once since I started sailing in '87. The radar flakes out in so many ingenious ways that I would replace it if I could. Even the Kenwood ham radio is showing signs of accelerated decrepitude.

My VCR stopped working recently, because a single drop of salt water made its way onto the surface of an important polished cylinder inside. This cylinder spins very fast, carrying along with it two magnetic sensors that pick the video signal off the tape. The drop of water produced a spot of corrosion that kept the cylinder from rotating fast enough. I tried to polish the spot, but nothing worked. Fortunately I acquired a spare VCR while I was in Hawaii, the last location where U.S.-style television equipment was available.

In spite of these equipment failures I am beginning to enjoy sailing more and more. In fact I wonder how easy it will be to go back to normal life after this voyage is over. I know one thing – when it's over I am going boat shopping. This boat has the worst interior woodwork I have ever seen in any boat or house. The wood is not durable, and nearly everything is glued together. Where screws were used, they generally didn't reach through one piece of wood to sink into another, so everything looked sound until I entered the tropics, where wood glue is known to give way. Pieces of trim fall daily from their places. When one or two pieces fell off, I used to glue them back into place, but now I chuck them overboard in handfuls of six or eight.

The other day a countertop lifted off its mountings. It was another example of screws too short for the job, and a small dab of glue was the only thing holding it in place. I couldn't do without the countertop so I mounted it as it should have been in the first place.

Now that I have enough experience to know how to look at a boat, I am going to shop for a better one. I have visited some boats whose interiors were entirely of hardwood, and the quality of work was obvious.

This boat really does have a teak interior, which is the stupid question I asked before buying it, but not all teak is created equal. Old-growth teak may be hundreds of years old, and very strong – but that wood is gone. Now they have commercial lots where teak is grown as fast as possible, and has the strength of cardboard.

I will probably buy a boat of more conventional design than this one, so I won't always be the last boat to arrive. This boat is heavy enough to be comfortable in perfectly awful weather, but I pay a high price for that the rest of the time.

My next boat will have to be bigger also – only because I can't fit enough sails, supplies and toys in this one. Also if I met someone I wanted to sail with, she would have to be completely immune to stressful situations to stand the cramped quarters on this boat. The forward berth is completely full of things I couldn't fit into existing lockers, so there's no private space except out on deck.

I would like to have gone shopping just once for a boat and kept it for a lifetime, but I didn't know enough about boats, in spite of all my advance reading. In ten years the interior of this boat will be completely dissolved, through a combination of bad wood and workmanship, and the many leaks at the seam between the hull and cabin moldings.

October 22 – Day 16

I am going fast! I should reach Cocos Keeling in two days at this pace. Yesterday I averaged 7.1 knots (including the effect of current). The wind is aft of beam on the port side at about 15 - 20 knots relative, an ideal wind. All three sails are up and I've been adjusting the speed with the roller furler. If I have too much sail up, the boat begins to wallow back and forth over about 60 degrees, a very uncomfortable condition and hard on the sails. So I tune the sails every couple of hours for a speed just below the point of discomfort.

The sea is getting smoother and my sleep has consequently improved. Plenty of dreams.

I've been planning my life after this sail. I'll buy a very fast computer of the latest generation and install a graphics adaptor in it. Then I'll make some more pretty computer graphic images, get invited to graphics conferences, and meet interesting people. This is something I was doing before I started sailing, but the available machines were slow and expensive. Things are changing fast in the computer world – more computing power for less money.

I'll buy a better boat, roomier, suitable for more than one person, and sail the San Juans in the summertime – I'll invite friends for week-long outings.

I'll stock my camper van with supplies and visit the desert – or if it's wintertime I'll drive to Utah and ski in some of the resorts out that way.

These are the immediate plans, ones requiring no great stretch of the mind. Then there are notions like selling my house in Oregon and living full-time on a boat, or buying a country house on high terrain and building a great ham radio station.

That's an advantage of sailing – the elements of your life, usually too big to think about clearly, become as manageable as chess pieces, that you move around an imaginary board as you sail and dream.

This evening I saw something I've never seen before. I was sitting out in the cockpit, enjoying the stars and the boat's glowing wake, when I noticed some glowing trails in the water. Then I heard surfacing dolphins – and I realized the trails marked their paths through the water! I went forward to the bow to watch the show. As the dolphins swam about, they disturbed the water and set off a glowing display called bioluminescence, just as the whitecaps and the boat itself do. It was pretty and mysterious – for an hour I watched an intricate dance of six to eight dolphins, all seen by way of glowing pathways left behind in the water. I felt as though I could follow their motions better than in daylight, when they can only be seen near the surface.

It was like visiting a spirit world – I didn't actually see any dolphins, I only heard the sound of their breathing, and saw their glowing pathways. Then I wondered how much reliance dolphins themselves place on these glowing wakes, as well as their better-known senses, to make their way through the nighttime sea.

November 9 – Day 9, Cocos Keeling to Sri Lanka

Cocos Keeling was so great it seemed almost sinful to leave it. Some things were difficult, like getting supplies, but the environment and the people made even these tasks more enjoyable. For example:

How I mailed my *White-tipped Reef Shark* letters in Cocos Keeling ... a true story.

Our story begins at 5 AM. I get up with some difficulty (unaccustomed to thinking of 5 AM as being part of life as we know it) and have breakfast. I pack my letters and my laundry in a waterproof bag. I decide to wear my foul weather gear, since it's blowing over 20 knots and I will be motoring my dinghy against the wind.

I take off in my inflatable dinghy, and make about 100 feet before the engine quits. I fix the engine and take off again. I am anxious that I should get to nearby Home Island on time to catch the ferry to West Island, where the post office and laundry are. During the crossing from the anchorage at Direction Island to Home Island, I discover that all the good-sized waves seem to have my name on them. Each one comes splashing into my dinghy as if invited, and gives me a big, salty kiss. Soon I am drenched under my foul weather gear, and I begin to think I would be more dry if I had worn nothing.

As I come into the lee of Home Island, I notice the wind and waves begin to diminish and my speed picks up. I had been warned to stay in the center of the channel while heading for the pier, because of coral all around. So I line myself up between the channel markers and motor on.

About halfway in I smack a coral head. My propeller's shear pin rescues my motor by breaking. I am too far out to row, also the wind is still strong, so I throw out my little anchor and repair the propeller. Available for this task are a Swiss Army knife, some extra parts attached to the outboard motor by its clever manufacturer, and a world-class vocabulary of swear words. Fortunately for me, the wind direction prevents my ingenious oaths from being heard by the schoolgirls who by now are boarding the ferry and watching the antics of the nut-case stuck out in the channel (Later I was told that yes, there are some coral heads within the channel, but everybody knows about them and steers around them. Except the first time).

I manage to repair the propeller, row away from the coral head, start the outboard and continue in. About 100 feet from the pier I run out of gas. I row the rest of the way. I tie up, throw my drenched possessions ashore, and run for the ferry, which has been waiting.

During the ferry ride from Home to West Island I sit outside, sorting through my possessions and trying not to look conspicuous, even though I am thoroughly soaked. I untie my waterproof bag, put the letters in my backpack and repack the laundry, which I set inside away from the spray.

When the ferry reaches West Island I jump ashore and start walking to the settlement, about 6 kilometers. About halfway I realize I have left my laundry on the ferry. But by this time I am so taken with the beauty of the place that I have a hard time getting very anxious that my laundry has been abandoned among strangers. I decide I will mail my letters, do some shopping at the market, walk back for the ferry's next appearance, retrieve my laundry, and return to town. A lot of walking, but a lot of beauty.

Anyway, I finally got to the post office. I furtively passed my damp letters through the little window into that mysterious outer world. Later I found my laundry just where I left it. I had been told that theft is almost unheard of, and certainly not someone's laundry from a sweaty 20 day sea crossing.

There was one very windy day in Cocos Keeling, so I launched my wind surfing board. The reef kept the wave heights down, but nothing stood in the way of the wind, so I went very fast, probably more than 20 knots. It is hard to imagine how I could have gone faster. I would hang from the harness with all my weight, the board moving so fast that it just touched the wave tops, and sometimes the wind would gust a tiny bit harder – and I would be pulled across the board and crash into the water. Quite a ride.

This passage has been very difficult – until today I have been too tired or busy to write. There are squalls all around, and they do funny things to the wind (see below). My constant attention is required. I can't just sit in the cabin reading, expecting the boat to carry me automatically to Sri Lanka. I actually have to work for a living out here.

Squalls have their own local wind pattern, usually blowing radially outward in all directions from the center of the squall. So if I pass to leeward of a squall, its wind is added to the overall wind. Big gust. If I pass to windward, the two winds sometimes completely cancel each other out. Start motor. If I happen to be aimed right for one, I might find myself trying to run straight up into a 25-knot wind.

I began in the Southern trades, moved to the Inter tropical Convergence Zone where there was almost no wind, and am now at 3 degrees South, in the Northern hemisphere's wind domain if not actually in the Northern hemisphere yet.

I am sailing as close to the wind as possible, and still can't make a course directly for Sri Lanka. I can only hope the wind changes direction well before I get there. Take Two is sailing farther off the wind, therefore faster, but they will have more lateral course error to make up later.

The Inter tropical Convergence Zone is the place where the Northern and Southern winds collide. It is near, but not necessarily on, the equator. The wind in the "zone" is variable in direction and velocity, sometimes there's just none – that's called the "doldrums" and was the great fear of old-time sailors, who sometimes drifted for weeks. And there are plenty of squalls and thunderstorms, since it's usually very hot and winds are often light – perfect conditions for a thunderstorm.

The air is clearer here than in the Pacific, which makes the sunsets spectacular. I think the Pacific haze comes from the Americas – long-range pollution from the U.S., Mexico, and Brazil, where they are burning the rain forests. Sometimes a volcanic eruption produces a global reduction in air quality and visibility – when Mount Krakatoa in Indonesia blew up in 1883, temperatures in Europe were abnormally low the following few winters (the Thames river froze) and sunsets were oddly colored around the world.

Some days here the sun makes it all the way to the horizon without being obscured by a cloud or haze. So I have resumed my quest for the

"Green flash." Supposedly the moment the upper limb of the sun passes through the horizon you sometimes see a green flash. I haven't seen one for sure, but twice I think I may have seen it – once in Hawaii and once here in the Indian Ocean, but on both occasions it was not a dramatic green color, so I am waiting for a more conclusive example before I decide it's real. I have a theory about it – it's actually a green "afterimage" produced by one's eyes, caused by watching the red sun until it disappears into the horizon, leaving one with the complementary color of green or "un-red."

But green flash or not, sunsets are spectacular here. Usually there are some cloud buildups by late afternoon, which (apart from how much trouble they cause me) are transformed from dull cumulus lumps at 4 PM into ingeniously colored fairy castles, complete with pennants flying from each balustrade and tower, by 6.

And one look isn't enough, and one direction isn't either. You must occasionally look in the opposite direction from the sunset, see pinks and reds in the region just vacated by the sun, then scan the horizon to your own sunset. I have given up trying to capture these afternoon episodes on film – the results never approach the actual event, and the camera distracts me anyway. I miss too much while trying to decide when to press the shutter.

I have been thinking lately about my experience of sailing, in particular how it has changed. When I made my crossing from Brookings to Hawaii, I was more alone than ever in my life. I could have yelled my head off or danced naked on deck – I could have fallen off the boat and no one would ever find out what happened. Completely alone, completely self-dependent. All that is still true, but in the months since then I have come to feel in touch with the world in spite of the distance. I talk to Bob and Ursula on the radio every day – we share experiences and views. I tune in the B.B.C. and hear the latest world events.

I still enjoy the solo sailor's self-dependence and aloneness, but part of me isn't having any of that, and that part builds connections through ritual. Writing letters while underway. Listening to the B.B.C. as if the events they describe could have any significance to me, sailing here on the Indian Ocean between two places each about 700 miles away. Watching a sunset, thinking I'll tell someone about it, next chance I get.

I am also thinking about my halfway point – the "Antipode," the point opposite my starting place. Fifty-eight degrees East longitude is opposite my home in Oregon, but I'm going back to Hawaii before returning to the West

Coast (it's easier that way), so 25 degrees East is the other antipode, perhaps the "real" one. Besides, if I think of it that way I can have two silly milestones to notice as I sail. On my route, 58 degrees is in the Arabian Sea between Sri Lanka and the Red Sea, and 25 degrees will be smack in the middle of the Mediterranean.

After I pass my antipode, all my sailing will have the effect of bringing me closer to home.

November 25 – Notes on Sri Lanka

Formerly named "Ceylon," Sri Lanka looks like a tear falling from the Indian subcontinent. Not only is it not like anything in the Pacific, it is unlike anything I have ever experienced. It is so densely populated that only the basic good nature of the people prevents utter chaos.

Sri Lankan market

Notwithstanding that good nature, a civil war is going on, mostly in the Northeastern provinces. A minority group, the Tamils, occupy the lowest rung in Sri Lankan society. They are dominated by the Sinhalese, who own most of the businesses and hold most governmental positions. In a separatist drive, Tamil rebel groups attack symbols of authority such as police stations, post offices, and any officials so unlucky as to cross their path. Sinhalese rebel groups also exist, they attack the Tamils and/or the designated authorities.

Two days before I arrived the government forces located and killed a key rebel leader, Mr. Rohana Wijeweera of the JVP (Sinhalese People's Liberation Front), and several others in their hideout. Accounts of the event vary – in one account Wijeweera gave himself up and offered to take the government forces to the hideout, and as they approached it one of his lieutenants opened fire, precipitating a firefight that resulted in the death of all rebels present. The local B.B.C. correspondent described this version of the events as "implausible." Other accounts have been offered, but the single incontrovertible element in all the accounts is that Wijeweera's body was cremated by the government immediately after death, without examination.

This setback for the rebels does not seem to have reduced the level of violence. Attacks on buildings and individuals continue to be reported, police stations being the favorite target.

Contingents of the Indian Army have been on the scene for some time, originally at the invitation of the Sri Lankan government, but they are now being asked to submit a timetable for their departure. Apparently they turned out to be sympathetic to the Tamils and their presence has not had the intended effect of reducing the level of violence. In fact, occasionally a story appears in the local press in which a Tamil group is found to be armed with Indian weapons.

It's educational to read accounts of the conflict in the local press. I can only conclude that strict controls have been placed on the way news is reported – for example, after some days of confusion about her whereabouts, Wijeweera's widow is described as placing herself "in the protection of the government forces." Lengthy newspaper accounts describe how Mr. Wijeweera was led astray by dogma, choosing a path of violent change and bringing shame to his family.

The rebel forces are by no means united. Accounts of division between them are, naturally, reported at length. In a recent story the LTTE (Liberation Tigers of Tamil Eelam) accuse the TNA (Tamil National Army) of being lackeys of, and supplied by, the Indian Army. This accusation could scarcely have escaped the attention of the government, since it simultaneously indicates division among Tamil rebel groups and misbehavior by the Indian Army.

Street scene, Sri Lanka

One need only travel by road to discover that wartime conditions exist. Roadblocks halt traffic several times between Galle and Colombo, and occupants of vehicles are individually searched. People in the employ of the government travel with several bodyguards. The status of a soldier is instantly obvious from his armament – while a rural policeman may be armed with an ancient and worn Lee-Enfield from colonial days, a member of an elite unit of the Sri Lankan Army proudly bears a new Soviet AK-47 that looks as though it has just been unpacked. But no one who wears a uniform, or has governmental responsibility, travels unarmed.

Apart from the fact of the war, travel by road can only be described as terrifying. The roadway is about 1 1/2 times the width of a single vehicle, so when two vehicles pass, they must throw themselves against the sides of the roadway in such a way as to swing past one another by centrifugal force. This maneuver requires substantial speed, for to slow down is to invite disaster. From time to time a truck smashes into a building in attempting this maneuver, and one can see several pulverized buildings on the roadway between Galle and Colombo.

The range of vehicles and velocities is astounding. From pedestrians, ox-carts and elephants through bicycles all the way to huge trucks, each seems intent on passing all obstacles on both sides, on a smoky, rainy, darkening roadway. I have yet to see a dog make an aggressive move toward a car, in fact dogs here have a profoundly haunted look, as if they don't expect to live beyond their own short-term recall. And they seem especially nervous when passing a restaurant.

The level of poverty here is extraordinary, in my limited experience of such things. This was brought home to me the first day, when I saw local people queued up near the dumpster used by the yachts, taking turns going through the garbage. At the end of the day the dumpster was empty.

A visit to the town marketplace is a quick education. It is more than just an open-air mall filled with struggling mortals – it is a world that operates on different principles. You may stand and slowly examine the pineapples if you wish, but you are likely to find

Ursula, snake, beach near Galle

yourself in the converging paths of an ox-cart going West and a three-wheeled motor ricksha going East.

I see people moving themselves and their wares in an amazing variety of ways. Balanced on the crown of the head. Pulled by an ox, who, even though surrounded by a fantastic amount of motion and noise, seems nearly asleep. Propelled by a lawn-mower attached to a converted ox-cart. A bicycle caught my eye – it was a complete fish market, with several kinds of fresh fish, a scale, and a proprietor who also pedals.

It is no accident that the Sinhalese are the merchants. Their methods range from the ingenious to the criminal, although the latter perhaps not by local standards. If someone offers to help you find a particular shop, you will pay about 30% more when you get there because the shopkeeper must pay your "guide" that amount after the purchase. Sometimes when you enter a shop you discover you are the center of an entourage of five, all of whom try to impress the shopkeeper with their relevance to your entry.

The range of individual well-being makes an American marketplace seem sterile. From the most prosperous shopkeeper, sipping tea between visits by well-heeled customers, to a legless man who, with neither wheelchair nor wheeled cart, must drag himself about with his still-functioning arms. At noon each day this man crosses the street from the morning to the afternoon shadows. When he makes his way across, the traffic doesn't stop, instead it parts. Big trucks, smoky buses, rickshas, ox-carts, bicycles, pedestrians, all make the smallest possible course corrections necessary to miss him. I think it took him about two minutes to cross the ten meters of road, but to me it seemed an hour.

This marketplace is an organism that thrives by its own rules, and the rules are complicated. I leaned over the counter of an open-air electronics shop, surrounded by heat and noise, and asked "Do you have a watch like this? It has five alarms." The proprietor looked up  *Sri Lankan girls on the beach* from his newspaper. He glanced at my watch and then at me. A small smile. "Buy five watches."

December 24

The political situation has deteriorated somewhat. The government's confidence after the capture and killing of Wijeweera has evaporated as the result of a new round of late-night violence. Here in the South most of the fighting is between factions of the JVP and pro-government vigilante groups. To cover their tracks, the rebels burn the bodies of those who are killed in the fighting, usually on a stack of automobile tires.

The rebels recently blew up the power lines, so there is no electricity or water pressure in Galle. In the anchorage we are rationing our water, collecting rainwater with awnings and buckets, and the bay is too polluted for swimming. I plan to raise anchor about January 5, good timing for the Red Sea.

{ 7 }

Sri Lanka to Tel Aviv

January 16 – Day 8, Sri Lanka to Djibouti

I have read most of five books so far during this passage: "Hotel" by Arthur Hailey, "Wired," about John Belushi, "Ragman's Son," Kirk Douglas' autobiography, a book about Robert De Niro called "The Hero Behind the Masks," and Elia Kazan's autobiography, "A Life." I didn't realize that "Wired" dealt so much with the Hollywood-L.A. scene, and that Elia Kazan was a film director – I thought he was a writer. Consequently I ended up reading four of these books as though they were elements of a set. In "Ragman's Son," Kirk Douglas even mentions two of the other books, and talks about Robert De Niro as well.

There's not much to say about "Hotel" except it's well-written and a good story. I saw a film rendition with Rod Taylor, who was regularly picked for that kind of story in the early '60's. Interestingly, in the movie Karl Malden – you know, "Streets of San Francisco," "American Express – don't leave home without it" Karl Malden – plays a cat burglar. I liked it, so when I saw the book in a hotel bookstore in Sri Lanka I grabbed it.

"Wired" (Bob Woodward) is written in a dry journalistic style, in which the events are expected to produce their own drama, and the author's personal views are kept to a minimum. It's very depressing. John Belushi shows how much trouble a million dollars can buy.

"Ragman's Son" must overcome the burden of its cutesy beginning, in which Issur Danielovitch (Kirk Douglas as a child) talks to his adult counterpart in trendy italicized passages I will bet were added at the insistence of an editor. I think Richard Bach popularized this device, in which you hold an interrupted dialogue with your younger, more callow self. The book gets better after that, although I think Mr. Douglas reveals more about himself than he knows.

"Robert DeNiro – Hero Behind the Masks" (Keith McKay) is just as bad as the title leads you to believe. I would very much like to read a good book about Robert De Niro. But this isn't the book.

I have greater expectations for Elia Kazan's "A Life." I haven't read enough to judge this fourth movie book, but at least the man knows how to write.

I am in the Arabian Sea, between the land masses of India and Africa. After a miserable start, with winds from every direction and velocity, and many freighters, conditions began to live up to the predictions of the guidebooks – steady Northeast winds, kind seas, sunny weather. I will want to remember these conditions when I get to the Red Sea, an area that is reported to be as trying as this is enjoyable.

I have been trying to decide what to do about this boat. Yesterday I tried to pull out a drawer, but the front of the drawer came off in my hand instead. I would like to strangle the master craftsman who built this interior.

Maybe I'll shop for a new boat in the Mediterranean. That might expose me to some boats and prices I might not otherwise see, but the drawbacks are great. I would have to purchase, equip, and shake down a new boat when I could be visiting pretty places instead. On the other hand I hate buying replacement gear for this boat and doing maintenance, because I know I'm not keeping it. My heart just isn't in it.

If I don't buy a new boat in the Med, I will be selling this boat as soon as I am back on the U.S. West Coast. I want a boat that sails faster than five knots without requiring extraordinary efforts, that doesn't leak everywhere, that doesn't destroy electronic gear with water and mildew (I am on my fourth VCR in two years), that doesn't paint brass and wood surfaces green when the sun is hidden from view.

I am not one of those prissy sailors who has to have a bristol (supremely orderly) boat to feel all right about the world. But having one-half a drawer come off in my hand is too much even for me. People whom I would like to impress come on board and say (or silently think) "Did a tree die in here?"

January 22 – Day 14

I have passed one of my landmarks – 58 degrees East longitude, which is exactly halfway around the world from Ashland, Oregon (122 degrees West). I had intended to write in my journal two days ago, when I was at the landmark, but it was blowing 30 knots and everything was wet and uncomfortable.

Now I am between Ethiopia and Saudi Arabia in the Gulf of Aden, approaching the Red Sea. I am going to stop in Djibouti for a while and monitor the Red Sea weather reports. I will try to choose a good moment to enter the Red Sea, which the most optimistic guidebook authors describe as very challenging and frustrating. The shopping in Djibouti is supposed to be good also.

I'm going to tell you another boat story. I met the crew of a boat named "Esprit" in Darwin (I've changed all the names in this story). John, the English captain, was looking for people to sail with him and share costs – he wasn't looking for paid crew, he wanted people willing to pay for the experience of sailing.

While in Darwin John met Jennifer, also English, a zoologist who occupied her time stealing eggs from salt water crocodiles.

A digression. Australian salt water crocodiles are huge and have the moral comprehension of reptiles – meaning if they like you, they eat you, and if they don't like you, they tear you to pieces and let the birds eat you. So you survive by not coming to their attention, just like with governments. And nothing annoys them quite so much as taking their eggs.

When I visited Jennifer's house I saw a photograph of her holding aloft two large crocodile eggs, while two assistants stand guard with oars. The idea of the oars is that if you hit a mama croc in the nose, she will be stunned for a bit and you can make good your escape. If this strategy were to fail, Jennifer could draw the .44 magnum revolver conspicuously resting on her hip. It's a dramatic photograph to happen upon, particularly stuck to a refrigerator.

Anyway, John met Jennifer and soon they were thinking of themselves as a couple. It was a foregone conclusion that Jennifer would come sailing on John's boat, as soon as she acquired her Australian residency visa, so in the fullness of time she could come back and steal more crocodile eggs.

John also met two Canadians, Linda and Philip, from the Vancouver area, and they arranged to join him.

Linda is an absurdly good-looking 19 year old. As to describing Linda I can only point and grunt, prosaically speaking. Linda is one of those people that makes me doubt Einstein's homily that "God is subtle but not malicious." She attracts attention wherever she goes – in Australia, where she worked in a bar, she heard comments about her chest often enough that she wanted to throw up. This is not to say that she is merely buxom, but among certain Australians that seems to have been the primary focus of her anatomy.

On New Year's Eve, in Sri Lanka, Linda engaged me in a serious, person-to-person talk, aided and abetted by alcohol, in which she revealed something I hadn't guessed: she finds sex disgusting. Her constant companion, being male and twenty-six, has tried from time to time to interest her in this activity, but without success. But that evening she was plagued by doubt – she wanted me, an older man, to say whether I though she was "all right."

Now consider the situation in which I found myself. It is New Year's Eve on a rather pretty beach in Sri Lanka, and a conversation is taking place between a very pretty young woman and your reporter, who, although predisposed to think, has been known to respond to chemical

Sri Lankan fishing boat on the beach

imperatives from time to time. Possible silly replies are rushing unbidden through my mind – "You've been cheated until now. It will be different with me, sweetheart..." – "I can't offer an opinion from this distance – I need to get closer to you" and so forth.

But none of these replies made its way to the surface of my mind and rode out into the darkness on my tongue, for the simple reason that I wasn't nearly as drunk as those around me. So I told her she would be better off having our conversation with an older woman, but since she asked me, my opinion was that she should pay as little attention as possible to other people's criticisms about her sexuality. If she wasn't interested in sex, that was that, her energies should be directed elsewhere. If, on the other hand, she were to give in to peer pressure, she would win a kind of acceptance, but it wouldn't be her who was being accepted, so what would be the point?

That's what happened – outside. Inside, I was thinking blasphemous things – "God, you slime – how could you create this beauty and leave out such an important element?" I felt a moment of sympathy for Philip, her companion, whom I had found somewhat frustrated and touchy – had I only known. And, on a different plane, I thought this another vote for a morally neutral universe, both with regard to the mischief wrought by a malicious "creator," and how unlikely it will be that Linda will have worthwhile relationships with men (through a fault in men, not Linda). However unimportant that might ultimately be, it seemed important to her – half of all the warm human bodies on the planet, unable for very long to resist a natural force, and thus produce in her a feeling of disgust.

But I digress – I was telling a story about Esprit. Jennifer decided to surrender to the moment and join the cruise, without waiting for her residency visa. The two Canadians had no schedule conflict – they were ready to go. John made a final addition to the crew, an Australian, Kent, someone with actual sailing experience. Also a cat, who, each sunset, would run from one end of the boat to the other with seeming abandon.

You will remember I left Darwin and had to return because of a broken shroud. I was then eager to get underway because the Southern Hemisphere typhoon season was about to begin. So I repaired my boat as fast as I could and cast off my lines. As I left, Esprit was still there, waiting for parts.

The story goes that she waited another week, then cruised at a leisurely pace to Christmas Island, then headed for Sri Lanka. But by then the season of dangerous weather had begun, and, sure enough, in the first week of the season a typhoon blew up and converged on them. The storm arrived with 60 knot winds, then moved off, then recurved and hit them again, over a period of five days.

Eventually Esprit showed up in Sri Lanka, somewhat the worse for wear. John started to plan the next leg of the journey, but there was a certain amount of grumbling among his crew. Apparently John is a perfectionist, or an endless criticizer, or something. You know – a captain story.

During the four week layover in Sri Lanka things went beyond grumbling. First Kent fell ill and flew to England to be operated on, which would seem to have eliminated him from the continuing journey. Then Jennifer decided John didn't have such a white horse after all, and regretted leaving Australia, in particular without having first gotten her residency visa.

Then Jennifer met Roger (say that with a French accent – rrrojhay), a kind and gentle French sailor, and decided to sail with him instead. I must confess to having argued with Jennifer in favor of Roger, after hearing some of her stories about John. But I'm not a journalist – I can meddle.

Then Jennifer's decision became pivotal for the Canadians – they weren't going to put up with John all by themselves. They flew off to Thailand.

This leaves the cat. John had planned to leave it in Sri Lanka anyway, never thinking how poignant that would be once everyone else left him. He offered me the cat, but I decided not to take her – I thought she would eventually fall off the boat and I would feel horrible. Then my friends Bob and Ursula agreed to take her on.

Yesterday, during our daily radio chat, Bob told me the cat went over the side. In a moment of boredom and frustration she made a jump for the whisker pole tied onto the rail. I think the whisker pole was more slippery than she expected. Bob and Ursula released the man-overboard package, a pole with a flag and a life ring, then turned the boat around, but couldn't find the cat. It takes a surprising amount of time to turn a sailboat around, and a cat is a small object in the water. Also with rare exception *felis domesticus* doesn't swim very well.

When I heard about the cat, I remembered a party on Esprit in Darwin. Ursula had arrived before me and announced that I was looking for crew, a wild exaggeration. As a result a young woman who was almost completely free of practical skills was trying to corner me at the party and get me to take her sailing. She tried to impress me with her qualifications – "I don't know much about sailing but I can cook." For myself, I was trying to talk to Jennifer, once I realized she was the woman about whom I had heard, who snatched eggs away from angry salt water crocodiles. Later I met the Canadians, noticed how Linda would draw her hair back with her fingers, as if attention needed to be directed to her face. And John, who, notwithstanding his behavior as a captain, is skilled in the art of conversation.

There they are, the players in my little story, now scattered like leaves before the wind. Kent, now in an English hospital post-op ward. Philip and Linda, likely having an argument somewhere in Thailand. Jennifer, sailing with Roger (remember, say it in French), probably by now realizing that all captains have things in common, and maybe by now Roger's horse isn't so white either. John, who, after his crew had abandoned him, visited Selene and talked in a startlingly humble way, about how supposedly there was something about his personality that drove his crew away. And the cat, the most energetic and certain of any of us, now sleeping in the stomach of a big fish.

January 25 – Day 17

My LORAN receiver has started to work. I didn't realize there was a LORAN system here until I heard the signals while playing with my short-wave radio. So I turned on my LORAN unit, and voila! This is a good omen for the Red Sea passage – I can use LORAN's continuous position data to hug the side of the Red Sea, steering between the freighter traffic and the shoals. Another advantage of LORAN is it gives true velocity and direction "across the ground." An ordinary knot meter tells you how fast you are going through the water, but can't account for ocean currents, or "leeway," a sailboat's sideways movement through the water.

This morning, as I watched the sea go by, I began to think about my time in elementary school. I remembered one of my teachers, Mr. Meyers, who thought more of me than I thought of myself. I can still see him, surrounded by dust and boys, organizing a baseball team in a field behind the school. Like so many things from that time, I am only now coming to understand what he represented, his field of grass, his baseball game.

I once took it for granted that a group of people picked at random will have many values in common, perhaps a majority. I now think this isn't true, a change of view that took many years. When we (men in particular) talk to each other, mostly using intellectual skills to convey intellectual notions, we produce a sense of unity, of common values. We acquired our intellectual notions in a uniform way, mostly in classrooms. Where we are different is in the realm of emotion. Emotions are not transmitted to children the same way ideas are.

In the lives of children, there is a way in which ideas are the province of the state, and emotions are "the private sector." The state has a vested interest in seeing that certain ideas about governments, about the social contract, are transmitted to children. It is in this area that we think ourselves alike. The process is helped along if a person has an emotional affinity for membership in a group. But this affinity, if it exists, originates outside the school – emotions aren't the business of the classroom.

That is one way in which we differ, in an otherwise homogeneous society. For example, I know about myself that, because of the circumstances of my childhood, I never acquired a feeling for the worth of groups. Therefore, if the value of a group is accepted, I am a lower creature than you.

I didn't arrive at this realization quickly or without pain. But I am sure of it. I am accustomed to having people spell out for me the value of groups as if I were a moron, and, with respect to this particular matter and a handful of others, I really am a moron. I prove this by asking stupid questions about hallowed traditions, for example, marriage. I am a lower creature.

I was a lower creature when I met Mr. Meyers. The other boys had been part of a group since birth, so competing for a place on Mr. Meyers' baseball team was not very difficult – if a particular boy was too small, or there were too many boys for two teams, or there weren't enough baseball mitts to go around, someone would have to sit out the game, "be rejected." It wouldn't kill him, it would be an isolated rejection in a life of acceptance. But it would have killed me. I was a lower creature.

I didn't understand any of this at the time – I only had my feelings and a handful of words. In the time I am remembering, Mr. Meyers was choosing his teams, surrounded by boys calling the name of their favorite position. There was plenty of dust and excitement – after all, this wasn't arithmetic or Palmer Method handwriting, this was baseball – something real.

I stood some distance away, but my toes weren't happy: the impulse to join a group of rowdy boys had become a raw power, a force conveyed by chemicals, that could move the sneakers of a lower creature.

Mr. Meyers liked me, I know that now. He knew I was a misfit, appealing but ill-equipped for life on earth. Now he waved to me, saying "Come on, Paul. Come play! Play second base for me!"

I shook my head, as I always did, but then something strange happened. All at once the playground's sights and smells invaded me and forced my words aside. For a moment of time I saw the world with the eyes of a real person, not a lower creature. Mr. Meyers began running toward the baseball field, beckoning his boys to follow – I saw him moving through a world built of groups, families, baseball teams. His smile, the gestures of his hands were a force of nature like gravity, by which all things were turned. I couldn't struggle against it: I knew I was looking at the clockwork of the earth.

That night I turned and turned. Mr. Meyers' exuberance and generosity might be the behavior of a normal person. His boys might be the earth's rightful inhabitants, all of nature their playing field.

How could I have failed to notice that my friends possessed an emotional resilience that I lacked? Those boys believed they had a right to Mr. Meyers' attention. Mr. Meyers believed it too. He didn't exact a terrible price for his companionship. In the grassy field they ran, they played, and no one was destroyed.

By morning I realized my parents were dead people. They moved about the world, but they were dead. And, by way of consistent and diligent application, they had produced dead children. This idea was painful at first, but its advantages were soon clear. If dead people don't love you, it isn't because you aren't lovable, it's because they're dead. Best not model your behavior on that of dead people, you will be thought dead yourself – find something else.

In the time that followed, I became a kind of amphibian, a being of two worlds and of neither, a lower creature posing as a smartass kid. And as I crawled from the sea onto the dry land, I would sometimes see Mr. Meyers as I did that day, a living, warm, dusty union of man and bouncing sneakers. He would look at me from the world of the living, he would wave to me. Come on, Paul, come play.

February 3 – Djibouti

The people are very good looking here, and interesting. Women wear long dresses of beautiful patterns and colors. Friendly, cosmopolitan people. When they discovered I was American some politely inquired whether the race problems had been solved in my country.

I must admit I was torn between a measure of loyalty to my country and a wish to tell the truth. But I told the truth – I explained that racism still exists and is a fact of life for African-Americans. And the biggest change brought on by the Civil Rights Movement of the '60's was a sense of guilt – it was now possible to shame people into acting fairly by pointing a television camera at them.

As I had these conversations I couldn't help thinking a visit to Djibouti would be a great punishment for an American racist. I personally think the only explanation for continued racist beliefs in this environment would be organic brain damage.

Bob, Ursula and I rented a car and drove through a beautiful desert. In one place a row of camels was being loaded with salt from a saline lake. In another a geothermal vent blew steam over a moonlike landscape of lava.

February 15 – Day 11, Djibouti to Port Suez

I have anchored at Marsa Fijab, a small bay on the West side of the Red Sea, in the Sudan. My main reason for stopping was to perform a list of repairs, but this environment is so beautiful it sort of takes you over.

Looking West from the boat I see desert and mountains. Some sand dunes have been blown against the base of the mountains. The mountains are entirely dry, no sign of vegetation, and are colored shades of brown – "brown tones" as they say in California. After marveling at the view for a while, it slowly came to me that I was probably seeing more than 100 miles. The air isn't always clear in the Red Sea, but when the wind backs off there is less airborne dust, and there isn't much pollution to limit one's view.

Except for an occasional Sudan Army truck on the coast road, it is completely silent. At the moment there's no wind – it is 11 AM and the nighttime land breeze hasn't yet given way to the afternoon sea breeze. I like the stillness after two weeks of very windy sailing, almost all upwind.

This is a different kind of sailing – more like the Med is supposed to be. I can sail for a couple of days, and, if the wind is too strong or I just want to sleep without interruption, I can landfall on the Western coast for a while.

Many things are being held in abeyance for the Mediterranean. My diesel motor is in very bad shape, in fact I may have to be towed through the Suez Canal. I have gone through all the usual things trying to fix it, but no luck – it just doesn't put out enough power any more.

Sailing upwind has meant heeling over a lot, and this has revealed more bad things about this boat. One water trap in the head isn't located high enough, so when the boat heels over on that side, water passes across the top of the trap, into the toilet, over the top of the toilet, and thence into the various lockers where all the supposedly dry things are stored. Also the sinks on the galley are mounted too low, so water rises out of the drains and over the tops of the sinks with heel angles of 30 degrees or more. It's entirely stupid that someone would design a sailboat that must heel over to move, and not think about the consequences.

I used to try to remind myself which lockers might get wet. Now I have a very short list of places that don't get wet – all the rest get wet in either rough sea conditions or in rain.

I wrote a sailing analysis program that reads the LORAN positions (a wire connects the LORAN receiver to the computer) and comes up with some interesting things. For one thing, after about five minutes of data collection it tells me exactly what direction I am heading and at what speed. It also tells me how much of that speed is applied to my destination – a quantity called "velocity made good."

My program reveals a lot. To begin with, if I am well heeled over and going fast, I might be drifting sideways in the water about 1/8 of my forward speed! That's because this boat doesn't have a very deep keel, in order not to hit things in shallow water. Another way to put this is to compare the boat's compass heading and the course revealed by the program – they are sometimes different by 20 degrees.

All this math revolves around a central issue of sailing – you can only get so close to the direction the wind is blowing, and exactly which angle you choose, and how much sail you use to move the boat, is crucial. This program shows me I have been using too much sail, heeling over too far, and drifting sideways in the water too much – something called "leeway."

When you travel North in the Red Sea, the wind blows at you from your destination. So sailing here requires good planning, and some frustrations just can't be avoided. For example, sometimes the wind blows a little off to one side. When this happens you take the opposite tack and you have a higher "velocity made good." But eventually you get to a coast and have to turn around and sail the less favorable tack, at which point you may literally be going away from your destination!

So my new plan for this sail is to anchor whenever the wind blows stronger than about 20 knots – it's just too hard to sail efficiently beyond that. Besides, there are some pretty places here. Because of weather I don't want to get to the Med before April anyway.

February 23 – Day 19

I am about 2/3 up the Red Sea now. This will be the longest sail I have undertaken until now, over the shortest distance. The diesel motor is getting worse, now barely running, and the propeller's drive shaft has fallen off repeatedly after each of my efforts to repair it. So I really have no motor at all. When I anchor I have to approach and leave on wind power.

How I discovered this is a story of its own, and another in my collection of anchor stories. One afternoon I entered Marsa Abu Imama in Sudan to do some repairs and just rest a while. I was able to sail in all right, with the wind on the aft starboard quarter, and then drop sail and anchor at a small reef.

Then I reconnected the propeller drive shaft to the engine and tightened the screws. If only I could have known then how much time would be spent playing with this coupling, and with how little effect. But it seemed secure, and I wanted to test it. So, like a fool I raised the anchor and tried to motor around the marsa. Within 90 seconds the drive shaft completely fell off the coupling. There I was, drifting in a tiny bay in a brisk wind, reefs all around, no motor, no sail.

I realized I was going to have to sail upwind through the bay to the anchorage, so I put out some of the jib and tried to turn the boat into the wind. But the tiller wouldn't budge – the drive shaft and propeller had fallen off and were jamming the rudder! So, thinking fast, I rolled up the jib to reduce my rate of drift and jumped into the cabin.

I removed the engine covers and crawled over the engine to the location of the drive shaft coupling, thinking I would pull the drive shaft off the rudder and hold it with something. But it had fallen too far aft and I couldn't get a grip on it. Now in a panic as the boat drifted closer to the reefs, I jumped into the water and pushed the propeller forward. Then I went into the cabin again, dripping wet, located the vise grips and crawled over the engine, then squeezed the vise grips onto the drive shaft, so it couldn't slip back.

Then I resumed my sail with the jib, tacking on one side until the reefs came too close, then switching sides, slowly making my way up to the anchorage. When I got to the anchorage I took care that I didn't get on top of the reef and hang up – I only needed to get into a depth of twenty feet, strike the jib, run forward and drop the anchor. But in striking the jib I lost too much time, drifted too far, and the anchor never found the bottom. So I had to raise 120 feet of anchor chain and sail upwind again.

This time I was too tired for caution. I let the boat sail until I could see the coral heads clearly, then struck the jib. As the boat turned away from the wind, making its way to the right depth for anchoring, it hung up on a coral head. Let's see, I thought, this is the third time in two years I've smacked coral. I have no motor to remove myself, and for all I know the tide is dropping. I could be quite well stuck. So I used the sail to force the keel off the coral, then ran forward and dropped the anchor.

At the time all I could think about was saving my boat, but later I realized I was in a country in the midst of a civil war, and those soldiers watching me from the coast road might have had more than an academic interest in me and my boat. They had no way to get to me on the water, but if I had gone aground they wouldn't have to.

Aren't my anchor stories becoming more baroque as time goes by?

There's more risk in this sail than I am used to – if the wind dies, as it sometimes does, I have no way to get out of the way of the many freighters in these waters. And the Gulf of Suez is smaller and more crowded than the

Red Sea. The nearest place for repairs is Tel Aviv, so I may have to be towed through the Suez Canal and then sail the rest of the way, all without motor power.

February 27 – Day 23

There isn't enough wind to enter the Gulf of Suez, so I have sailed into a place on the coast of Egypt called Hurgada. I was hoping to reconnect the drive shaft to the engine, to be able to motor when the wind isn't blowing, but the drive shaft and the coupler are just too worn – they won't stay connected more than a few minutes.

But I'm glad I stopped here – there is something about this place. First, the approach to the town is a series of shallow bays, sheltered from the Red Sea but sharing tidal flows with it, meaning they are rich in marine life and clear as well. The coral is beautiful, and there are fish everywhere. I saw the anchor hit bottom in 30 feet of water.

The town of Hurgada looks somewhat fairy tale right now, a row of lights beneath a clear evening sky and thin crescent moon. I would have liked to visit the town but the risk of approaching it without motor power is too great – at any time the wind could drop away and leave me at the mercy of the tidal currents.

March 1 – Day 25

Yesterday, my diesel engine stopped running completely – the fuel injection pump has failed. I haven't found a simple remedy to bring it back to life. A diesel's injection pump is the single most complex thing on the engine, and so far I haven't even figured out how to take it off the engine.

To put it mildly, this is a new situation. When the wind stops blowing, I stop moving. Also, the windmill and solar panels are now the only sources of electricity, since I can't use the engine to charge the batteries. So I have to be careful how I use power. If the wind isn't blowing more than 18 knots at night (something not usually wished for), I can't use the radar. So I have to sleep in the cockpit and wake myself at intervals to watch for boats and things. I can't nurse the boat into an anchorage using the motor.

I am in the Gulf of Suez now – the Red Sea part of this sail is finally over. But the gulf is narrow, and full of freighters and oil derricks, so I have to be especially watchful.

Yesterday I decided to anchor and sleep, instead of trying another night of sailing, watching and sleeping, none of those purposes being well served. So I started toward the Egyptian town of Tor, where I heard there was a nice harbor. But just before sunset the wind died, and I was dead in the water.

I rolled up my sails and sat down. To the West the sun was setting behind a row of oil derricks and refineries out on the water, each of which was lit by many lights, and each burning off natural gas in a spectacular display. All this was under a crescent moon that seemed to have been cut from ice by a sculptor. To the East was the town of Tor, at the edge of a desert that slopes gently upward to Mt. Sinai, very red in the sunset. Mt. Sinai, however you may picture it, is very rugged and dry.

And I thought: This must be the antipode of my travels – the true opposite of my normal environment. What could be more distant from Oregon than being adrift between a biblical landscape and a group of alien mechanical beings, who seem to be wading through the Gulf of Suez, lighting their way with smoky torches?

I get a peculiar sensation watching a big factory at night – as if I am fated to be only a visitor, meant to gaze in windows but never go inside. This time I certainly didn't want to get any closer while drifting on the tide – one of the risks I faced was hitting a gas pipeline, breaking it with my boat and blowing up.

But I thought about the floating factories. I thought: Do you guys really want to collect all that oil, in this relentless way, burning up all but your favorite parts? What will your grandchildren use to light their lamps?

Later a small wind started up and, it being too dark to approach shore and anchor, I set sail and moved slowly past these behemoths. It was as if they were trying to tell me something, standing fat and brightly lit on their spindly water legs, the roar of their torches carrying across the water. There was a sense of power and absolute certainty about them – as if their effect on the world would stand the most critical muster. They seemed to me, sailing past in my tiny boat, to be castles of the time of oil, creating a sense of reassurance by their very size, a reassurance, just as in medieval times, mostly of illusion.

March 12 – Port Suez

I have been busy since arriving. First I discovered I wouldn't be towed along the canal, at least not very soon or at any reasonable cost. Then I saw I would have to fix the injection pump myself, there being no local mechanics skilled enough for this task. The manual for my engine bluntly instructed me not to try to take it apart, but I had no choice.

What was fixing the pump like? Try to imagine working on an old-style Swiss mechanical watch that's been filled with dirty black oil. When I got done the entire boat was covered with crankcase oil, including me. But I did fix the pump – some dirt had jammed one of the

City skyline, Cairo, Egypt

pump pistons in its cylinder. I wanted to remove the dirt without taking away any metal, so I used a toothbrush and toothpaste. This stunt worked.

Now the engine was running again, but without much power. I continued to ask to be towed along the Canal, but with no measurable effect (you can't simply transit the Canal under sail power). So I reattached the propeller drive shaft, tightened things as much as possible, genuflected, and announced that I was ready to go. The act of a desperate man.

The next morning, what may be the sorriest boat on record tried to make its way up the Suez Canal against a 20 knot wind. I was making about 1 1/2 knots, the engine was overheating, and I was very cold. After only seven kilometers, the drive shaft fell off again, and I was towed – back to Port Suez.

Bedouins traveling in the desert

That was four days ago. Since then I have been trying to figure out why the engine has no power. The "best local mechanic" made an appearance, but after two hours of effort couldn't suggest anything except that the engine needed to be overhauled.

Then, after a suggestion from one of the boats now in Tel Aviv, I realized I hadn't inspected the pipes that lead the exhaust gas out of the boat, admittedly a long shot, and difficult to get at. I removed an elbow of pipe that had been in place since the boat was built, and examined it. Both openings looked normal – a thin black coating of carbon. But I was running out of ideas to fix my engine, so in desperation I tried to run water through the pipe. It was completely blocked!

After struggling the pipe elbow open, I used a hammer and screwdriver to remove a huge obstructing mass having the color and density of brick. I then reassembled the engine and started it. The engine ran perfectly – in fact, it appears this blockage has been building since before I bought the boat in 1987, and my complaints about the engine, the propeller, how the boat is too heavy for any engine, etc. were brought on by this undiscovered fault.

The moral to this tale? You must do it yourself. No one, no matter how well paid or expert, will uncover any but the most trivial faults, and the expensive solutions will be applied first. I have been consulting mechanics virtually since the day I bought this boat, and have bought a lot of expensive, unnecessary parts, because this – this mechanical equivalent of constipation – went undiscovered.

I started out as a sailor not caring much about diesel motors – after all, this is a sailboat. But now I've sailed the Red Sea without motor power, a 27-day undertaking, and am stopped dead at the mouth of the Suez Canal. As a result I am halfway to being a decent diesel mechanic, out of dire necessity: I had to fix my engine or apply for Egyptian citizenship.

So now I am waiting for a new drive shaft coupler to be built locally, after which I can try the Canal again, with an engine that runs normally, and maybe a propeller that won't fall off.

Meanwhile, I took a day to visit the pyramids. The largest of the pyramids at Giza, as impressive as it looks now, was once covered with finishing stone, so that it had a smooth and symmetrical appearance. Since then most of the finishing stone has fallen off or been removed for use elsewhere. It requires some effort to imagine how it looked when just completed, huge, shiny and symmetrical, but I can see how it might have produced instant belief in a Sun God.

When I visited I quickly shook off the guides who wanted to tell me all about the pyramids, and walked on my own around each of them. Some of the finishing stone lay in piles at the base of the largest, and I confess if I had found a piece small enough, I would have grabbed it. I am becoming a shameless tourist.

I realized the Great Pyramid could be restored for the cost of a single Stealth bomber. This is a complex subject – some might argue that the pyramid is a historical artifact and should be left as it is, others would rather have the bomber. Weathering and the

The Giza Plateau near Cairo

decay from pollution is much more severe on the exposed structural stones than they would be on finishing stones. But fixing up the pyramids is not the most serious problem Egypt faces.

One evening I visited the town of Port Suez with my agent's son (in Egypt each sailboat has an agent that represents it with the authorities). We went to a social club, drank Egyptian tea, and played dominoes. As we played, he told me something I hadn't realized – many Egyptians regard Anwar Sadat as one of the greatest Egyptian leaders of all time. I had gotten the idea Sadat wasn't very popular, partly because a dissident group in the Egyptian army assassinated him. But that would be like believing John Kennedy wasn't very popular because Oswald, a former U. S. Marine, shot him (if we accept the persistent rumor that Oswald acted alone).

I then visited Cairo and saw the Sadat Memorial, a beautiful and architecturally impressive structure, with guards in perfect uniforms, and an eternal flame burning at the tomb. In case I might have missed it, my driver stopped the car and pointed it out, making me understand with gestures and a few words of English that a great man was buried there.

Next Day –

Egypt has been a trying experience – I would have been out of here 12 days ago, towed behind another yacht, except the Egyptians long ago figured out such towing would reduce the profit made by tugboats, so they made a rule that one boat can't tow another, unless their hulls are of different materials. Then, to close another loophole, a tugboat towing a disabled boat always takes it back to its point of origin, no matter how close it has gotten to the other end of the canal. And finally, it is nearly impossible to arrange to simply be towed from one end of the canal to the other. And should it be made possible, it costs about US$4,000.

Parts are impossible to order and nearly impossible to have built here. After two bad starts I now have a reasonably decent drive shaft coupling. For this one I made detailed drawings and stood over the lathe while the part was made (and the machinist I found was first-rate).

In exchange for this unplanned 15-day stopover, when not struggling with my boat I met some interesting people. I never saw a nicer group of people so totally at the mercy of a corrupt and ineffective government. My agent says the authorities take possession of a yacht from time to time, and if they could they would sell the sailors as well as the boat.

If I had known the policies of the Canal authorities, I would have made absolutely sure my engine and drive train were in perfect condition. In my own defense I will say that my motor was okay in Djibouti, the last major stop, and any major repairs would have had to be accomplished in Darwin.

Take Two and the other European boats I have been traveling with are in Tel Aviv now – I talk to them on the radio. I think I will haul this boat out of the water in Tel Aviv and paint it again. I have a list of repairs I can make there also.

Israel & Egypt Notes –

Israel and Egypt are both Middle Eastern countries with similar climates, located close to one another. There the comparison ends, for Israel lives in the 20th century. Before you decide this view arises from my Western origins, I must tell you the Egyptians themselves made this comparison for me. In a single breath one young Egyptian told me how much he hated the Israelis, and how it was impossible not to respect their accomplishments.

With one exception, every person having an official position in Egypt asked to be bribed, for which the term is "Baksheesh." No one knows the price of anything until they have been paid off, then the price is higher. If you refuse to pay, things disappear from your boat.

The first of the two pilots I was required to have on my boat to transit the canal spent his time yelling at me in Arabic and demanding more money. The second, who I call the "gentleman thief," spent most of his time asking for more money, or videotapes, or alcohol, or sex magazines. If you are a single hander it is more difficult, because then you must steer the boat while the pilot plunders it.

The one exception I mentioned was a uniformed officer responsible for seeing me out of the Port Said entrance and into the Mediterranean. The second of the two regular canal pilots had just debarked with his bag of booty, mostly groceries he felt justified in taking. Then the official came on board, informed me that bribery was a criminal offense, and asked me whether anyone had asked me for anything during my stay in Egypt. I would have laughed at him, but this might have greatly complicated my departure. I could have told him of every demand for payment, but this would surely have taken a huge amount of time, since I had been in Egypt 18 days and had been approached at least once a day by someone with his hand out. Besides, I had paid nearly every official who demanded payment, just to protect my boat and hasten my departure, so didn't that make me a criminal also?

Then the official departed and I was free to sail out of Port Said. About five minutes later a steel boat came alongside and a very raggedy crew tried to make me believe they had some further official duties to perform. I told them to stand off, since by this time I was offshore and the water was too rough for close maneuvers. So they asked a bunch of questions, all of which had been asked by a dozen other people, then the most motley of them held out his hand and said "Do you have a gift for me?"

Those who travel to Egypt as normal tourists, arriving and departing by air, may think this picture exaggerated. But I realize now that if I hadn't sat down and fixed my diesel engine, my boat would eventually have been confiscated by the Egyptian authorities and I (with some luck) would have been deported.

When I think about these thieves in positions of authority, my heart goes out to the powerless Egyptian citizens, in particular the women, who, in silence and fertility, are the greatest victims. I think in particular of a group of schoolgirls I met in the marketplace, arms laden with books, eyes dark with wonder. Before they were shooed away they asked some questions, which showed they were braver than I was – I suspect if I had dared to say what I wanted to, I would have been put up against a wall and shot. Instead I just answered their questions. Yes, I owned a house and a car. No, most people in America don't live like the people on "Dallas," an American television program popular among Egyptians. Yes, many women have their own jobs, sometimes their own houses.

An Israeli recently told me the Arab birthrate is five times that for Jews in Israel, and that eventually Arabs will be in the majority within Israel. This is one of my clues that the situation in Israel is not only more complicated than I imagined, it's more complicated that I could have imagined.

Israel is the most militaristic country I have visited. In old Jerusalem, I saw some West Bank settlers strolling near the Wailing Wall, looking very much like American hippies – beards,

Western Wall, old Jerusalem

backpacks, casual dress. Except that they carried Uzi submachine guns.

Visiting old Jerusalem has had a profound effect on me. The old walled city of Jerusalem sits largely unaffected by its modern surroundings, so I found I could move from a twentieth-century avenue through a large gate, and suddenly be walking a narrow cobblestone path in a marketplace not much changed since biblical times. In the early morning hours, bags of spice are unrolled for display, their scents filling the air beneath the arched stone ceilings.

Jerusalem was probably the first, or one of the first, truly cosmopolitan cities. A city of our time is cosmopolitan because ideas travel through the air at the speed of light. Jerusalem was cosmopolitan because nearly everyone had a reason to go there, and then to maintain their right of access. For Jews, Jerusalem was the site of their early temples, artifacts of which remain. For Moslems, the rock from which Mohammed is said to have risen to heaven is now enclosed in a shrine. Christians, who have a comparatively recent stake in this ancient city, can use parts of the Bible as a tour guide to Jerusalem.

I would like to see a comparison of all the administrators of Jerusalem, a need the existing museums only partly meet. Maybe there should be scores for each regime, depending on how dreadful they were. Around 1000 C.E. (that means Christian Era, the Jewish term for A.D., about which term Jews aren't so crazy), some crusaders rode down from Europe and stormed the city by the North wall. They cut up everybody on whom they could lay hands – Jews, Moslems, and others. But the idealism of their quest, and the ferocity with which they laid waste to everything in their path, was so completely at odds with the forces that sustain a city that they were obliged to abandon it, after a mere 200 years. They get a zero, only because my rating system doesn't have negative numbers.

Spice shop, old Jerusalem

Around 1500 C.E. Suleiman the Magnificent, who evidently wrote his own curriculum vitae, completed the wall begun by others that now surrounds old Jerusalem. Then he magnanimously allowed all interested parties access to the city. I give him an eight.

This account is hardly encyclopedic, since there were so many occupiers about which I don't know enough – Babylonians, Persians, Greeks, Romans, Seljuks, Mamluks, Ottomans. Even Britain, from 1917 to 1948.

Masada, Israel

The Israelis, who captured Jerusalem in 1967, allow Moslems, Christians and others access to the city and its shrines, so they may get a high rating, but their record is still being written. I will let history decide.

There is something about the history of this area that isn't well understood among lay Christians, something diplomatically hinted at repeatedly in the museums of Israel. At the time of Christ the Romans were making things very difficult for the Jews, and this naturally increased their anxiety about the coming of a messiah, a prospect that is embedded in Jewish beliefs. When Christ made his appearance, he didn't simply claim to be the son of God, he presented himself as the messiah for which the Jews had been waiting. Only much later was Christianity perceived as separate from Judaism, and an enmity between Jews and Christians begun.

I have never been able to get very excited about conventional religions. I have come to the view that the most profound religious and spiritual experiences are individual ones, without guides or interpreters. This makes me a poor candidate for an army of wall-stormers and infidel-hackers. It also makes me stand in awe of the history of Christianity (just as an example), in which a simple dispute about whether Christ was or was not the Jewish messiah devolved into a blood feud lasting, so far, 2000 years.

But in my naiveté I think the close association of Christ and the Jewish society of which he was a part should reduce the animosity to manageable proportions, when in fact there is ample evidence to the contrary – I'll call it the principle of trivial difference: the closer the beliefs of two groups, the greater the animosity between them.

(April 16)

This week I went on my third trip to Jerusalem. I visited a museum where some of the Dead Sea Scrolls are on display. These scrolls were hidden in a cave in some big earthen jugs, about 130 C.E. There was a rebellion going on about that time, between the Jews and the Romans. The Jews were being led by a guy named Bar Kochba. Some of his followers said he was the messiah (although he did not) and would free the Jews from domination by the Romans. He didn't succeed, and the Jews were (yes, again) scattered all over the place by the angry Romans. But the scrolls remained hidden until 1947, leaving a legacy of great detail about the rebellion as well as the daily life of that time.

Wow, I thought. This guy Bar Kochba and Jesus Christ have more than a little in common. The more I studied the events, the more I realized it was quite by chance that Bar Kochba didn't have his own messianic cult later on, or attract the attention now focused on someone else.

I sat around in the museum looking at the scrolls, thinking what history would have been like if Bar Kochba's life had precipitated the division that Christ's life did. Maybe "Christian" history would have been more warlike, if that can even be imagined. But at a more practical level, if I hit my thumb with a hammer, I think "Bar Kochba!" sounds better than "Jesus Christ!" We've been cheated by history out of a great easy-to-say oath, a matter of great interest to sailors.

Now that I have explored old Jerusalem and heard its history, and in particular after walking the wall that separates the old city from the new, I think no one can visit this city and come away unchanged. Only through a great effort of will can one walk its narrow passages, hear the voices of spice traders, old people, children echoing between the ancient stones, and believe himself separate from all who have walked here before.

I expected to have my boat hauled out for painting and repairs right away, but two weeks went by for various reasons. Then the boat crane's cable parted and dropped a boat, which reduced my enthusiasm for this boatyard. By the way, when the cable parted the boat dropped into the water and the keel struck the bottom. The owner decided not to haul the boat back out again, instead sailing to Cyprus. Yesterday the boat, with many people on board, sank, fortunately with no loss of life. Naturally rumors are flying that the boat was damaged when it was dropped and this caused it to sink, but the owner won't be able to collect insurance because the boat wasn't hauled out again for inspection.

But I digress. When I was finally hauled out, using a different crane, I saw a huge scar on one side, below the waterline. I remember smacking something very hard one night in the Indian Ocean, probably a waterlogged freight container, but I inspected the boat inside for leaks and damage and found nothing. Later I dove on the boat and saw a cracked area, which made me even more eager to haul out.

Now with the boat out of the water I could see three large cracks radiating from the impact point to a distance of about eight inches. And a pattern of oval concentric cracks in the paint showed that the entire hull had flexed at the impact, remarkable because the hull is greater than an inch thick at that point. I think the only reason the hull wasn't punctured was that the container hit the boat near the beam, just a "grazing blow."

So now I am back to being glad I have a heavy, poky boat, in spite of the things that annoy me about it.

Telling jokes in Israel was a surprise. I tell jokes everywhere I go – I always have at least one joke for a given situation. For example if I meet a couple who are both computer scientists (this actually happened recently), I tell my computer-scientist-couple joke (they get into bed and the woman says "So are we on line tonight or what?").

At first I found the Israelis to be a tough audience. I was prepared for some differences – only the truly brain-dead think Jewish humor is the same as any other kind. But over time I adjusted – I began to tell fewer straightforward jokes, those that depend only on surprise or a play on words, and instead told a handful that I personally like but don't get to tell very often.

I also found that, unless I invented a joke on the spot, they had heard it. I also noticed they preferred jokes that (1) spoke to the human condition or (2) required some depth of thought. Here are some jokes I told, and heard, in a group of Israeli boat-owners one afternoon in Tel Aviv. I started with an ordinary one, that relies on the element of surprise (it's my own):

A. Professor Gedachtnis, when did you first realize you had total recall?

B. It was ... It was ... Er ... Umm .. wait ...

They laughed, mostly because they hadn't heard it. Then I tried this one, from a Woody Allen movie:

A. But sex without love is an empty experience!

B. Yes, but as empty experiences go, it's one of the best.

This also relies on the element of surprise, but is very good. Most had heard it, but they laughed anyway.

A laugh-meter would be wasted in Israel, because some of the best jokes, those requiring some thought, receive a grunt or a nod as high praise. Now my friends told this one:

Two men are at dinner. The waiter brings two plates, one generous, one skimpy.

A. You choose.

B. No, you choose.

A. Okay. (takes the big one.)

B. How uncivilized! If I had chosen, I would have taken the small one!

A. So? I chose, and you got the small one. Why complain?

Definitely category (2). This next joke appears in another Woody Allen movie, "Crimes and Misdemeanors" that I saw in Tel Aviv (my apologies for not recalling the exact words):

A. I hate to tell you this, but [the subject for your interview] has killed himself!

B. I'm shocked! Where I grew up people never killed themselves – they were too unhappy.

This line got a small laugh from the theater audience, but after a moment, a round of applause. It definitely falls in category (1). This next one belongs in both category (1) and (2). It is a little complicated and I rarely tell it anymore, because I usually end up having to explain it:

Two businessmen are sitting in a train station between Minsk and Pinsk.
A. "Where are you going?"
B. "To Pinsk."
A. (thinks for a minute) ... "You're lying! You *are* going to Pinsk!"

Not for the faint-hearted, but most of the Israelis got it right away. One had heard a different version, which he proceeded to tell.

Then I told this one, and perhaps I shouldn't have bothered, since people had already heard it, or if they didn't they guessed the punch line themselves. One person described it as "very Jewish":

For his birthday, a mother gives her son two ties. The next time he visits, he's wearing one of the ties. She says "You didn't like the other one?"

I almost never heard the kinds of jokes popular in the U.S., those that make their point in five words, or that have no point, or that disparage a nationality or ethnic group, or that require an elephant, a light bulb, or someone Polish. I wanted to sip my wine and watch the sun go down as the conversation rolled on, but I hadn't heard most of the jokes, many were worth remembering, and the Israelis had heard them all before. So I took notes.

{ 8 }

Tel Aviv to The Caribbean

Larnaca, Cyprus was my first stop after Israel. It was one of those prosaic nautical experiences in which a particular town is supposed to have every imaginable kind of store and supply one could wish for, then when you arrive there is nothing.

Overlooking a port in Cyprus

I was told there was a sail maker in Larnaca, fortunately I decided to have my sails repaired in Tel Aviv, thinking, a bird in the hand, etc. There was no sail maker in Larnaca.

I was told there was a Yanmar Diesel dealer in Larnaca. I heard this as far back as Egypt. I made up a list of the parts I damaged during my makeshift repair, as well as all the spares one might wish to have. When I got to Larnaca, I found the phone number of the "dealer." After some struggle, I discovered that he had no shop, no parts, and no knowledge. If you went to a particular place on a particular day, and he wasn't busy, he would be there too, and (if you brought your own part numbers) he would take your money, order the parts from Japan, then ninety days later deliver them to you and charge you retail. Even if I had wanted to do this I didn't have any part numbers, and I certainly didn't want to spend ninety days in Larnaca.

I delivered my life raft to a shop at the marina that advertised itself as being an inspection service. It turned out that the life raft inspection was carried out at a shop in another town (Limassol) whose schedule was very relaxed. I stayed an extra week trying to recover it.

On the bright side, a group of boat people and I rented some motorcycles and toured Cyprus. We planned to have eight people on four bikes. I thought it would be nice to have a big, comfortable bike, so I chose a Honda 650. If I had known how far I would be pushing it I would have selected a more modest size. The rental agency provided approximately one teaspoon of gas, just enough to propel me out of sight of the rental shop. I pushed the bike about 2 kilometers to a gas station and filled it up.

Later in the day the battery began to act up, so that the bike would stall if allowed to idle, and the electric starter wouldn't work either (on many modern bikes there's no kick start lever). So if I stopped at a light and didn't keep the engine revved up I would have to push the bike, jump aboard, and start it. Then (while I kept the engine screaming) my passenger would get aboard and we would dart off.

That night the bike died completely, probably as a result of my foolishly wanting to use the headlight. After a three-hour wait the rental shop brought a replacement bike, which, when unloaded from the truck, couldn't be started. A mechanic was called in and the bike was brought to life about midnight.

The rest of the group had by now gone to a monastery in the hills near the town of Pafos (named Agios Neophytos) which provides overnight accommodation for free (the guests are supposed to figure out that donations are accepted). I didn't really get to see the monastery that night, wishing only to fall asleep, but on waking I thought Scotty had beamed me up by mistake.

The monastery overlooks Pafos and the Mediterranean, but the buildings are so well constructed and beautiful that it is hard to decide which direction to look. Behind the modern monastery is an older section built into the face of a cliff. The entire site is absolutely clean, plants tended and watered – a place where sweat holds entropy at bay.

From time to time one saw a monk, say, watering a plot of flowers, or moving from one room to another, head bowed. It was unsaid but clear that we outsiders should not interact in any way with them.

I enjoyed the visit but finally I thought it a mistake to go there. I realized no donation could balance the negative effect of an invasion of eight laughing, motorcycle-riding, casually dressed tourists. When the cameras inevitably came out I wanted to object, but I realized the explanation would be very long-winded and probably produce more heat than light, so I didn't start.

The remainder of the trip consisted of rides through a landscape very reminiscent of central California as it might have looked 75 years ago, and several hair-raising episodes involving certifiably insane truck or bus drivers, and some equally nutty behavior on the part of the other motorcycle drivers. I kept falling behind because I didn't want to die nearly as much, or as soon, as the others. I always thought the reason for a big bike was to have a comfortable ride, not to see how fast you could pass a top-heavy truck full of live pigs on a narrow mostly-dirt road with a cliff on one side.

Today is June 1. I arrived here in Finike, Turkey (site of ancient Phoenicus) early this morning, after a two-day crossing from Cyprus. I had not intended to stop in Turkey but a number of people said nice things about it, so I've decided to include it. I'm glad I planned it this way because the wind has started blowing with gale force (gusts of 45 knots), and I reached this port just in time to seek shelter.

The exchange rate is 2600 Turkish Lira per U.S. dollar, which makes transactions seem peculiar for a while. I filled up my diesel cans and discovered they wanted 102,000 lira. At first I thought I was being raked over the coals, not able to make the conversion in my head, but when I got back to the boat it turned out to be two dollars a gallon – usurious but not criminal.

As usual, an expectation wasn't met, but this time it was a pleasant surprise. A number of people remarked on the formidable Turkish bureaucracy and the time it takes to clear into the country. I guess some changes have been made, also in this marina the taxi drivers know the routine. For about four U.S. dollars they zip you around to the various offices and do some interpreting as well. The procedure took about an hour and a half, which is much better than average for this part of the world.

I'm not crazy about the anchoring and mooring practices here in the Med. When I arrived this morning I decided to anchor away from the marina inside the breakwater instead of trying to slide between two boats. Later, as the wind picked up, all the local charter boats returned at once and tried to slip into their berths. Several collisions took place, mostly because the wind unraveled some well-intended maneuvers. You know it's bad when you can hear the hulls crashing together across the marina, and see masts whipping back and forth.

I'm not staying long enough to launch my inflatable dinghy with the outboard engine, so I rowed my hard dinghy ashore several times this morning for fuel and clearance, to the amazement of the local sailors, who travel between marinas and rarely use a dinghy. I am completely alone on the far side of the bay – I hope I find places like this elsewhere in the Med. I think the extra distance is worth it.

(June 5)

I have just spent a couple of days at a place called Kale Koy, an area dominated by a castle on a hilltop. There are two small towns separated by a bay. One has the castle above it, the other offers more shelter from the wind, and, since the wind was blowing 35 knots when I arrived, I chose shelter. The next day I hiked around the bay to the castle.

After I climbed the hill and sat down in the ruins of the castle, I tried to imagine who built it and why. I can't imagine building a castle as a weekend project, a fling – there must have been a group wishing to preserve their goods or lives against some other group. And, because of the forbidding terrain, the "other group" would have to arrive by sea. The castle has high walls and a very large inside area, but no internal buildings, so I guessed that during an attack the entire village temporarily took shelter inside the walls.

Beneath the castle's walls, Turkish girls row wooden boats between the village and the boats riding at anchor, offering scarves for sale. They are invariably dressed in bright-colored pantaloons and scarves, and they are invariably pretty. When they get done with you, you may or may not own a scarf, but your heart is certainly broken.

I have noticed the majority of the yachts here are German, so I am once again using some of the German I learned from Bob and Ursula. The Turks I meet are much more likely to speak German than English as a second language, so I find myself speaking German to the Turks as well as to the other boat people.

When I noticed this preference for German among the Turks I remembered a special relationship exists between those countries dating from the opening days of World War I. In August 1914 a German warship escaped its British pursuers and made its way to Istanbul, in a masterstroke of diplomacy that effectively allied Turkey with Germany, with far-reaching effects. The British pursuers, thinking more in military than diplomatic terms, couldn't figure out why the German ship was racing East instead of West. By the time they discovered the ship's destination it was too late,

Turkey permitted Germany access to its ports and thus to the Black Sea, and Germany was able to attack Russia from an unexpected direction. The terrible waste of Gallipoli was a later attempt to undo this damage, and the British, looking for a scapegoat, sacked their First Lord of the Admiralty, a young man named Winston Churchill.

Today I am in Kas (pronounced "kash"), my last stop in Turkey. Kas is somewhat dramatic, even though it doesn't have a medieval castle. The earth rises almost vertically behind the town, and some sarcophagi (burial sites) are hewn into the cliffs very high above the town. When I saw these I thought it's one thing to accept that the departed have gone to heaven, it's quite another to carry them halfway up.

(June 17)

I have been on a two-day stop in Rhodes nearly two weeks now. I had been told there was a dealer for my autopilot here, and, as usual, there is no dealer in any meaningful sense of the word. I thought I would just pick up some extra electric motors and return my two broken autopilots to service.

A brief explanatory note: an autopilot is the device that steers my boat through the water. Without an autopilot I would have to sit and steer the boat by hand, a practical impossibility for more than about eight hours. The key mechanical element in the autopilot, and the part the wears out fastest, is a small electric motor worth about US$10. The entire autopilot costs US $800.

It turns out that the company that makes the autopilot won't provide spare parts. I had heard a rumor to this effect but I couldn't believe a company would hold their customers in such contempt and manage to stay in business. But it's true: if something breaks, you may (1) return the unit to England for repair, or (2) buy a new autopilot. Option (1) would make sense if I wasn't sailing anywhere for six months. Option (2), which I am now exercising for the fourth time in three years, should be easy but isn't. The first marine store I approached was a dealer for my autopilot – but in name only. They had no autopilots, no catalogs, and no knowledge. They were willing to take my money and order a unit from England, then charge me higher than retail price. Reminded of the Yanmar "dealer" in Larnaca, I declined.

The second dealer assured me that there was an autopilot like mine in Athens, it would be simply a matter of getting it from Athens to Rhodes, at which point in the conversation he couldn't resist saying "it will be here tomorrow." That was almost two weeks ago. It turns out the Greek Customs people are responsible for delivering things between the islands, to prevent anyone circumventing either the import duty or the 13% value added tax by shipping something directly to one of the islands and claiming it as a shipment within Greece.

But the Greek Customs people get paid the same salary whether their packages arrive on time, or late, or never. As a result late arrival is dearly to be hoped for, because on time almost never happens, and never almost always.

A friend, a more experienced sailor, used a different method. He called a vendor in the U.S., placed his order and requested air freight shipment. When he told me his plan I thought it was the silliest thing I had ever heard: an item from a company in England, about a thousand miles from here, is flown halfway around the world to the U.S., taken off one airplane and put on another, again flown halfway around the world to here, where it miraculously appears at the local airport's freight window, marked with the magic words "Spare parts for yacht in transit," to avoid problems with Customs. When I ridiculed my friend's plan, he looked at me with an expression normally reserved for brain-damaged children. He got his parts and left a week ago.

Rhodes is a pleasant enough place, apart from the artificial anxiety brought on by owning a boat. At one time there was an enormous bronze statue of Helios the Sun God that is said to have straddled the port entrance. Called the "Colossus of Rhodes" and counted among the wonders of the ancient world, it unfortunately was knocked down by an earthquake in 227 B.C.

A large, imposing and very charming castle dominates the skyline of Rhodes. Naturally this well-defended structure inspired people to attack it, in that adversarial logic for which humans are notorious. Principal among the attackers was Demetrius Polioketes, who fancied himself another Alexander the Great – we'll call him Demetrius the So-So. Anyway, he built a fantastic siege machine, nine stories high, weighing around 125 tons, that sheltered troops, delivered them over the castle walls, and catapulted huge stone balls against the defenders. Piles of the stone balls he used lie about the castle today – I tried to move one, and quickly realized I wouldn't be able to help Demetrius the So-So storm the castle. Later I did a little math and estimated that each ball weighs 360 kilos (800 pounds).

After I proved mathematically that I couldn't get the ball onto my shoulder, I sat down on it and thought about history instead. Someone once said that all history is lies. Certainly most of it is intended more to direct you to a particular outlook than to report events objectively, but even the comparatively objective parts tend to be swept away by the more dramatic events and people. That is why military history is dominated by battles in which many people got killed, regardless of their military significance. My favorite example is Douglas MacArthur's campaign against the Japanese during Word War II.

MacArthur used an interesting strategy against the Japanese-held Pacific islands: he would discover where the Japanese had most of their people and equipment, i.e., where they expected an attack, and he would leapfrog around that island to one behind it. He would attack this less-defended island, cut off communications and supplies to the more forward island, and the Japanese would have to abandon it.

The Japanese tended to be fairly rigid in their thinking, so MacArthur successfully used this strategy again and again. As a result he was able to keep his casualties down to about 60,000 men in a campaign lasting several years. By comparison, in Europe the Allies lost 100,000 men in The Battle of the Bulge, a single battle that lasted only a few weeks.

But history largely overlooks MacArthur's achievement – the casualty rate wasn't very high, therefore nothing important could have been going on out there. The effect of this kind of history is to plant the idea that you win battles by massed frontal assaults, an idea that should have been abandoned for all time in 1918.

The most dismal aspect of this kind of history, one reinforced every day in the evening news, is that ordinary people and events don't count. In the U.S., largely because of television and the realities of prime-time broadcasting, people who aren't famous aren't anything. A town will never be mentioned until a tornado rips it to pieces. A man will go unnoticed until he shoots up a schoolyard.

I have a story about this famous-or-nothing way of thinking, with a bit of "the only real poets are dead poets" mixed in. Once John Cheever gave a poetry reading, then opened up to questions and comments from the audience. One woman raised her hand and asked "Were those real poems or did you write them?"

(June 26)

The autopilot never arrived in Rhodes and I finally left. A local sailor sold me an actuator, the only part I needed, so I think I have enough spare parts now.

After the town of Rhodes I visited Lindos, then Simi, and now Kos. There are many places in the Med with the same names – it becomes confusing. But there are other confusing similarities, like the many postcard-cute towns, each dominated by a castle. Lindos and Kos both have castles, parts of which predate the Christian Era. Simi had no castle, but in exchange it was picturesque and vertical.

Lindos is on the South coast of the island of Rhodes (not to be confused with the town of Rhodes) and its castle is spectacular. One gets the impression that every Greek town wanted to have the biggest, highest castle, and the original reason for the castles, to repel invaders, was forgotten.

I had heard nice things about Lindos, mostly having to do with the combination of architectural and human beauty one finds there. In the past it was a gathering place for young people, but now that overnight accommodations exist the average age is increasing. Lindos has more bars per square kilometer than anywhere I've yet visited.

Most beaches in Greece are topless in principle, many also in fact, some are bottomless as well. Some behavioral rules exist that are never spoken out loud but everyone understands. The first is the border between the taverna and the sand – on crossing this border one covers up or uncovers depending on direction of travel. The second rule is the same for nudist gatherings everywhere: no staring. Men being men, this second rule is obeyed reluctantly, and certain devices are employed to permit discreet peeking, or perhaps discreet staring might be more accurate.

One lazy day I sailed about the beaches of Lindos with my sailing dinghy, and saw many interesting things. At one place there was a nice flat rock area, away from the main beaches, perfect for sunbathing - but what's that? As I sailed closer I saw a row of older men sitting in the shade, each armed with a paperback book, facing the sunbathing area, um, reading.

Kos seems to have as many young people and bars as Lindos, as well as an international airport. According to some of the Europeans I talk to here, it is a preferred spot in the Greek Islands. Loud music in the evening, many people meeting each other.

When I sailed in I thought I would fill my tanks with water. Imagine my surprise when I found every water tap locked up! In Kos, ouzo is literally easier to acquire than water. I took my jerry cans ashore and prevailed on a sponge vendor to unlock his tap, which he graciously did. Later, wanting to show my appreciation and to assure a future supply of water, I bought one of his sponges. Then I wondered whether I might have insulted his generosity by seeming to pay him for the water. But I wanted to send a signal that yacht people aren't all exceedingly uncivilized and cheap, a general impression in the Med. I eventually realized the sponge man probably goes through the water-barter ritual every week and I was probably making too much of it. Besides, it's a nice sponge.

Now that I am in the Med I have been trying to behave like a regular person, in the hope of meeting people and defeating loneliness. I noticed some time ago that I feel a lot more lonely on land than while sailing – I think the proximity of people does it. So, since Mediterranean night life centers on bars, I go to bars. They are less sordid here than in North America, being mostly out in the open, with nice furnishings. Even civilized, a word I rarely apply to bars.

But let's face it, I am sort of a misfit in this environment. I make interesting conversation, a minor handicap. I am older than the fathers of about half the people I meet, definitely a major handicap. And there are some language difficulties, even though everyone knows at least some English. I can make myself understood in German, French and Spanish, but a normal conversation is out. I am the only American in town – there was one other but he sailed away.

I remain practical to the end. I expect to fill my evenings with conversation, but just in case I remember to take a book. If I'm not talking to anyone or walking around people-watching, I sit and read my book. Seems natural enough to me. I expect people to think "How interesting! Someone reading a book!" but sometimes I think the reaction is more like "Check out the geek with the book!"

I discovered something when I sat down to read the other night. The bar attendant came by and told me two things – one, to stay I had to buy a drink, and two, they had only alcoholic drinks for sale. I am the sort of person who will drink in company but I don't like to drink alone, so I walked around until I met someone.

Later I thought how peculiar that system sounded to an American. A combination of serious social problems brought on by alcohol in the United States and a tendency to sue anybody for anything, makes it necessary for bar owners to have coffee and other non-alcoholic drinks handy, and to stop serving people obviously drunk. But I haven't seen anyone ridiculously drunk here (maybe I haven't stayed long enough in bars or visited enough islands yet) so perhaps Europeans are more self-controlled than Americans would be in the same situation. I am quite sure if a group of Americans were exposed suddenly to this Greek drink-or-go-home system, they would be quickly reduced to a sodden, limp, incoherent, barfing pile of groaning bodies.

I recently fixed the computer system on the boat of some friends. The captain wanted to write letters and print them, he wanted to send and receive text messages over the radio, he wanted to be set up as Selene is, and he had all the necessary hardware. But the system had been installed wrong, it couldn't be used as it was, I was the only person who could do it. It took half a day and every test device I own, but I fixed the system.

I enjoyed the task, and my friends have a working system now. I thought about it later and was struck by the fact that I have a completely upside-down life: my work is my leisure, and my leisure my work. Taking care of my boat, deciding where I am going to go next, visiting the offices of government officials, protecting my boat from people who can't sail, this is work. Fixing somebody's electronic problems and then being invited to a great dinner, this is leisure.

I was to have sailed North today, but the wind has started to blow really hard, naturally from the direction I want to go. Oh well, I guess it won't kill me to have another sample of Med night life.

(July 14)

I feel as though I have visited every island in the Aegean. I have visited 11 places since Kos, most after motoring a small distance against the "Meltemi," a strong wind that blows from the North much of the time. After I visited Lesvos I got tired of beating against the wind (which seemed to be getting stronger), so now I am turning back South and using the sails again.

I seem to have adjusted to the summertime Aegean. I move the boat just often enough to maintain a kind of sun drenched rhythm of pretty places, whitewashed towns asleep in time, or bays of bright green sand. I have been dividing my time between towns, where one finds conversations, magazine stands and Greek salads, and isolated anchorages, where one recovers from the towns.

(July 18)

I am learning that the bigger towns should be avoided! I thought I would visit Mikonos to get fuel and water and to see whether the night life was as great as rumored. Even though the overall wind was moderate, the terrain at Mikonos produces gusts of hurricane force right in the marina. This is something you find out by going there, the guidebooks don't mention it. I managed to shred may favorite sail on the way into this "shelter."

But the fun had just begun. In the marina, people who chartered their boats three days before were bashing each other and the rocks, crossing up their mooring lines and anchor rodes, and generally making a mess. I took one look at the scene and departed, realizing that even if I succeeded in single-handing my boat into a mooring without hitting something, I wouldn't last two hours in there. There were twice as many boats as moorings – frustrated, inexperienced sailors motored in circles like sharks.

So I went up the coast about 5 kilometers to a small indentation in the coastline. It didn't deserve to be called a bay, it was just a place where the wind was blocked by a hill, and the waves were not quite as high as in the open sea. I anchored and got ready to make a fuel run in my dinghy. I put on my wet suit for this trip – there was no way I was going to make a trip in 60 MPH winds on the open sea without getting soaked.

It was the most miserable trip. Huge waves blew across the dinghy and me, and I could scarcely see for the spray. But I got my fuel.

Then I changed into dry clothes, beached my dinghy and took a bus to town – to arrive dry, you see. After all, the point of visiting a town in the Greek Islands is to sit down and have a Greek salad, and maybe get into conversation with people for whom a sailor is an interesting creature.

That evening, during just such a conversation, I kept being distracted by salt water that had been injected into my ear during my wild, wet ride and would probably require surgery to remove. I thought about my poor shredded sail – my favorite! – and how tired I was. But I kept this to myself, after all, I wanted to make sailing sound interesting, in which you cross an ocean without having to drink a good percentage of it. I didn't weaken and complain about my life on the sea, it was a nice conversation – I lied.

(July 22)

After two days in Ios I think it fair to say it is a pretty Greek island thoroughly spoiled by tourism. It has a reputation for free living and caters to the youngest tourists, a recipe for trouble.

As usual I declined to enter the marina, where people are packed porthole to porthole for the privilege of hearing disco music until 5 AM. I have anchored out in the middle of the bay next to the town, a good place to launch my wind surfer in the afternoon.

Ios is geographically divided – the old, "real" village is on top of a hill with a pretty cobblestone path called the "donkey trail" leading from the modern part of town up to the old village. And yes, donkeys still make their way up the path. All the nicer restaurants and bars are in the old village, in particular a place called "Club Ios," perched on the highest hill, best visited around sunset when they play classical music for the gathered sunset-watchers. On my first day here, sitting among the sunset crowd, I believed I was in yet another Greek island town where tourism coexists with traditional village life. But then the sun went down.

My version of a night on the town, an interesting conversation with interesting people, has no place in Ios. The probability of even a coherent conversation, much less an interesting one, floats near vanishingly improbable in the early hours of the evening, to later drown in a sea of alcohol.

From a philosophical standpoint Ios stands as an extreme embodiment of the human mating ritual. Young women, endowed by nature with an absurd perfection of beauty, appear at the beach in a spectrum of clothing that ranges between nothing and almost nothing. Young men, confronted by this sight, and surmising that it might be too good to be true, steel themselves with alcohol against the prospect of rejection before, during, and after visiting the town's public meeting places, which happen also to sell alcohol in many of its more lethal forms. At the height of the evening, people of both sexes, drunk, no, poisoned by alcohol, can be seen trying to steer their bodies from place to place among the narrow cobblestone paths, pausing here and there to throw up.

(July 25)

Thira is the site of a large island, the center of Minoan civilization, that blew up about 1400 B.C. and, according to prevailing theory, single-handedly destroyed that civilization. It is also coming to be recognized as the source of the Atlantis legend told by Plato.

The rim of a crater is all that remains, with a small central island of lava and ash that is still volcanically active, last erupting in 1926. The town of Thira is located high on the rim of the crater, so high that a cable car is used to lift people arriving by sea. The views are nice, both from the town at the top of the crater and at my boat, anchored at the bottom.

I hated leaving the boat at the anchorage because it is entirely open to the West, but I wanted to visit the town, so I put out two anchors. The town stretches along the rim of the crater and is perfect for touring on foot, which I did. After a long walk I had dinner with four American college-age women on holiday.

They saw me sitting alone in the restaurant and, being entirely modern women, invited me to their table. Fortunately for me they thought sailing was a highly romantic occupation, and they asked lots of questions. How did I find my way across the water? Did I see sharks and whales? Was it lonely out there? I don't know what impression I created, but they charmed me to death. They were smart, resourceful young women who had plans for themselves.

We then moved on to subjects besides sailing and I realized they knew something of the world – they weren't limited to conversation about Prince and Madonna. They wanted to know where I stood on abortion, the draft, gun control. And they were too classy to ask whether I was married or how I could afford to sail around the world. As the evening went by I stopped wondering whether they could prevail against the world and began wondering whether the world could prevail against them. They showed class and poise, and they broke my heart.

(August 2)

It may sound silly, but now that I have sailed away from Greece I realize more than anything else I am going to miss their salads. It speaks to the unpredictability of travel experiences that I will probably remember the salads longer than the donkeys or the cute fishing boats.

A typical salad served in a small Greek island town has tomatoes – lots of tomatoes – cucumbers, onions, bell peppers, olives, a slice of feta cheese, and a small bit of lettuce buried beneath. Usually everything in the salad is produced within 20 kilometers of the restaurant, so everything is fresh and there are local differences in content. But always great tomatoes.

To appreciate my enthusiasm for the Greek tomato, a tomato grown slowly and painfully in soil enriched with goat droppings, you would have to visit an American supermarket and sample the uniformly red artificial spheres offered there. You would also have to understand the place of salads in the American diet. In my childhood, salad was a punishment. If you were bad, if you were overheard saying a bad word or caught feeding the goldfish to the parakeet or vice versa, you got salad for dinner.

By "Salad" I mean a monotony of iceberg lettuce, perhaps broken here and there by a radish. Or a bell pepper. Which is why salad dressings are so elaborate in America – spicy, creamy, thick dressings, delivered in a bottle bearing a picture of someone famous, a meal in itself, can make even iceberg lettuce edible. By contrast, a Greek salad is dressed in the plainest way – oil and vinegar – so as not to hide its beauty.

In a Greek restaurant you are provided with small bottles of oil and vinegar, but it is understood that you will act responsibly. If you pour, rather than sprinkle, the vinegar, the proprietor may wither you with a stare. When I first arrived in Greece I acted toward a salad as a fisherman toward a fish – kill it, then eat it. But I have mended my ways. Would you grab a bottle of ketchup and attack an Italian chef's pasta and sauce? Okay, then.

(August 5)

Oh, my poor jib, my favorite sail. A sail that, when acting with greatest efficiency, also takes a pleasing shape. Torn from leech to luff now, lying in a disordered pile here in Malta. I have asked the sail person to assess whether these rips mean the fabric has lost its strength, or repair is worthwhile. I can't have a new sail built here, only repair the old.

I knew the Aegean was windy before I went there, but nowhere in my guidebooks did I read of 60 mile per hour winds. Or that, when gale force winds are predicted, harbor officials are known to physically prevent charter boat clients from leaving, lest they lose more than a sail. I, as a foreign yacht, was free to do as I pleased, and I did, and now my sail lies broken.

I think one must approach Malta by sea, as the forces of Suleiman the Magnificent did in May of 1565, to understand its basic character and history. On approaching Grand Harbor at the town of Valletta one is confronted by a series of walls rising from a rocky shore. This enormous fortification is The Castle of St. Elmo, ingeniously designed by the Knights of St. John. Suleiman came here with 40,000 men, laid a siege and several attacks against the castle and, after several months and the loss of 30,000 of his men, gave up and sailed away.

In another battle, one perhaps less romantic from a modern perspective, Italian and German airplanes tried to pound the island to dust in the 1940's. These attacks also failed, and submarines and airplanes from Malta continued to haunt the shipping lanes from Italy to North Africa. One of the more fascinating stories of this battle involve three small cloth-covered biplanes that had been left behind in crates by an aircraft carrier early in the war, assembled by the Maltese, christened Faith, Hope and Charity, and then used to hold off the Italian Air Force.

Here I am describing "important battles" again, as if armed struggle was the essence of history. But I think Malta is an exception, a place whose history is quite literally a series of attempted invasions. But apart from this, Malta grabs you and won't let go. The steep town of Valletta is located on a narrow peninsula – one can look down its streets in three directions and see boats sailing by. One is reminded of San Francisco, except for Valletta's greater sense of history and permanence.

Listen: anybody who visits the Mediterranean and passes up Malta needs reality therapy.

I have been thinking about time lately. If I want, I can think of Valletta as a relatively young town, by comparing it to Jerusalem. As an example, cannons were included in the design of the Castle of St. Elmo. Smooth-bore iron cannons that could fire on ships approaching the harbor – that isn't so different from modern technology, not really. On the other hand, to an American Valletta can seem ancient, because it was built before the Beatles appeared on the Ed Sullivan show. Five hundred years before, but, you know, before.

When I was young I held in contempt all history before the invention of electronics. How did people function without radios? Suppose you had an urgent message, what did you do, send someone running through the night? I would pose this question with the sarcasm I thought appropriate to the idea of someone carrying a message by hand from place to place.

But some things have occurred to me since then. One is the charm of a world in which messages must be crafted with great ingenuity and care, to justify the effort of their delivery. And some of history's messengers literally raced against time and death. Consider the story of Pheidippides, who ran from the Plain of Marathon to Athens, a distance of some 26 miles, to deliver news of the Greek victory over the Persians, then fell dead.

The other is the tyranny of modern communications, in which perfectly awful images are transmitted through space at the speed of light. My favorite example of execrable bad taste was the television coverage of the Challenger disaster, in which the all-seeing cameras panned from the fireball to the faces of the astronauts' relatives, who watched the spacecraft blow up and realized their children were dead.

In my time as an engineer I designed part of the Space Shuttle, and fought a few personal battles to improve the safety of the craft (a story I will tell later), so I was already devastated by news of the explosion. How could the President allow a schoolteacher aboard a dangerous spacecraft? Did he actually believe the NASA rhetoric, that it was a bus that went into space?

But then I watched the TV version of the event and saw the quick cuts between the fireball and the tear-stained faces of the relatives. I remember jumping up in my empty house and shouting at the screen, "Stop this! That schoolteacher is someone's mother! Leave those people alone!"

On the other hand, TV brought Americans the Vietnam war, and made us so sick of ourselves that we stopped it. So television's relentless, prying gaze and instant response can be put to good use.

I envision a committee, in some mature world yet to be, that evaluates new technologies before admitting them into general use. The committee asks two questions. One, what is the best use for the technology? And two, what mean, petty, small uses can this technology be used for? But committees create problems of their own. Maybe a television etiquette will come into being over time, naturally, that will make our TV programming seem as silly as the turn-of-the-century practice of stringing electric light bulbs absolutely everywhere.

Malta has brought something else home to me. Valletta is an absolutely charming town, with magic streets and buildings, the air thick with history. It reminds me, as Jerusalem did, that no amount of personal awareness or wonder can ever be enough. The experience of such a place overflows the capacity of one's senses. It has come to me that to experience this place as it should be I need the capacity for wonder I had when I was 12.

This may seem the beginning of yet another lament about my ridiculous childhood, but bear with me. I just have to accept this as an example of my upside-down life. At a time when I was biologically and intellectually ready for the Mediterranean and its rich history, I was being told to get serious, to suppress my more imaginative impulses. Now that I am 45, a time when most men are becoming fixed in their behavior and views, I need the openness to new experience of the young. So I do my best. My favorite ploy is to try to see a place as if I have no childhood experiences, as if I have just landed from nowhere. For me this is an effective mental tactic, besides being almost literally true.

There is another invasion taking place in Malta, and this time the castle isn't holding back the invaders. Over the tops of the classic stone buildings one sees a forest of television antennas. Sicily is only 60 miles North, and the Maltese have discovered that a tall antenna picks up Italian TV. But the forest of metal poles looks terrible. I asked a local person whether any consideration had been given to tearing them down and installing cable. He told me that a contract had recently been signed to do just that.

But the invader has carried off the young people. I didn't need a government pamphlet, only my walks around town in the evening, to discover the young have emigrated to wherever those slick images come from. Most young people seen here are tourists.

(August 15)

I hadn't intended to visit Italy – one can't visit everywhere, after all, unless one makes a superficial whirlwind tour. But after Malta the wind got mean and I had to stop in Sardinia to refuel. I am glad I stopped, even though only for a day.

Cagliari is a port near the Southern tip of Sardinia, not really a town for tourists, which made it more interesting. Almost no one spoke English. I quickly learned the Italian for Good Day, Good Evening, Thank You, Yes, No, and Help!

After I got a supply of lira and restocked my boat with diesel fuel, I decided I had better make a walking tour of the town, lest I visit Italy and not even see it.

The first thing I noticed about the people was they were almost all good-looking. I searched a sea of faces for one as homely as those of my relatives, but had no luck. I tried not to stare too much, but it was shocking to see so much human beauty so indifferently carried about.

The second thing was the friendly and relaxed atmosphere. People you looked at looked back, sometimes smiled. Of course in Cagliari with my red hair and beard I was as out-of-place as a Martian, apart from being a foot taller than the average, so I should have expected to be looked at as often as I looked.

Being in Italy, I decided I should have a plate of spaghetti. I don't know where I get these silly ideas, these algebraic correspondences of mine, like Italy = spaghetti. After walking around for about two hours, I realized a couple of things. One, spaghetti isn't very special. Italians who go out to eat want something out of the ordinary. So not all restaurants have it, or necessarily want to serve it. And two, it was August, holiday time, and most restaurants were shuttered for the month, the proprietors sunning at the beach.

If you own a restaurant in America, you move heaven and earth to be open during a holiday – you know, when people are out looking for a restaurant. So you take your vacation some other time. In Italy, if you did this you would have the beach to yourself, but you would miss your friends. So I discovered nearly all the restaurants were closed, at the height of the evening, hungry people wandering about.

But I found a restaurant that was open, and had spaghetti. I sat down and waited. Half an hour later I hadn't succeeded in attracting the attention of the waiter, who was in animated conversation with his friends, so I left.

But I didn't mind. I saw the town and its people. I was happy with my walk. So I went back to my boat, had chicken stew from a can and watched Italian TV.

Even Italian TV was a surprise, especially late in the evening. In America, television networks have a department called Standards and Practices, which decides what's acceptable to show all those impressionable youngsters out there – in Italy I think the Mafia rubbed them out. On TV some people were taking off their clothes. Others looked as though they hadn't worn clothes in a long time. They were even touching each other, without any clothes on. They appeared to be enjoying themselves.

Of course I was disgusted, and I fully intended to leap up and switch off the TV. But I realized that, if I was going to write about Italian TV, I would have to observe it for some time, otherwise it would be like criticizing a book without reading it. This sad thought was quickly followed by another – it wouldn't do to watch just one channel, I would have to watch all of them. It was my duty.

I decided I liked the people in Cagliari – they seemed to have mastered the delicate art of living. But my favorite story about the Italians comes from Malta. During the war the Italian Air Force would fly over from Sicily loaded with bombs to drop on Malta. But they knew the Maltese were going to shoot at them, maybe even knock down some of their airplanes. Somebody might get hurt or killed. So they would fly within about three kilometers of the coast, the Maltese defenders would start up the air raid sirens and the guns (which could be heard in Sicily), then the pilots would drop their bombs in the ocean, turn around and go home. They would report to their commanders they had left Grand Harbor a smoking ruin and go home. Not so the Germans, who came to Malta later and lost almost

2000 airplanes and pilots.

I write this as Saddam Hussein is leading a huge army into Kuwait, and American forces are gathering in Saudi Arabia. We need more Italian common sense.

(August 23)

There's a big church here on Mallorca, a Spanish island off the mainland coast. A big church? – I might be trying too hard to avoid my tendency toward exaggeration – okay, I will go for balance. Let's see. I first spotted it 50 kilometers away, in spite of the normal August haze. I think you could stand a 747 jumbo jet on its tail inside.

Ingenious sundial, Mallorca, Spain

It has all the classic elements – stained glass, statuary, monster columns. Anyone who visits – a lifelong Marxist, who believes religion to be the opiate of the masses, a revolutionary Muslim who sees Christians as infidels – is going to experience a moment of complete disorientation upon entering this enormous chamber. It seems the designers intended to overcome the defenses of the most skeptical visitor, deliberately, with malice aforethought, leave them standing lost, saying "Oh, My God / Ach, Mein Gott / Dios Mio."

I think a child entering this place would be struck down in an emotional sense, and, depending on your view of the capital-C Church, placed beyond later meaningful reclamation. A skeptical adult, while not necessarily converted instantly into a believer, could not escape the emotional message of the space, that someone sure as hell believed something to put this up.

I accept intellectually that there are some larger cathedrals farther North in Europe, but my imagination is short-circuited at the moment, so I won't consider visiting them. Or until I have a chiropractor fix my neck.

(September 5)

Before I came to Spain I thought I knew a little about bullfighting. I read something by Hemingway once, but it seems I forgot some important details.

I had this idea that the bull came out from his dressing room and chased a bullfighter around for a while, then after getting hot and sticky, he would go back in the shade and drink some lemonade. Call his stockbroker. You know.

I was wrong. I was never so wrong about anything in my life.

First, the matador always kills the bull. Always. When the bull comes out the little door, he is dead. No going back through the little door, no lemonade. Second, they stick things in the bull of various shapes and sizes until he bleeds to death.

When the bull first comes out, he is extremely dangerous. He has all his blood still inside him, he isn't overheated, he wants to crash into something with his horns. At this stage everybody hides behind wooden barricades. I saw one fresh bull go completely nuts, drive straight into a wall, break his neck, and fall dead. He had been in the ring less than thirty seconds.

Then some toreros and a matador (a torero fights the bull, the matador kills him) come out and challenge the bull to charge them. The toreros are usually understudies of the big star. You know they aren't stars yet because their capes are big. If I go in the ring I'm going to bring my mainsail, that's how confident I am. I'll paint the sail red and wear dirt-colored clothes. And running shoes.

Pretty soon a horseman called a picador comes out and sticks a spear in the bull (the horse is protected by armor, sort of a medieval jousting outfit). When I first saw this I thought the bull should be allowed to chase the toreros around for a while longer before getting poked and starting to bleed. But then I wasn't in the ring.

Then the bullfight begins, the part most Americans would recognize right away from television or those velvet paintings at K-mart. The matador holds his cape out, and the bull, with an I.Q. of 3 1/2, charges through it again and again. Every once in a while another guy races out and pokes these little decorated spears called banderillas into the bull's back. The spear guy has to be fast: he has no cape.

Aren't they being mean to the bull, I thought. There are four banderillas hanging off him, he's bleeding a fantastic amount, he seems dazed. He'll probably fall over any second. As I thought this, the bull jerked his head a little to the right and threw the matador into the air.

The understudies quickly moved in and distracted the bull, and the star got up. Fortunately he was thrown by the bull's head, not his horns. He decided to continue the fight. I'm glad it wasn't me in the ring – I would have wet my pants and been laughed out of Spain. I almost wet my pants anyway.

In the final stage the matador tries to kill the bull with a long, curved sword. The matador waits for the bull to charge and, from a position directly in front, thrusts the sword out and down through the animal's back. Sometimes the matador must charge the bull to accomplish this, in any case it's very difficult and dangerous. Sometimes the bull gets annoyed by the matador's charge and charges at the same instant, sometimes the bull tries to turn away and snags the matador.

But the sword went in and the matador jumped away. Now the toreros gathered around with their capes. The bull made a few more charges, then sank to the ground.

I thought that was all. But after that bull had been dragged away by a team of mules, another matador took a position in the middle of the ring, on his knees, with his cape directly in front of him. I was told later this man was talented but relatively unknown, and wanted to prove himself. A fresh bull loped into the ring, spotted the matador and charged him.

The bull, now racing, seemed determined to squash this kneeling man. At the last moment the matador took the cape in his right hand and swept it across to the left, and the bull leapt toward the moving cape in mid-charge, missing the matador by the width of a coffin lid. Then I did wet my pants.

(September 10)

My first week in Palma de Mallorca I had a new sail built to replace my worn-out jib. But I ended up spending three weeks there, mostly waiting for a piece of exhaust pipe that never arrived (sound familiar?). I couldn't run the engine without it, so I had to wait. And wait and wait. I finally realized it wasn't coming and asked a shop to build one from scratch. It was $260 for what would have cost maybe $30 if the diesel engine dealer actually stocked parts.

A truth about long-distance sailing is that you spend a lot of time waiting for parts, or doing repairs – probably more than sailing. Which brings me to my next anchor story – this one stretches over three days:

I left Mallorca and sailed to Ibiza, another of the Balearic Islands off the Spanish coast. As night fell I anchored in front of some hotels on the East coast. In the middle of the night the wind began to blow very hard from the East, a peculiar wind direction for this season in the Med. So on waking I found myself in the wrong place at the wrong time. I struggled to raise the anchor and sailed for the town of Ibiza, thinking there would be a sheltered bay.

The sail was enjoyable, Ibiza being one of the prettier islands in the Med, and the anchorage at the town looked well-sheltered. But the bottom was all grass, something anchors don't hold onto very well. On the other hand there were about five boats already anchored there so I decided it couldn't be too bad.

I am strict about anchoring. I always test the holding by running the engine at full throttle against the anchor to see if the boat moves. But at this place the holding was so bad I ended up cruising around the other boats, dragging 400 pounds of anchor and chain behind me, hoping to find a spot the anchor liked. I'm sure the other boats had me marked down as a nut-case by the time I found a barely acceptable spot.

I wanted to go ashore and see the town, but the wind kept getting stronger and I didn't dare leave my boat. I decided I would go ashore the next morning, usually the time of least wind. I got my dinghy ready and then read a book.

At dawn a thunderstorm approached and the wind hit 60 knots. Every boat dragged on its anchor – from the smallest charter boat to a big 80 foot motor yacht – all were blown out of the anchorage, fortunately in the direction of a big bay. A schooner didn't have enough motor power to fight the wind and required the help of a tugboat.

I had anchored away from the other boats in the bay, so when I dragged I had time to gather up my anchor without hitting anyone. After the wind died down I decided I would take shelter in the marina. I had just spent 21 frustrating days trying to get my boat out of another marina, but I was very tired – all I could think about was securing my boat and getting some sleep.

I don't know why I thought the holding inside the marina should have been any better than outside. I got into a row of boats, all with anchor out and stern tied to the dock. I performed my usual test and decided the anchor was secure. Then I paddled ashore and set my stern lines.

I was trying to decide whether to have breakfast or take a nap when another thunderstorm approached. The wind came up and my boat dragged again – just like outside. But this time I was tied to the shore, so when my boat was blown against the dock I couldn't just motor away. I called for help at the top of my voice in English and Spanish. Someone came and untied the shore lines and I gathered them out of the water (so as not to snag the propeller) and then started motoring. But someone had left his own personal mooring line floating just beneath the surface (so no one else could find it but him) and my propeller snagged on it. The propeller wound up this line very fast and tried to drag the boat backwards, but instead the drive shaft was ripped off the engine.

So now I had no anchor and no engine, and the wind was blowing me against a concrete dock. Some people came and pushed the boat against the wind, and I put the outboard motor on the dinghy. I took the second anchor into the dinghy and motored out as far as I could and threw it into the water. Then I dragged my boat off the pier by winding up the anchor's line. I didn't expect the light anchor to hold the boat by itself, so I reset the main anchor.

It was then that I found out why all this had happened to me – the main anchor was stuck inside an automobile tire. The anchor had dropped into the tire when I first set it. The anchor's point stuck into the bottom when I tested it with the motor, but when the wind came up, instead of digging deeper the whole thing came loose and dragged. This marina was really a wet junkyard.

So I moved the main anchor farther out – now I had two anchors out at great length, the boat was off the concrete wall, and I could try to fix the engine. First I loosened the coupler, the thing that attaches the drive shaft to the engine. Then I dove in the water and pushed the propeller and drive shaft back into position (thinking of my identical Red Sea experience). Then I tightened the coupler, or what is left of it.

That's as close to the town of Ibiza as I got. The wind kept blowing, I couldn't think about approaching the shore again, so I did what I should have done the day before – I gathered up my anchors and sailed away. The wind was still blowing hard, but I just put out a little of my new jib and had a nice sail out among the big swells. This pleasant sail took away some of the humiliation I experienced at being completely out of control of my boat, tangled in lines, bashing the dock.

My boat has always liked being out on the sea, disliked the land, and hated marinas. There's a saying about houses, something like "we shape our houses, then they shape us." I think this goes for boats too – I am being shaped by her, I am coming to prefer the sea to the land, even when the weather is awful.

Am I beginning to sound like one of those single handers that loses his way on the reality road map and starts talking to his boat? Well, nothing is simple if you examine it closely – I am by nature a scientist, my boat is really only plastic and wood, but – but she is as alive as any person I have known, and more alive than some.

Look at it this way. If you are rewarded for diligence and punished for misbehavior by a piece of plastic, someday it will come to you that the hunk of plastic meets the basic condition we use to distinguish people from things – coherence and consistency. This means two things: we have silly ways to tell people from things, also a good boat can pass a test that some people might fail.

But you want to be a rational person, you want to keep your scientific outlook. So you say "She is just a piece of plastic" and you smile.

I had a pleasant windy sail, but I still needed to sleep. So I sailed around to the West side of the island and found a nice bay, clean sand bottom, sheltered from the wind, good anchoring. No town, no people.

This little bay opens to the South, so I decided to perform one of my favorite experiments – comparing the sextant position with the satellite navigator (satnav). I started this voyage relying on my satnav for positions, but I packed a cheap plastic sextant, just in case, you know. Then in the South Pacific, as Bora Bora disappeared in the East, the satnav died. I was obliged to find my way to Fiji with the plastic sextant.

The results weren't great. One day I was 18 miles from where I thought I was. So when I got to Fiji I bought a better sextant made of metal – and a new satnav.

A sextant is just a fancy gadget to measure angles. If you are on the ocean and have a clock and a sextant, you can figure out where you are. You just measure the angle between the horizon and something in the sky – the sun, a planet, or a star. Then you either measure something else or wait for the first object to move some distance and measure it again. I usually measure the sun in the morning and again in the afternoon.

We live on a ball in space (right here I had intended to write the most lucid paragraph ever written, at the end of which you would know exactly why measuring the sun's angle twice in a day tells you where you are on the earth. The paragraph kept getting longer and longer as I tried not to leave anything important out. After all, not everybody is a rocket scientist. But when I found myself starting with "we live on a ball in space" I knew I was done for).

I wrote a computer program that takes my sextant angles and times and figures out where I am. It's just like the old-fashioned paper-and-pencil method but it's fast. Also the program knows where the sun is, any date and time. This program is so easy to use it makes me picky. I usually take three sights in the morning and three in the afternoon, and average the results.

The books say position accuracies better than ten miles on a small boat are good, because the sextant operator gets bounced around a lot, also he is close to the level of the water, which means waves sometimes get in the way of the distant horizon. By comparison, a big ship gives you a higher viewpoint and rocks a lot less.

So I sometimes find a bay that faces South and anchor there. The water is usually calm and the boat doesn't rock. Under these conditions the only errors are my own – not holding the sextant steady, not reading the angle scale correctly, not being patient.

My test took all day (with digressions for swimming, washing clothes, eating, stuff like that). I turned the satnav on and let it collect positions, which I then averaged (since satnav positions are not perfect either). Instead of using a wristwatch to record the times of my sights, I connected a push-button to my computer and pressed the button to mark the times. That way, when I saw the sextant's image of the sun touch the image of the horizon I could just push the button.

In the past I have tried to look from the sextant eyepiece to the watch really fast – a very tricky business. Either you swing your head without moving the sextant, which may leave you permanently scarred, or you push the sextant out of the way really fast, which means after you write down the time, you have to go diving for the sextant to find out what the angle was.

Well. After taking a lot of sights and computing the results, I found the satnav position agreed with the sextant result to less than 2/10 of a mile (850 feet, to be exact). This is good, if I say so myself. In fact, to do any better I would have to measure time in fractions of seconds, because one second of time changes the result by one-quarter mile.

On long crossings I sometimes take sextant sights just to pass the time, and I have wondered how accurate a sextant is under controlled conditions. Now I know it is as good as a modern electronic wonder like satnav (some old-time sailors say "better").

(September 17)

I visited Granada while traveling the coast of Spain, on the strength of a rumor that they had a nice castle.

The "nice castle" is called the Alhambra, which marks the Western reach of the Moorish empire. It sits on a hill overlooking Granada, the traditional capital of Spain, and the resting place of Ferdinand and Isabella.

I can't compare the Alhambra to anything I've seen before. Over a period of eight centuries monarchs competed to possess, and then to add to, this high fortress. Most of the architecture is Moorish, although some Western influence can be seen in recent additions.

I kept moving from place to place within the outer walls, and seeing more fountains, gardens, and palaces – walls covered with the most beautiful and delicate stucco and tile patterns. After several hours of this, I sat down in a stupor and glanced at my guidebook. The book told me I had spent my time in a part of the fortress devoted to administration in those far-off days – there was another palace, across a ravine, where people went to enjoy themselves.

This is unbelievable, said I. This place is a heaven of rooms and gardens, tended by invisible keepers whose greatest joy in life is to find an untrimmed cypress, an unswept walk, a fallen gum wrapper. How could that green land across the footbridge be more beautiful than this?

But it was.

(October 2)

I am in Gibraltar, the place the Greeks called the Pillars of Hercules. To be more precise, I am on Gibraltar, as windy and exciting a piece of rock as I have climbed. I can see North Africa and Spain in one glance, with a strip of water between. Beyond is the Atlantic, the last major ocean I haven't sailed.

When I pass through the Straits of Gibraltar, for me, a modern sailor, it will be just another blue place on my charts, another step toward home. But I want to imagine the thoughts of the great ocean explorers, for whom Gibraltar was the end of the known world.

Author with the Barbary Apes in Gibraltar

When I was young I remember a row of trees that marked the end of my world. Those trees were as far as a rusty bicycle would carry me, and the land beyond them stood unexplored as I languished behind panes of glass, pale and mute, waiting for a bell to ring. Any bell.

I knew there was something beyond those trees, apart from a fence and a hill. But I would be thinking about something else. I pedaled up to those trees and turned away so often that they became a pretty solid barrier.

One Saturday a Navy fighter plane blew up over my neighborhood. The plane's entire load of jet fuel, scattered across the sky by an exploding turbine, burned up with a thunderclap, and stopped a conversation I was having about marbles.

A flashing red light warned the pilot that something unpleasant was about to interrupt his flight, and he ejected himself a second before the explosion. My friends and I saw the pilot as a tiny black dot, then the parachute canopy opened above him. We saw the broken airplane, trailing orange flames and black smoke, falling to the ground. To an adult, this would have been a dramatic event, a reason to turn off the television and go outside, but in my glassed-in life it was a wake-up call from God.

The plane crashed on the hill that was just beyond the end of the world. I jumped on my bicycle and rattled and clanked my way to the row of trees, now made small by a pillar of smoke. My friends and I clambered over the fence and moved as close to the wreck as we dared. I tried to pick up a bit of metal, but it was too hot.

I had to remember to breathe. An airplane, one of those dull punctuation marks in the sky, had broken and fallen to the ground, had become orange fire. While falling it had traveled as far as I cared to pedal my little bones, I mean until then. It was a metal death bird, and its rider was lucky to have escaped it.

Then some Navy people appeared and made us leave, without any souvenirs, and I turned back toward my neighborhood, suddenly small behind the trees. The contour of that hill was now part of my map of the known world, along with burning airplanes. In my dreams of the following weeks, more airplanes burned up than could possibly have been supplied under the Navy's budget.

So who am I to laugh at people who turned cold at the thought of passing the Straits of Hercules, or at Columbus' sailors, terrified at the prospect of falling off the edge of the world? Until an airplane fell out of the sky, I pedaled my bicycle up to that row of trees, carrying two peanut butter sandwiches in a brown paper bag, and turned away toward the school, day after day, for years. I displayed the curiosity of a turnip.

(October 12)

I am in the Canary Islands now, making arrangements to fly to Germany to visit Bob and Ursula, my friends from "Take Two" whose voyage has now ended, and who are making an uneasy reentry into normal life after several years of sailing.

It's a good time for a side expedition. The best time to sail from Gibraltar is before the end of September, but one must wait until the end of November to continue across the Atlantic, to avoid the hurricane season. Most people wait in the Canaries.

(November 8)

My friends Bob and Ursula live in Staufen, a small town near the French border in Southern Germany. The Black Forest and the Rhine River are close by, and many of the German wines are produced there. For two weeks I explored the area by bicycle and on foot, mostly in the

My friends in a French town

forest and among the vineyards, but with some visits to towns and households thrown in.

The countryside is a study in beauty and order. When you come to the edge of a town, the last house goes by and you are in the country – no suburban developments, no billboards, just a fence and then open land. And no litter, either, not so much as a bottle cap. When I asked Ursula "how come there's no litter?" She just looked at me and said, "They shoot you."

I knew Ursula well enough to get her meaning. She says that kind of thing for two reasons. First, she knows Americans will do anything that won't get them shot, and second, she likes to make fun of Americans' view of Germans. We've seen too many war movies, too many Nazis from Central Casting. We expect to see Germans in the town bakery shouting military commands at each other.

But Germans are also preoccupied with history. Some would like to get a divorce from their own past. In America when I was young I heard about the "Good German," the obedient citizen who heard of atrocities but paid his taxes and did nothing. Since Vietnam I hear that expression less often.

One day we had lunch at a schoolteacher's house. This man spoke several languages including English, and he kindly tolerated my German. He was also a good cook, and brewed wine from the grapes in his garden.

After lunch and wine the German conversation got too fast for me to follow, so I picked up a photo album. I happened to be turning the pages from left to right, that is, from the present toward the past. Soon the countryside picnic scenes gave way to snapshots of the war. The schoolteacher's father standing next to a crashed airplane. A group of soldiers, posing for the camera as tourists do.

The schoolteacher's daughter pointed out her grandfather in the album, then wandered into the TV room. I must have appeared to be idly leafing through the album, but my mind was racing. Can this man take pride in his father's war service without sanctioning the policies of the era? Who gets responsibility for the crimes of that time? All Germans? The military? People with political power? Obedient followers? The schoolteacher's daughter?

I realized I was posing questions rapidly that Germans probably pose to themselves over a period of years. And, I hope, Americans as well, now that we've experienced Vietnam. From the perspective of the couch I sat on, I decided that trusting a state is dangerous, and outright obedience is disastrous.

I think America's track record is comparatively good for such a large and powerful country, and I think I know the reason. We usually stay out of trouble by electing only morons to public office. If we accidentally elect a non-moron, we usually don't trust him or do what he says. If both these safeguards fail, we can be made to feel great public embarrassment, even shame, to a degree not possible in a mature European country.

Germans are loyal and efficient, and these qualities produced a disaster without parallel in human history. But Germans have long memories – today's students know the names, dates, and events of the Thirties and Forties, and show a healthy degree of skepticism about public affairs.

So I closed the photo album and rejoined Bob and Ursula, and we walked home through a pretty vineyard. As I walked I thought, I'm no more afraid of the Germans than of the Americans. And no less.

November 25 – Day 5, Canary Islands to Caribbean

You can sail your boat in the Canary Islands, but it is tricky. There are few natural anchorages, and none is entirely safe. Most of the nice bays have been taken over by dreadful marinas that offer small shelter from the rough water, and charge you for the privilege of being there.

As I prepared for my visit to Germany I discovered that all the boats in Las Palmas marina would have to leave, to make way for a fleet of boats taking part in a transatlantic race. So I had to find another marina on the island, move the boat, then bus back to Las Palmas to catch my plane.

When my trip was over I found my boat bashed and broken. The only marina with space available offered only slight protection from the swell, and the people there didn't care about the boats as long as they got their money. My stainless steel bow pulpit had been smashing against a staircase, and my rail against a concrete wall, as I sat drinking wine by the Rhine River. I would have been better off leaving my boat in Las Palmas at anchor, outside the marina, an idea that seemed irresponsible until I saw the aftermath.

I was able to bend the pulpit back into shape with block and tackle, but I felt shame anyway, as though I had betrayed my poor little boat. Until I flew to Germany I hadn't left the boat anywhere for longer than a day, afraid that something bad would happen. I found a marina, tied the boat securely, but something bad happened anyway.

When I got back, most of the fleet of transatlantic racers had arrived and filled the Las Palmas marina to overflowing. Many of the racers hadn't crossed an ocean before, and some were at the extreme level of inexperience. Every race year a few boats run out of food or water in the relatively easy Atlantic crossing. Can you imagine planning an ocean crossing and not packing a few extra cans of beans?

I overheard a conversation as I walked alongside the boats – a little girl asked, "Mommy, how do I start the stove?" and her mother, visiting a nearby boat, called out "Just turn the knob and find a match, dear." An ordinary conversation, unless you know something about boats. You see, propane is heavier than air and sinks to the lowest place it can find. In a house it just runs out below the kitchen door and annoys your dog. On a boat, a big plastic teacup, watertight and airtight, the gas collects in the bilge. Eventually there's enough gas down there and the boat blows up.

Elaborate precautions are taken to keep the gas from escaping unburned and collecting in the bilge – electric safety valves, warning alarms – but if you turn the knobs on the stove, the gas comes out, just like at home.

So did I butt in and lecture these hotshot sailors on the dangers of propane? Not on your life. Some likely outcomes flashed before my eyes – The woman emerges and bawls out her husband for enticing his family onto a boat that is dangerous even while tied to the dock. Or, she confronts me and says "My daughter and I have circumnavigated the globe three times, you miserable sexist. We just haven't lit the stove yet." Or the daughter, match in hand, lifts a bilge hatch and says "Gas? I don't see any – " *boom*.

By the way, I have a kerosene stove. It smells bad and is hard to use, but my boat won't blow up.

Anyway, their boat didn't blow up, or if it did, I didn't notice with everything else that was going on. Would-be sailors crowded the marina, petitioning boat owners to take them across the big water. They even commandeered dinghies and rowed from boat to boat, pleading to be taken sailing.

There are a number of arrangements between boat owners and crew members. In one, the crew are professional sailors, cooks, etc., and they are paid. This is the usual arrangement on big yachts. In another, people agree to work for free, for the experience of sailing. Finally there are boat owners who make you pay to sail with them. At first I didn't realize people were that desperate to sail, but plenty are, although they are usually the least experienced sailors and many regret the arrangement almost before casting off.

The bulletin board at the marina made interesting reading. Some male boat owners had posted notices asking for females to apply for crew positions. Did I say "Qualified female sailors?" No, and neither did they, just "Females." I thought this rather blatant, but I actually saw one female in the act of applying. She approached a boat and asked "Are you seeking crew?" The owner bounded out of the hatch with somewhat more than the minimum effort required, and spied the applicant, an Englishwoman of about fifty years, conservatively attired in an ankle-length flower-print dress, straw hat, and practical shoes.

She was female, the only listed requirement, and she bore herself with quiet dignity. For all I know she was supremely qualified, had done postgraduate work in navigation theory and been a sailor from a tender age, but I also know what this skipper wanted to see, and she wasn't it.

The skipper lived a frozen moment with his mouth hanging open, a fish caught in his own market, as he realized he wouldn't be able to explain his requirements to this serious, dignified woman. If truth in advertising were required on bulletin boards, his notice would have said "Nut-brown, smoothly muscled young females desired for Atlantic crossing. Applicants should be stupid or brain-damaged, cooperative, and physically appealing. Previous experience not necessary or desirable."

But I don't know what happened next, I was just walking by. And I set sail the next morning for the Caribbean, sort of on a whim. It turned out my timing was good, I had decent wind for the first few days. Many of the Atlantic race boats are in that area now and they have either no wind or contrary wind. They were part of an organized event and so they had to leave on a predetermined day – no whims allowed.

I remember how anxious I used to be at the start of a long crossing. Now I find myself relieved to be underway. I can organize my thoughts, review where I've been and where I am going. Write in my journal. Make plans. And watch the sea go by.

This morning, probably because of the smooth seas, I was thinking, what's the biggest wave I ever saw? How did I figure out what to do with it?

I think you learn the basic lesson of the sea by watching a wave bash a sea-wall. After that you know what must be done. You give the sea what it wants. You mustn't give too much or too little, and it must be on time. You either wake up and change the sails or the sea rips them for you. There's no hearing, no appeal, no excuse.

And no jury. If the sea takes you, you can't blame a corrupt system of justice. Maybe you bought the wrong boat. Or you sailed when storms are likely. Or, worst of all, you were disrespectful. I think you can learn to have a flawless lunch with Queen Elizabeth more quickly than pass muster with the sea. Meaning no disrespect to the Queen.

December 14 – Day 24

It's been a beautiful sea. When the wind stopped for a few days, I just drifted around. The noise of the engine would have spoiled the perfect blue silence. I went swimming and checked out my boat. Then I looked down, following the boat's shadow into the deep. The water is very clean and very blue.

The next day one of the Atlantic race boats came by. I saw him coming and prepared a gift – I tied a float to the end of a long line, and tied a bottle of wine onto the float. The I let it float aft. That way they could collect the gift without having to come too close. They caught on fast – by the time they had hoisted my bottle they had one ready to give me. I was a little embarrassed – I sent over a bottle of ordinary Spanish white wine and got back a bottle of champagne.

I've been hearing the race boats on the radio – some of these boats are way too much for their owners. One guy has hydraulic steering and can't make it work – so he can't steer his boat. He's been having long radio chats with people who know about hydraulic steering.

Another boat started taking on water. I don't know the whole story yet, but the crew just got onto another boat and watched theirs sink.

I'll give them the benefit of the doubt and assume they had a leaking rudder post. That's one of the nastiest problems you can have. On modern boats, a rudder post sticks through the bottom of the hull and connects the rudder to the steering gear, usually a wheel in the cockpit. But if the rudder hits something, the watertight seal can break and water starts coming in. Sometimes the seal breaks without waiting for a special reason.

There are some remedies. The most effective is not to have a rudder post. On my boat there's a big stick called the tiller, which runs off the back of the boat and attaches to the top of the rudder – so I don't need a rudder post. It's an old-fashioned, even ancient arrangement. Nobody thinks I have a race boat, but I have one less hole for water to come in.

Another trick is to have a tube inside the hull, surrounding the rudder post and rising with it above the waterline. So if the rudder seal fails, the water can only fill the tube, not the boat.

The most dramatic solution, assuming you are stuck with a rudder post, is to disconnect the post from the steering gear and let it drop out the bottom of the boat, then – quickly! – plug the hole. Now the boat won't sink, but you can't steer it either.

If you sail long enough, you think of ways to keep your boat from sinking. I have some wooden plugs that look like big bottle corks. If one of the through-hull valves broke I would hammer one of the plugs into place. But what if the water was already too high inside to find the place where it's coming in? That's easy – just dive outside the boat and plug the hole from there. Unless it's dark, unless the wind is strong, unless, unless.

All I'm saying is I would try very hard – but I can think of things that might sink me anyway. Like the container that hit me in the Indian Ocean. In Tel Aviv I saw where the scar was and realized it had only hit a slight, glancing blow. Even so, it pushed the hull in several inches before bouncing off. If it had poked through, it would have made a big hole and I would have had only a few minutes to try a repair or launch the life raft.

If I was really mean (or really meaner) and wanted to know whether someone would lose his boat easily, I would ask him how quickly he could be touching the bottom of his keel. I remember that windy day in Hawaii when I stupidly fouled my prop with the dinghy line and started drifting ashore at Molokini. I took my Swiss Army knife out of my pocket and jumped into the water. I didn't sit down to think it over, or talk on the radio. I got in the water.

I have to admit the Hawaii story happened only because I didn't take the time to think about what I was doing – I should have shortened the dinghy line or moved the dinghy abeam before trying to motor – and suddenly I didn't have any time left to think.

You aren't required to know anything to go out sailing, at least in the United States (many other countries have a certification program). The American policy toward boats is consistent with the cowboy mentality: You are on your own. If your boat breaks, maybe you drown, but nobody else gets hurt.

Actually, as I get older I have more respect for this way of thinking. If only one person is at risk, and he fails to train himself properly, he gets what he deserves. Unless innocent bystanders are involved, I think it's better than an expensive certification program that may not be very effective.

Like the one for pilots. Before 1949, in order to be licensed to fly, you had to know how to spin and recover from a spin. A "spin" is when one of the airplane's wings is flying and the other one isn't. So the one flying wing races around the fuselage really fast, the other one doesn't, and the plane falls with a corkscrew motion.

The airplane manufacturers complained that the spin requirement was scaring too many flying students away. Some pressure was put on in Washington and the requirement was dropped. You don't have to spin around while pointing at the ground anymore. You don't have to do anything scary to become a pilot.

Now, over half of small-plane accidents involve a stall and a spin. This usually happens during a final approach to a runway, near the ground. The pilot makes the plane fly too slowly and one wing stalls (stops flying). The pilot panics and tries to bring the nose up by pulling back on the controls, which makes the stall into a spin.

If the pilot was spin-trained he would know exactly what to do. But there would be fewer pilots, and fewer airplanes would be sold. So, just like in a boat, you are on your own – except innocent people live near airports.

The first time I heard this story was during my pilot training, so naturally I asked my instructor to train me in spins. He happily did, and my first solo spin was my second scariest experience.

My scariest experience? The first time I jumped out of an airplane. But that's another story.

(December 26)

I enjoyed the Atlantic crossing an indecent amount. Even when the wind wasn't blowing I liked being there – I didn't want any noise so I just drifted about until the wind came back. I read books, wrote little computer programs, enjoyed the sea. I didn't want it to be over. I wanted to move slowly across the water and never get anywhere.

Moonrise on a windless mid-Atlantic day

One windy day I saw a small whale inside a wave. The waves were steep that day and I saw a grayish object in the blue – it was a whale swimming along, inside the top of the wave, looking me over. The whale would ride to the top of each new wave and eye my boat, as if in a passing railroad car of water.

My radar has stopped working. Fortunately there weren't many boats along my route. I tried to wake myself each hour or so and look out, but as the days went by with no sightings I got lazy. I am going to try to find parts for it here in the Caribbean, but I suspect I'll end up having to do without radar from now on.

I have to leave the Caribbean in February to assure safe weather in the Pacific. It's too bad, the people here are very enjoyable. They are content and self-possessed, and from time to time they gently remind their Northern visitors that everything will turn out all right.

I have been traveling with a boat called "Tamure," from Connecticut. Scott and Kitty are making their second circumnavigation, this time with their children Alex, 14, and Spencer, 12.

I first ran into Tamure in Tel Aviv, and we have crossed paths repeatedly since then. During the Atlantic crossing we called on the radio every day, talked about the weather and the sea, as I did with Take Two in the Indian Ocean.

During long crossings Alex and Spencer make model boats, sometimes very complicated affairs with fishline rigging, plastic-bag sails, wind vanes for steering. Sometimes while at anchor I will see them rowing about in their dinghy, putting their models in the water, letting the wind carry them away.

I have been getting around in my sailing dinghy more lately. My big dinghy, the inflatable with the outboard, is

Looking up from my anchor

a lot of trouble to set up and take down, and unless I am taking on supplies it's hardly worth it.

These little sailing dinghies aren't like the big boats that carry them – if the wind blows hard they have no ballast to keep them upright. You must shift your weight to keep afloat and sailing. If you make a mistake or lose your balance while moving about, or if a power boat passes too close, you get wet. Sometimes these little boats lose patience with you and fill with water. Usually they don't sink all the way but it's hard to get them high and dry again.

I have sunk mine several times. The first time I was sailing in a little bay in the San Juan Islands in Washington State in 1987, my first year as a sailor. I was taking pictures of the big boat with a rather nice camera. A little gust of wind came along and I wasn't ready – suddenly I was in a pile of floating debris, oars, sails, "boaty bits" as they say in Australia. And the camera was ruined. I had to collect all the pieces and swim them ashore to refloat the boat, and I learned never to carry anything I didn't want to get wet.

I think I've learned more about sail trim and balance in the little boat than the big one. And quicker, too. Things happen fast in a sailing dinghy.

Tamure has a sailing dinghy as I do, and one day on the island of Antigua Alex, Spencer and I decided to explore our bay with the little boats. Spencer managed to borrow a third dinghy, so we had a fleet of miniature sailboats.

First we had sort of a race, and discovered my boat was faster when sailing upwind but Spencer's was faster when running downwind, because it had the biggest sail. Then we began exploring the shore. Sometimes we would find an opening in the mangroves and sail into little dark bays, surrounded by brush and roots. Then we would see whether we could sail out without having to grab the brush and push the boat free. We found out if you are willing to play constantly with the rudder, you can sail exactly backwards.

In the afternoon the wind fell off and we drifted about, sailing on tiny breaths of air. I would find out whether I was moving by watching a leaf pass by in the water.

Then the wind died completely, and I decided I would sail just with sunlight – the pressure of light on one side of the sail would push me along. This is what happens when you spend too much time in the tropics – it's called "going troppo." But when I put the sail in position, the boat actually started moving – and I realized the hot side of the sail was heating the nearby air and pushing me a tiny bit.

It was that kind of afternoon. Alex and Spencer tolerated the presence of a grown-up and I had the benefit of their company. The bay was kind to all of us. We saw giant spiders in the mangroves, fish came by, people laughed when they saw our little navy.

January 22

There are some beautiful little islands here, most well away from towns. A few rival the beauty of the Tuamotus in the South Pacific – classic tropical islands, a central knot of trees and brush surrounded by sand.

Yesterday evening I stood on the shore of one, waiting to take a sunset picture. But as the air cooled I came under attack – thousands of "no-see-ums" bit me all over. I quickly snapped my picture and got away from the shore, but today

Caribbean sunset

I am all bite and no bark.

I thought about it and realized insects hadn't been a problem in the South Pacific, and I figured out why. There are very few people there, so there aren't any "no-see-ums" either.

Most of the sailors here are boat charter clients, and many can't sail or anchor. When I first got here I assumed that, if there were thirty boats anchored in a bay, that meant the holding was good. But the average holding in the Caribbean is poor, usually a thin layer of coral sand over rock, and there are too many charter boats for the good anchorages. So people anchor anywhere, and drag a lot.

The bigger charter companies instruct their clients in anchoring, and pass out charts showing approved anchorages, places that will take hold of a boat even if the client just throws an anchor off the bow. The best anchorages are sheltered from the wind, the average day isn't very windy, and there is a huge number of charter boats trying to squeeze into the approved anchorages. From a distance their masts look like a forest of denuded trees.

A charter client typically motors to an open spot, drops the anchor off the bow, and waits five minutes. If the boat stops moving, end of procedure, go inside. The more experienced of them know better than to drop their anchor directly in front of another boat, but others do not, and one sees many "charter tangos" danced out when the boats inevitably crash together.

The nightmare of the charter companies is a big squall, with sustained winds over 25 knots. When this happens, a few poorly anchored boats begin to drag down on others and start them moving too. Even a soundly anchored boat can't hold back three or four others – so a chain reaction takes place and all the boats end up on the beach. The charter clients go home and tell stories about the "big storm," the charter companies untangle and salvage what they can, and the insurance companies replace the rest.

Among the charter fleet my boat is very conspicuous. People come by daily, asking what kind of boat it is, where did I charter it. I think they secretly wonder why anyone would charter *that* boat.

{ 9 }

The Caribbean to Oregon

January 28 – Day 2, St. Thomas to Panama

Today is the fifth anniversary of the Challenger disaster, and (within a few days) the 24th anniversary of the 1967 Apollo fire. I was just getting started in electronics in 1967, and later I worked on the Space Shuttle, so for me this date has special meaning.

The Apollo fire took place during a ground test, a sort of dress rehearsal of the moon mission, with the astronauts strapped into the command module. The command module was designed to be pressurized, so the astronauts wouldn't have to wear space suits while underway. Someone realized the spacemen could breathe pure oxygen instead of air, and the pressure of the oxygen would only have to be one-fifth as great (because air is only one-fifth oxygen). The spacecraft would only have to withstand one-fifth the pressure, it would weigh less, the booster rocket could be smaller, and so on.

When the spacecraft was on the ground, they had to make the inside and outside pressures the same, so they raised the oxygen pressure to normal air pressure. This was a terrible mistake. Pure oxygen, at the pressure of air, is very dangerous. In an oxygen atmosphere you can touch a flame to a piece of steel and it will burn with an unearthly white light. Almost anything will burn. Now: Try to imagine putting out a piece of burning steel.

They say a brief short-circuit made a spark, and the spark ignited nearby materials. Everybody was in a hurry to get to the moon before the Russians, so people were taking shortcuts – for example, using ordinary wire instead of the approved fireproof kind. In the investigation that followed the fire it was discovered that a lot of things that were safe while in space (at one-fifth pressure) would burn on the ground. And there were some things in the spacecraft that weren't safe anywhere.

By the way, the Russians were also racing somewhat recklessly into space, and they had a disaster of their own a few years before. While trying to launch a Mars probe something went wrong, a group rushed onto the launch pad to repair the booster, and it blew up. Many of their best scientists and engineers were killed.

I was a young, idealistic technician at the time, and I wanted to be an engineer someday, maybe build part of a spacecraft. When I heard about the Apollo fire I swore I would never cut corners, never risk the safety of astronauts.

Years later I got my wish – I designed some electronic devices for the Space Shuttle. And I got to see the politics of space first-hand.

I have to tell this story carefully, since the people I worked with are still in the aerospace business, and I don't want to single out anyone for what is normal industry practice.

But back to my story – my design was nearly finished, and met the strict safety and reliability requirements for manned space flight. Then some officials appeared and told me the voltage on the Shuttle would sometimes be higher than they originally thought – my design would experience greater stress than anticipated – could I reassure them no problems would result?

Within my company I let it be known that I would have to make some changes to keep the electrical stresses within safe limits, to prevent the possibility of smoke and fire. But there was another contract coming up and the managers in my company didn't want to make waves. So they overruled me – the managers intended to announce there was no problem.

Does this sound familiar? After the Challenger disaster it certainly did to me – it turned out an engineer had tried to warn NASA not to launch, that the solid rocket boosters were dangerous, but his managers overruled and silenced him.

My story has a better ending. After I was overruled, I wrote a letter of resignation. In my letter I explained the risks and said I would rather resign than allow dangerous hardware onto the Shuttle. And I pressed my letter into more hands than absolutely necessary. The embarrassment level got pretty high and the managers backed down – I was allowed to make the necessary changes.

Does this make me a hotshot, a moral person? Not really. I wasn't married, no children to support, I could afford to lose my job for a principle. Besides, I was able to imagine what would happen to me if I caused a Shuttle failure – kids on the street saying "There's the guy who killed all those astronauts and the schoolteacher."

I didn't become an engineer just to design things. I wanted to design them right. I was a bit too idealistic for the engineering profession, whose motto is "Ship it." So I changed careers – I got into computer science.

January 30 – Day 4

The wind gets above 30 knots every day and the wave heights are amazing. And the sea is too rough to go fast. I had been trying for better than six knots, but that was too greedy. A gust came up this morning and broke a sheet block.

I reduced sail after the block broke. Now I have the smallest sail plan I've ever used on a downwind sail – just the staysail on the starboard side and a small bit of the jib poled out to port. The ride is slower but more comfortable.

These are the conditions this boat was built for. Huge seas approach from aft and the canoe stern usually rises up and parts them. A flat transom boat would be shipping most of these waves aboard. Even this boat gets some of the bigger, breaking waves, so I have to stay inside a closed cabin most of the time. Sometimes my electronic tiller doesn't react fast enough and the boat gets twisted beam-to. Then the closed portholes momentarily fill with water, but the boat recovers on its own.

Last night a flying fish flew right through the overhead hatch and landed in my bed. He started thrashing about, wishing he was somewhere else. Then I woke up, felt his greasy little body on my stomach, and wished that too.

I am getting used to these seas, but I am missing a lot of sleep. It could be worse – I could be sailing upwind.

February 3 – Day 7

Last night I took a huge wave aboard, which rolled right into the cabin. It was the sixth night of the passage and I was beginning to suffer from lack of sleep.

I realized I was getting into a dangerous situation – the wind kept getting stronger, finally peaking at 45 knots, and I was sailing toward a coast that is continuous, with no large bays or passages. If I missed the entrance to the Panama Canal I wouldn't be able to turn about and sail against the wind, and I would be forced against the rocks.

Because of the wind and seas I had begun to spend more and more time inside the closed cabin, to keep the water out. But about midnight the waves seemed to be going down and I wanted to look for the entrance lights with the binoculars (remember my radar is out). I opened the hatch, crawled into the cockpit and began to scan forward for navigation lights or the glow of cities.

Then the boat began to roll violently, a sign of a big wave. I looked over my right shoulder to see a wall of water approaching from the North. The wave grew steeper and began to break, and rolled the boat down so the port side rail went in. Just then another wave, a reflected wave from the nearby coast, broke across the port side and the two waves completely covered the boat. I was seeing (and tasting) the much-feared "rogue wave," the multiplying effect of two or more waves that meet and break at once. As I was lifted off my feet I wrapped my arms around a shroud and watched the water pour through the open hatch into the cabin.

In a moment the water receded and my feet found the deck again. I dove into the cabin and closed the hatch. Everything inside the cabin was wet. All my clothes, bedding, radios, charts, everything.

I very much want to tell you that I whistled a tune as I toweled off my charts and electronic gear, but I was just too tired, scared and angry. I was completely wet and I hadn't even made out Panama's lights for my trouble. I crouched in the cabin and screamed my frustration. I said unkind things about the sea. I used words normally reserved for women of low character, usually spoken by men of low character. I tried to invent new oaths.

This was different from several years ago. There was no terror, no respectful silence now. I was in the position of the child that knows it is loved unconditionally. I was disrespectful to the sea because I know she loves me. She will punish me, perhaps even kill me, but she will not stop loving me. I know this.

Later I found a dry quilt in a locker the sea had not reached. I took off my wet things, wrapped myself in the quilt and lay down for a while. As my anger abated I reflected that the sea, even in its worst moments, has been kinder to me than any person I have known. This made me angry all over again, because someday I want to meet a person as kind and balanced as the sea.

Yes, yes, I know what you're thinking – why is a grown man talking this way? For your answer, you must hear a minimalist composition performed by the wind, watch dolphins play in moonlight, and listen to the whales singing as you are rocked to sleep by the sea. If this happens to you once, you are still fit material for human company. If it happens to you every night for several years, you can visit the people who live on land, but you will not belong to them ever again.

(February 5)

I have visited enough offices now, filled out enough forms – I go through the Panama Canal in two days. I am anchored near the town of Cristobal on the Atlantic side. There aren't any marine stores here, but I have managed to repair most of the damage from the Caribbean crossing.

Panama's recent history is like a perversion of colonialism, which is itself a perversion. Ordinarily a small Central American country like this would have been liberated some time ago, and perhaps the Panamanians would have adopted a system like Costa Rica, their neighbor to the West: no standing army, few serious problems. But too many big and small players want a piece of Panama.

Cristobal is not so much a town as a camp for economic refugees – shattered buildings, piles of garbage, a sense of desperation even in daylight. Armed guards are everywhere. If there is something of value, a bank, a grocery store, there is a barricade and a man with a gun at the entrance. People are warned not to leave the marina after dark. Some boat owners recently disregarded this advice and went to town for dinner. The customers at the next table finished eating, paid their bill, then pulled guns and robbed them.

Yesterday I visited the bank to buy a stamp required by Immigration. As I walked back to the Canal office building I heard the sound of automatic weapons, a sound that startled only me. Later I was told bandits robbed the bank just after I left it.

Today I rode from the Canal office to the grocery in a taxi, and watched the town go by. I was struck by the terrible condition of the streets, and even more by the force of will and optimism in the faces of the Panamanians. I had seen this in other places – Sri Lanka comes to mind – people of such strength of character that they step over a pile of shattered masonry to meet a friend, push away a ruined environment with a wave of the hand, a shouted greeting.

These were real, living people, happy against all reason. They couldn't file a class-action suit, sign a consent decree, or sail away. I didn't have the strength of character to live as they did, nor even to witness their lives – in their wrecked streets I felt like a cardboard man. Then my vision started getting blurry for some reason. I didn't want my driver to think I pitied his people, so I paid him and walked the rest of the way.

February 12 – Day 3, Panama to Hawaii

I traversed the Panama Canal with a group of five sailboats, anchoring in Gatun Lake overnight. The boats are tied together in twos and threes in the locks, and then secured to shore with long lines, before the water level changes. Gatun Lake is fresh water, so as soon as the anchors were down everybody went swimming.

I didn't swim as long as the others because I had some chores to do before dark. As I sat in the cockpit planning my next move, I spotted a fresh-water crocodile about seven meters long, cruising slowly near the shore. I yelled "Crocodile!" And suddenly it was like the beach scene in "Jaws," people scrambling out of the water. Fortunately the croc remained visible, cruising along, his nose, eyes, and dorsal scales seen by all, or I might have been lynched.

As I motored along I remembered how much mechanical trouble I had at the Suez Canal. Then I began hearing an unfamiliar sound – but I decided it was my imagination. Later I checked and found a hole in the exhaust manifold, the same part that failed in Suez – but this is a new part that I had built in Spain, only six months ago. I couldn't fix it right then so I wrapped a rubber patch around it, held in place with some radiator clamps.

When I got to the Pacific side of the canal I found a taxi driver that knew the town and we spent several hours trying to locate parts. I didn't find the parts but I saw more of Panama. The driver pointed out an area that seemed to have been squashed by a big hand – it was Manuel Noriega's neighborhood. The story goes that Noriega drove out in a private car as the bombs fell.

This sail, between Panama and Hawaii, will be my longest passage, probably 40 days, possibly more. I had intended to stop in Costa Rica, but as I came near it the wind piped up and I realized I had better keep sailing, since this is an area of light winds and frequent calms.

February 15 – Day 6

I haven't gotten to the trade winds yet, so winds are light, and sometimes contrary. After dark a moderate wind blows from the North. After sunrise it weakens and shifts to the West, a small headwind, not enough to sail with. So I have to motor in the afternoon, in order not to go backwards.

I know this will be a long crossing, so I am trying to conserve my supplies – you know, fuel, water, cookies – the essentials.

I measured the inside of my favorite cup, then filled it with water by pressing the foot-pump. The cup holds 16 cubic inches and two presses of the pump filled it, so (skipping some math here) each pump is about 1/30th of a gallon. I have been counting how many pumps I use, and I find I'm using about six-tenths of a gallon a day. After I run out of sodas I think I'll probably need a gallon a day. I have 60 gallons on board. So I have enough water to make it to Hawaii unless I break my mast.

Did you know it takes eight times as much fuel per hour to make a boat go twice as fast? This is called the "Cube rule," because the fuel used per hour increases as the cube of speed (it's true for cars too, once air resistance becomes important). So when I have to motor I use the lowest throttle setting – I go only 2 1/2 knots but use a tiny amount of fuel. I have 70 gallons on board, a lot for a little boat like this. I packed it on board, mostly in jerry cans, before the Red Sea passage, only to lose my engine and carry a lot of fuel a long way for no reason.

That takes care of fuel and water. Now cookies. In my time as a sailor I have come to realize that cookies can sustain shipboard morale better than almost anything. So I packed an obscene number of cookies for this passage – oatmeal, chocolate chip, gooey vanilla filled, the worst examples of the baker's art.

In the evening, usually while watching a movie, I reach for a bag of cookies, resolving to have only a few. After the movie I sit in the cockpit, watch for freighters, adjust sails – and have some more cookies. Around midnight my hand is buried in an empty bag – It looks as if I'm designing an "Elephant Man" puppet.

But it's impossible to pack enough cookies for a long passage. About a year ago I tried saltine crackers instead – they lasted just fine, in fact I still have some of them – but I was a basket case. I mean, who wants to watch "Pee-wee Herman's Big Adventure" while eating saltine crackers?

I've been seeing plenty of dolphins and whales. One morning I had to steer away from a breeding pair of whales and two young, California Grays I think, sleeping on the surface. Most evenings some dolphins play around the boat. A few nights ago I watched phosphorescent trails of dolphins – like in the Indian Ocean – but this time there was almost no wind and the surface was calm, so I could see the outline of their bodies in glowing green beneath the surface. I went to the bow and called to them, and remembered not to whistle, and they came up and looked me over (I have noticed some dolphins think your whistle is a warning and swim away).

A few days ago a group of six birds (sooty shearwater, *puffineus griseus*) landed on the boat when the headwind was strong. I guess they wanted to go West like me and got tired of flying. In the evening they crowded along the bow rail and looked cute, so I let them stay. The next

Sooty Shearwaters on the bow

morning the entire boat was covered in bird droppings. Some of the flock had taken positions on the mast spreaders during the night and, well, do you know the term "carpet-bombing?" So I chased them off, then washed my boat.

February 20 – Day 11

The trade winds have started – the wind is becoming more steady in strength and direction. The ride is smoothing out, I don't have to change sails so much.

The sooty shearwaters are becoming real pests – every day they land on the spreaders and refuse to leave. They have figured out I won't hurt them – so my shouting and arm-waving has no effect. They carry on endless conversations using squawks, beaks and wings punctuated by, um, solid waste discharges. I

Shearwaters on the mast

tried to scare them by firing a shotgun round, just for the noise. They all crapped at once, then resumed their conversation.

Last night I was looking through the binoculars at the Andromeda galaxy and the nebula in Orion – both interesting objects and easy to see with binoculars. The Andromeda galaxy is a big spiral galaxy that is thought to have the shape of our own. But only a time-lapse photograph through a large telescope shows it as a galaxy – through binoculars it just looks like an oval of glowing gas. When astronomers first saw it, they called it a "planetary nebula" and thought it was a gas cloud close by. Now we know it is a galaxy in its own right, very far away.

The Orion nebula (located on Orion's "belt") really is a local cloud, a mixture of gas and dust, and astronomers believe stars are forming there. Supposedly some of the mixture falls together through the force of gravity, and as it comes together its density becomes very high. Then some of the atoms begin to fuse together and release energy. The energy radiates outward, preventing any further increase in density, and blowing any extra material out of the neighborhood – voila, a star.

Apart from being a star cradle, the Orion nebula is very pretty through binoculars, even on a rocking boat. As I watched I realized I hadn't seen this nebula or the Andromeda galaxy so clearly before – then I remembered it's usually cloudy where I live in Oregon at this time of year. Also there's (need I say) no city lights here to spoil the nice dark sky.

I put the binoculars aside and checked my sails. Then I saw something scary – my mast-head light had gone out! I've gotten adjusted to not having radar any more, but sailing without navigation lights is asking for trouble.

I checked the switches and circuit breakers with no result. I quickly realized there was only one remedy – I would have to climb the mast and replace the bulb. And it would have to be now, both because the water is calmer at night, and I didn't want to sail a dark boat even one night.

I took down the sails to slow the boat as much as possible, and put the ladder over the side (in case I fell off the mast and *wasn't* killed, I could swim back and climb aboard). But once the sails came down the boat started bobbing like a cork and the mast swung wildly.

I started up the mast, taking a step when the boat wasn't rolling and holding on when it was. I managed to get halfway up when two sooty shearwaters suddenly took flight with a squawk, almost hitting me with their little wet calling cards. These two miserable birds had been perched on top of my mast on either side of the navigation light, blocking it from view!

Little web-footed gangsters.

I want to talk about batteries. Normally one doesn't spend much time thinking about batteries, but on a modern sailboat it comes to you that you must be nice to them or you will be punished – you might have to hand-steer your boat, in complete darkness, without sleep, forever.

My wind vane doesn't work, so instead I use an electronic tiller. I have electric navigation lights. My satellite navigation receiver requires electricity. I even need electricity to take a sextant sight, only because I am lazy and make my computer do the math.

If I had a complete electrical failure, I have a plan to carry on, but it would be a painful, sleepless experience. I would sail up to the latitude of Hawaii using the North Star for guidance, then sail West. That's the oldest and easiest method for navigation, used by the old-time sailors until accurate shipboard clocks were developed. I would have to figure out how to steer the boat without electricity, but there are some tricks for that also. Finally, because I would have no lights, I would have to stay alert, so no sleep.

In Israel I met an American sailor who doesn't worry about these things – he has almost no electronic equipment, and he sleeps a lot. He crashed into a freighter in the Red Sea. His bow was squashed but he was all right. Hey man – no problem.

I am thinking about electricity lately because of the masthead light story, and because my alternator stopped alternating a few days ago while I was motoring. An alternator is a fairly simple gadget, some coils of wire and diodes, the engine spins it, it makes electricity. I mean usually.

I have three ways to charge my batteries – the alternator, a windmill, and two solar panels. Unless the wind is brisk the windmill won't keep the batteries charged. The solar panels help but even on a sunny day they can't do the job alone.

So I realized if I lost the alternator, and I continued to have no wind and little sunlight, I might as well have lost the batteries. So pretty soon I sat in a pile of alternator parts, checking them one by one with a meter.

Everything checked out. The nine diodes, the four coils of wire, the brushes, everything seemed okay. I reassembled it and tested it again, thinking I might have cured it by taking it apart and putting it together. But no.

Finally I realized it wasn't a broken part, it was how two of them were (or weren't) connecting. The field brushes, a couple of pieces of carbon, were pressing against the contacts for the field coil (the part that spins) as they should. The brushes and the field coil tested okay separately, but when they were put together there was no electrical connection between them.

It turns out a thin layer of enamel had formed on the field contacts, probably because of the salt air. The brushes couldn't connect to the field coil, therefore no magnetic field and no electricity. I cleaned off the enamel and the alternator came back from the dead.

But I digress. I was going to talk about batteries. If you own a car and it isn't too cold where you live, you probably think about batteries every other year. I think about batteries every day. Are they charged enough? Charged too much? Has something been left turned on that will discharge them? Do they have enough distilled water in them? Do I have enough distilled water on board for the passage?

When I bought this boat, there were a couple of ordinary car batteries on board. They say if you completely discharge a car battery about five times, or allow it to sit discharged for a while, it will be ruined and you might as well throw it away. I realized mine were dead, so I bought some new ones for my first passage to Hawaii.

In Hawaii I left the boat in a marina for about four months while I traveled back to Oregon. One day there was a big rainstorm. Some of the rain made its way into my bilge. The automatic bilge pump tried to pump out the water, but there was too much water and not enough battery, so the batteries died. When I returned I bought some new ones.

By the time I got to Fiji I had destroyed battery pair number three. By this time I had learned something about batteries, so I bought some "deep-cycle" batteries, the kind that tolerate repeated complete discharge. They were pretty good batteries and lasted about a year.

In the Caribbean I couldn't charge them any more so I went battery shopping again. One shop reassured me they had some great batteries and I should come by very soon. When I got there they discovered they had run out of the great batteries but they had some pretty good ones in the warehouse. When we got to the warehouse they discovered they had run out of the pretty good ones but had some good ones. Since mine were dead I decided good was better.

But, in spite of some glorious labels saying "deep-cycle" and "maintenance-free" and "24-month warranty," these batteries died in *one month* of sailing. Naturally by that time I was in a completely different island and country – I was on St. Thomas in the U.S. Virgin Islands. And I found a shop that actually did have some great batteries. They were unlike anything I had seen before. To begin with, there were no water caps on top. They could be mounted upside-down, it didn't matter. I had read about them in a magazine and heard favorable reports from other sailors. Two of them cost 650 dollars.

They're the best batteries I've ever abused. They charge in a shorter time and discharge over a longer time. I don't have to carry distilled water any more. They tolerate complete discharge, over and over. It came to me that if I had known about these batteries in the beginning, I would have saved money by buying them, at $650 a pair, instead of the five pairs of batteries I bought at about $200 a pair.

March 2 – Day 21

Today marks the halfway point of distance for this passage – as I write I am 2208.5 nautical miles from Morro Puercos, the final point of land Southwest of Panama, and the same distance from Hilo, Hawaii.

My average speed is increasing – the second half of this passage seems faster and I probably won't need 42 days to get to Hilo. And I hope I don't – by then cookies would be a distant memory.

For the last five days there's been a big storm to the Northwest, disrupting the normal trade wind pattern. Every day I pick up a weather chart on the radio, and in the area of Hawaii for nearly a week the wind has been blowing exactly backwards – from the West. My winds have been light but not contrary – I'm glad I'm not farther West right now.

I have been watching the ocean swell, and it gives ample evidence of the storm. Beneath the local wind-driven waves you can see a long swell with a height of about a meter, smoothed-out remnants of big storm-driven seas. But you can't feel the swell inside the boat, it is too gradual. You have to look.

I haven't seen a ship or boat in 18 days, which is all right with me. Early in the passage I saw a few freighters, then I realized I was in the middle of one of the great-circle shipping lanes. So I wrote a program that calculates my distance from each of the known lanes – I use the readout to avoid them.

I know modern ships use complicated methods to decide where to sail, but the average ship is still in the center of the lane. I have been steering to the South of the great-circle track between Panama and Hawaii, trying to keep clear by more than 100 miles.

I was thinking – at the moment I am more than 2000 miles from land in any direction (except a small bit of Mexico). That means (punching a few calculator buttons) an area of more than 12 million square miles of water, mostly empty.

The bridge on a typical freighter is 65 feet off the water. This means the visible horizon is (punch, punch) about nine miles away. So in my empty ocean with a radius of 2000 miles I can fit (punch, punch) about 38,000 freighters in such a way that they are invisible to each other, and me. I mean assuming they wanted to play my little game. Lucky for me, there probably aren't that many freighters in the world, and certainly not out here.

Let's see – a freighter is invisible nine miles away. That means a fast one, going 30 knots, can move from being invisible to being kissing close in 18 minutes. So if I wanted to responsibly watch out for ships, I would have to scan the entire horizon every nine minutes. Apart from getting no sleep at all, in 40 days I would have to look 6,400 times.

Forget it. I want to read a book, listen to the radio, and I absolutely must sleep. Instead I'll rely on the kindness of the sea – and probability.

March 7 – Day 26

The sooty shearwaters, the web-footed gangsters, have gone. Now the only birds I see are an occasional Red-Billed Tropicbird, and another, smaller bird that never comes near my boat. I sometimes see him speeding across the waves at a distance. This little bird looks and flies like a swallow, has the swallow's streamlined wings and forked tail, and flies very fast. I can't find any ocean birds like him in my book.

The trade winds are back – the normal Pacific High has reestablished itself to the North, the sun is out, and the wind has curved around behind the boat for the first time this passage.

Now that I'm within 2000 miles of Oregon, the radio link to my house is working again – I can send and receive printed messages. It's nice to hear what's going on in my neighborhood. I can read a bit of news and pretend I am there.

In my time as a sailor I have adjusted – completely – to being at sea. In the beginning the isolation of the sea was overwhelming, a matter of immediate and constant attention, even a little anxiety. Now I am simply at sea – if I want I can enjoy the look of the water, imagine the empty expanse of water around my boat, or I can tune in the B.B.C. or read a book.

It comes to me that I may have adjusted so completely to the sea that I will have an equally difficult adjustment to living on the land. Out here I can withdraw from the reality of the sea, but what will I do when the sea itself is no longer available to me? When the neighbor's dog is barking at 3 AM and I can't just sail away?

On the other hand, there are places on the land I miss – the desert most of all. I have been thinking about the desert today, remembering places I have visited.

I used to prowl the desert in Eastern Oregon in a Super Cub, an old-fashioned, rugged airplane that you can set down almost anywhere. I would leave in the early morning, fly East until the afternoon, then find an old jeep trail or dry lake to land in. I would bring a sleeping bag, water, some canned food. And a telescope.

From the perspective of modern times, the most striking thing about the desert is its complete economic irrelevance. Rapacious real-estate moguls yawn, their eyes glaze over, at mention of the desert. No one is about to turn it into condos and malls – there lies its magic.

In the desert you can read nature's unblemished handwriting. No signs tell you why an anthill is in a particular place – there are plenty of walks, none of them interpretive. And in a few days the silence of the desert gets inside you, infects you with a sense of eternity, and the certain irrelevance of all our works.

I think this comes to me now, while sailing, because the desert is the part of the land most like the sea. With this difference – the desert's silence is deeper.

March 14 – Day 33

The weather has been awful for five days – high wind and waves, rain, no sunlight. But Selene is riding here better than the Caribbean, because there are no land masses to reflect waves. So, even though the waves are high and sometimes break over the side, they don't engulf the cabin like before.

A night's high wind blew my radio antenna away, so I rigged a temporary replacement and raised it on the main halyard. This antenna broke, too, and that left the main halyard stranded on top of the mast.

The main halyard is the line that I use to raise the mainsail, and so far it's been too rough to go up the mast and recover it. Fortunately the wind is so strong I haven't needed the mainsail anyway. The weather has been so consistently windy I think I may get all the way to Hilo (four more days) without having to retrieve it.

But I have worked out a plan to retrieve the halyard, just in case the wind goes down. I would trail a line and a float in the water to grab onto in case I should fall. I would fly only the staysail, to keep the boat from rocking too much. It occurred to me the mast would be steadier if I flew all the sails, but the boat would move too fast – if I fell off there's no way I could get back on board, even with a line to grab hold of. At the other extreme I could take down all the sails and lie ahull, not moving through the water, but I tried that when the web-footed gangsters hid my light – riding the mast was pretty violent even though the seas were moderate.

There are two ways to go up a mast – steps and bosun's chair. A bosun's chair is a cloth seat attached to a line, the line is raised up the mast and takes you along. But normally someone must winch the line for you, so there has to be someone else on board. If you have steps on your mast you can climb them alone, so I put in steps when I got this boat.

When the weather gets rough, the mast is the least stable place on the boat. So if you must climb it you have to choose a good moment – and then hang on. If you are in a bosun's chair and lose your grip, you become the weight on the end of a pendulum (the line) and you crash into the mast again and again. I know a woman who broke her arm doing this. On the other hand, if you are on steps and you lose it, you fall – either onto the deck or the water.

March 17 – Arrival Day

The weather is still windy and cloudy – I can't see much. But I am so close that the Big Island has become a dark mass in front of me.

I am thinking today about arrival – how I adjust to the land. I remember the first time I approached this island – I tried to imagine sailing in, dropping my anchor, but I was still completely at sea, embraced by the timeless waves. Then a propeller-driven airplane passed overhead, and its droning announced the existence of land activities: governments, armies, populations of happy shoppers. In an instant I awakened from the sea, became a citizen of a western country with certain privileges and responsibilities. After the airplane passed there was a silence that had not been there before – the machine had spoken and I had heard it. I was breathing but holding my breath.

Since then I have moved from sea to land many times, and I don't change so completely when I come to shore. In a way I don't yet understand, I am no longer a citizen – I am given over to the waves, even while on land. My experiences on shore have come to seem metaphorical – reefs and passages, risks and opportunities, and a sense that I must keep the boat moving.

But there is one difference between my experience of sea and land: when I am at sea, women are perfect. Perfect in form and thought, creative, ingenious, heart-stopping. I know this is a defect in my character, unfair to actual women, and it might be why I put to sea again and again.

Return to Hawaii (Selene at left)

The water is turning light green, becoming shallow. I see floating bits of wood.

(March 24)

I arrived in Hilo on the 17th, a very wet day, 35 days after leaving Panama. And 724 days from the day I left Hilo, in March 1989, to sail around the world. My little sea-level spacecraft has taken almost exactly two years to orbit the earth – the Space Shuttle covers the same distance in 90 minutes.

What if Selene really were a spacecraft – what kind of planet takes two years to orbit? If my boat made the same two-year circle in space that it's made on the sea, the central planet would have to be very small – just 350 miles in diameter, smaller than many asteroids. A planet with a surface area greater than Texas but less than Alaska. Standing on it I would weigh a quarter of an ounce. My boat, which on Earth weighs 16,000 pounds, would weigh one pound six ounces. A jumbo candy bar.

It's coming to me as I write this – I have sailed around the world alone. The earth is round, I can report this to you as personal experience – I wonder whether the Flat Earth Society will have me as an honorary, sacrilegious member?

I met a sailor here in Hilo whose rigging broke as he sailed from Los Angeles. His mast came down, after which he could only sail downwind slowly. Then he was hit by the storm I saw on my daily weather charts, the one with the backward winds – he was blown back toward California 300 miles. He ran out of food and water in his 89 day sail to Hilo. My worst passage was a walk in the park by comparison.

I have been shopping here in Hilo, and some products seem dramatically better, especially for someone who has been out of the country for two years. My new mountain bike is better, shifts easier, has more gears, and was $200 less than the salt-water casualty I threw overboard in the Red Sea.

I have always compared bicycles with my first, which I found in a junkyard when I was 12. I rode that bike until I was 18 and working. It was horrible the first day I owned it and as the years went by it got worse. It was uniformly rust-colored and I never had to lock it up. It didn't need a bell or horn – the sound of grinding metal was enough warning. I rode it to my high school, a place where some people had better cars than other people. My classmates dreamt about bigger engines – I dreamt about having a front fender.

If I had seen this new bicycle when I was 12 I would have started salivating uncontrollably and been put under sedation. I would have ridden it to school beside myself with joy – and I would still have been a complete misfit when I got there.

I like this new bike, but shopping in Hilo seems different from two years ago. But it comes to me that the town is the same – I have changed. I have a different view of what's normal. I visited the shopping mall to buy all the things that broke or wore out at sea, but I could hardly stand to be there – inside the building there was an atmosphere of relentless seriousness, an almost religious commercial fervor. The bright, colorful stores faced onto a drab corridor, like altars in a secular church.

I made my way to a bench in shock. I will confess that I was once an outright lover of shopping malls, but in spite of the muzak and the sound of beeping cash registers, there was no sign that this was a real market – no one arguing a price or visiting a friend, no food vendors with little carts, no dirt.

But I had to buy certain things to make my boat whole again. I had to stay and visit this place, so I tried to raise my spirits with memories of a more pleasant market. I remembered the fish vendor from Sri Lanka, whose entire commercial establishment – fish, balance scale, profits – fit on the back of his bicycle. A man who could be wiped out by a thorn, but who smiled everywhere he went.

I thought about the taxi driver on Cyprus who took me home for lunch – it was on our way, he was hungry, why not? And I recalled the day my friend Ursula and I shopped for a knitted cap in the Arab Quarter of Old Jerusalem – we knew we had bargained as low as we could when the proprietor asked us to leave his shop.

In America we have better goods in greater quantity than anywhere in the world. So why do we turn customers into robots, and markets into automated factories? At the mall I forgot where I was for a moment – I turned to a salesman and said "This is too much – I can't afford this – how about –" but then I saw the expression on his face, the curious look of an entomologist who has just found an alien bug.

(April 23)

The day I left Hilo I circled around the Big Island clockwise, one of my favorite sails, but one most sailors don't make because it's the "long way." Because the sail takes almost a day, I started in the afternoon so I would arrive at my destination in the light of the following day. As darkness fell I sailed past an active lava flow – lava comes out a vent on Kilauea and flows several miles to the sea. As the lava spills into the ocean it makes great clouds of steam, glowing red from inside. It is a fantastic, primal vision that cuts through you – you are watching the earth bleed.

The next day I sailed into a small bay on the Southwest of the Big Island, a beautiful, remote bay. It is one of the few Hawaiian bays still in a natural state, and the local people have asked me not to say its name. The coral is very pretty and almost untouched.

One afternoon I went for a free-dive, just fins and a mask. I would dive down about 10 meters, grab a rock on the bottom and listen to the whales singing in the distance. Some time ago I realized why I could only hear the whales in deep water – near the surface of the water the sound waves take the path of least resistance and escape into the air, but deeper the waves can't escape and travel horizontally a great distance.

Along with the whales, I could hear some dolphins nearby. As I came up for air, I saw them too – a pod of about eight spinning dolphins, so named because they sometimes jump into the air, spin around, and fall back in. At first I thought I would swim over and take a close look, but before I could act on this idea they swam over to me.

I was in such a remote place that these dolphins hadn't seen many people, and they were as curious as I was. They swam up and surrounded me, looking me over and squeaking their comments. One of the larger members of the group abruptly moved close and I touched him (or her), more or less instinctively, as one might do in a group of people. I know that spinning dolphins are quite shy and don't like to be touched, and I don't think this dolphin meant to move quite that close. But it was nice anyway.

The dolphins soon lost interest in me and began to swim away, and I followed for a while. It struck me how much they resembled a group of people as they moved along – a family or a group of friends, the younger, smaller individuals trailing behind, exploring, then sprinting to catch up to the group.

Looking up at passing fish

And each one so beautiful. I know what I think when I see a beautiful woman – call it a fascination with architecture – but the dolphins put us at a disadvantage. Let's face it – people are pretty lumpy and irregular. Funny little bits and pieces hanging off the oddest places.

As the dolphins left me behind, hanging in the water, wearing a mask to make up for my eyes, and fins to make up for my feet, a floating lump pretending to be a fish, I tried to imagine being a dolphin in love with another dolphin.

The "green flash" is real. For some time I have been watching sunsets, trying to satisfy myself that the phenomenon was real or some kind of optical illusion. One of my theories was that it might be something called an "afterimage," the result of staring at a bright light. If you stare at, say, a red light for a bit and then look away, you will "see" a green light in the same position. This afterimage is produced by your eyes' light sensors being temporarily overloaded, and this was my explanation for the green flash.

Several days ago, here at Puunoa Point on the West side of Maui, I again watched the sun drop below the horizon. This time everything was perfect – there were no clouds or haze near the horizon, the air was calm and clear. And as the sun disappeared, for more than a second the last visible part turned a bright emerald green.

This was impossible to confuse with an afterimage – it lasted too long and was too bright. So I think another of my explanations is correct – the atmosphere acts as a prism, breaking the sun's light into individual colors which take different paths to your eye, and the path for green happens to be the last to disappear. If the earth's atmosphere was completely free of dust and pollution, we might see a "blue flash," but the shortest wavelength of light in the setting sun is green.

I feel kind of silly, having sailed all the way around the world watching sunsets with the aim of proving or disproving the existence of the green flash, only to have a conclusive example presented to me here where I started.

When I visit the West side of Maui I always make a pilgrimage to Olowalu Canyon, a beautiful place in the Western hills. To get to the canyon you have to walk or ride a mountain bike through the sugar-cane fields that separate the narrow developed strip near the beaches from the island's high country.

The route into the canyon takes you across a farmer's land, the canyon itself is extremely rough, becoming nearly a technical rock climb in places, and it is very hot. But it's worth it – a display of rocks and foliage not to be seen elsewhere. And a stream runs through the rocks, augmented by small waterfalls along the way.

Life can be complicated for a farmer. He owns the land, you have no right to be there, but (inevitably) there is something on the other side of his land you want to see. He can't afford to let you think it's okay to cross his land, especially now that anybody can get sued for anything, but fences and signs are expensive, and it's a lot of work jumping up and down and yelling.

So you try not to let the farmer see you. You don't touch anything, you stay away from buildings and vehicles, you conduct yourself with respect and near-invisibility. This was a lot harder when I was 12, but I have more impulse control and sympathy for farmers now.

So I make my way into the canyon. I bring along some sodas and food and I usually stay all day. After I have made my way up to a particularly attractive swimming hole I sit down and take off my shoes. The water is a lot colder than the sea.

The canyon is about 15 miles from the population center of this part of the island, where about ten thousand tourists dwell on the sand. But I almost never see another person in the canyon – hiking in a hot, rocky place isn't part of the "package," the reason people come to Hawaii.

(May 19)

I am anchored in Hanalei Bay on the North coast of Kauai, near the Western end of the Hawaiian chain. This is my favorite island in Hawaii, a green and pretty place.

There are some nice bike rides and hikes here. One of the hikes takes you through a tropical jungle to a high waterfall and a pond – the water is cold but by the time you get there you don't care.

I have been fixing up my wind surfing board – there are some perfect windy beaches nearby, ideal for flying off the tops of waves. I'm about to move to one, so I can windsurf directly from the boat.

I have my summer planned out, and it is a bit more complicated than one would expect for a Hawaiian odyssey. You see, there's a solar eclipse in July, only visible on the Big Island of Hawaii, about 250 miles upwind from here. I've never seen a total solar eclipse, a peculiar situation for someone with a lifelong interest in astronomy, so I'm not going to miss this one.

I want to depart for Oregon in early August, and I naturally enough anchored in Hilo on the Big Island at the end of my crossing from Panama. Normally I would have moved slowly West during the summer and sailed away from Kauai for Oregon, a natural downwind progression – except for the eclipse. So, at the end of June I am going to sail back to the Big Island for the eclipse, which is why I am here at Kauai so early in the season – I didn't want to short-change my favorite island.

Because of the eclipse, people on the Big Island are going crazy. All hotel rooms are booked and have been for a year. They expect an additional 40,000 people, beyond the normal tourists and residents. Officials plan to handle the event as they would a natural disaster.

My plan is to sail to the Northwest part of the Big Island and drop anchor in a little-used bay I know about, then go ashore with my bicycle. But if things are crazier than I imagine, I will drift offshore and watch the eclipse from there.

Planning for the eclipse reminds me of what I realized in 1987 when I first visited Hawaii by airplane and rental car – it's a lot easier in a boat.

(July 16)

The eclipse trip turned out better than I imagined, in fact better than I could have imagined. Before I set sail for the Big Island, a wind surfing friend with an interest in astronomy discovered she couldn't get an airplane seat to the Big Island, so she asked if I would sail her there. She was an experienced sailor, also I had become rather sweet on her in my time on Kauai, so I said yes. I had just sailed around the world alone, thinking from time to time how nice it would be to have some company, so I was ready to try sailing with someone. My friend likes sailing, we knew we would get along, she was a perfect choice. As we began our sail I was in heaven – by the time we got back I was in love.

But I digress – this is supposed to be about the eclipse. We packed her bicycle with mine, bought some extra food and treats, and sailed. On the night of July 9 we crossed from Maui to the Big Island, arriving just after dawn. Before we left Kauai, people said the bay I had chosen was packed full with eclipse-crazed boaters, but that was just talk – it was scarcely more crowded than when I visited in May.

The sky was completely clear that morning, just 24 hours before the eclipse. The weather report called for clear skies – I chose to take this as a good sign, even though Hawaii weather forecasts are incredibly unreliable. We went ashore with our bicycles and toured the area, scouting for places to sit and look at the sky.

The eclipse was to take place at 7:30 in the morning, when the sun was just 20 degrees above the horizon, so I had to choose a spot carefully on such a mountainous island. But I had thought this out during my earlier visit – I was confident we would see the big show unless the weather flaked out.

And guess what? In spite of the weather report, it began to rain during the night. And rain and rain. My friend and I decided to be philosophical about it, maybe we would miss the eclipse – we were having a nice time sailing around, we didn't want to be greedy with nature.

Shortly after dawn we rowed ashore and pedaled our bikes inland a short distance. It was completely overcast. There was a park on the side of the road and I suggested we stop. I figured if we stopped then, we would conserve energy to chase sunbeams later on.

I learned later that 15 miles South of our little park, a group of eclipse watchers, organized by Honolulu's Bishop Museum, waited under cloudy skies. They had paid a lot of money to join the museum tour, and their site had been chosen by experts. Each was armed with a camera and a "sun peep," a little plastic filter that would protect their eyes from the sun's direct rays, assuming the sun ever come out.

During the next hour, my friend and I sat in the little park near the boat, watching the clouds dance and tease. About seven, when the sun was half eaten by the moon, the teasing stopped and a great hole opened up. Some of the people there had gone inside to watch the eclipse on TV, but the sunbeams playing on the ground brought them out again.

At 7:28 the moon gobbled up the last morsels of the sun, and a great shadow swept in from the West. The sky became dark – not black, more like deep twilight. It would have been completely dark except for two things: there were still some clouds around, scattering light from outside the moon's small shadow, and a volcano in the Philippines named Pinatubo had recently erupted, filling the high atmosphere with dust. This dust, which had been making pretty sunsets lately, also scattered some light into the cone of darkness.

But I must tell you – I saw the moon's black disc relentlessly eat the sun, finally blotting out all but a golden ring. We shouted, we said things that would have gotten us in trouble with the Church, then, as the darkness swept in we became animals, silent, primitive, all eyes. But some part of my brain was still working – I looked through my binoculars and saw beautiful purple streamers coming out from the sun, charged particles riding magnetic loops into space.

The show went on more than four minutes – a long time to be turned into an animal. Then the sun reappeared. I knew it was coming back – honest I did.

To the South, the several thousand people in the official Bishop Museum Tour, sun peeps in hand, waited under a total overcast. It became dark for four minutes, then it got light again. They put their sun peeps away and got on the bus.

(July 20)

I am spending my last few days in Hawaii back at my favorite wind surfing beach on Kauai. I have made more friends here than the other islands, also it's prettier and less spoiled. For now.

While in Hawaii I have been exposed to something called "New Age." I was originally going to say "New Age Thinking," but that would be a contradiction in terms. I think this New Age business came to full flower while I was out of the country, not that I could have done anything about it.

New Age is, among other things, crystals, pyramids, astrology, numerology, mysticism, UFO's, ESP, and channels. If you were born before the complete disintegration of reason, i.e., sometime around 1960, you might think these things are harmless and not very interesting. But if you have no training in reason or skepticism, these things aren't quite so harmless.

I heard some amazing things from the New Age people. Naturally I was seen as completely ignorant, after all, I didn't even have an astrological chart with me – how could people relate to me without my chart? So I was given some New Age books to read. And I read them, carefully, more carefully than their owners.

Normally – I mean, once upon a time – a book that presented a new idea did so by supplying: (1) A statement of the idea, (2) scientific proof that the idea isn't bogus, and (3) examples of the idea's usefulness to the reader. Each of the New Age books had (1) and (3) but no (2). One of them talked about blood types – supposedly if you know someone's blood type then you know all sorts of important things about him. Another extolled the magic power of crystals. Yet another explained pyramid power.

And, of course, a book about UFO's – you aren't really New Age if you haven't been contacted by extraterrestrials. Usually they grab you on a dark road with no witnesses, take you inside the UFO and examine you, and tell you things about their world. They won't let you take any souvenirs for proof, not so much as a space gum wrapper. You sneak some photographs, but later you discover the film has been fogged by the aliens so you can only see dark blobs, which the National Enquirer publishes anyway. Naturally the aliens are extremely advanced, and they tell you secrets so important you can't tell anyone else – except the President, who for some reason hasn't answered your letter. Yet.

And channels. Channels are people who are wired in such a way that they have regular contact with (usually famous) dead people. If the dead people were painters, then the channel can paint using their skills, if they are musical composers, then the channel plays for them. You get the idea. But it seems these channels only tune in famous people – I want to meet a democratic channel, who talks to a shoe salesman from Cleveland, someone so boring death was an improvement. Or a tax accountant – you visit the channel and he says "Mr. Ubergeist wants to know, did you file that extension yet?"

So I returned the books, and explained what I thought of them. I really wanted to say that when they were true they weren't interesting and when they were interesting they weren't true, but I thought this might be impolite, so I just said I didn't find any proof between their covers. The response startled me: "But they're books!" That was it – how could they print something that wasn't true? I remember believing this until I was seven.

But even then I didn't realize what I was up against. While visiting the New Age house of a crystal fanatic, I asked what material his crystals were made of. He answered "quartz." I know something about quartz, so I told him what I knew. I explained if you bend quartz, it responds by producing an electric field, and conversely if you apply an electric field the quartz responds by bending. It is this property of quartz, called the "piezoelectric" effect, that makes it useful in clocks – all those digital watches have a little bit of quartz in them, vibrating, keeping them accurate. And computers, and VCR's, anything that needs accurate timing.

By this time my friend's eyes were the size of flying saucers. He had no background in technology – it was all magic, and now I had made his crystals magic by association. I had hoped to show a normal property of quartz, and an everyday use for it, but all I had done was increase its mystery.

At first I was angry – believing in things that are untrue is wasteful and sometimes dangerous. Why would these people believe in things that had no proof, when they could select equally amazing things that were true? But slowly I realized it wasn't a rejection of science and technology – they simply hadn't been taught how to think. They couldn't distinguish between amazing lies and amazing truths – pyramids and penicillin were equally mysterious.

I know some of the reasons for this decline in thinking power. First, public schools tell you *what* to think instead of teaching *how* to think. In public school there's an answer to every question – it's simply a matter of consulting the right authority. In real life the most interesting questions have no known answers, or several answers of equal value. But public schools can't prepare you for real life because they are financed by governments. Governments prefer citizens who don't think for themselves, and absolutely love citizens that cannot think at all.

Another reason is the isolation of science from everyday life. Scientists once walked among mortals, but now they are paid by governments and large corporations to work on problems that often have no connection with everyday life. Only rarely does a scientist try to explain science, or scientific reasoning, to the public. Most scientists don't have the time, between teaching more young scientists and trying to conduct research. I worry that science will become something understood and practiced only by specialists, and the skeptical, rigorous scientific outlook will vanish from the lives of ordinary people.

There are other, more subtle forces at work. Once I gave a lecture in which I tried to explain some of Einstein's Theory of Relativity to a group of regular people. I used simple examples, mostly blackboard drawings, and no mathematical equations. The audience began to show signs that they were getting it – they started to understand how it was that the moon stayed up in the sky.

Then a specialist in relativity (who somehow sneaked into my audience) objected that I was making it too simple, I was leaving out a lot. He was right, of course, but I had achieved my aim – my audience wasn't terrified of relativity any more. Now they might open a book and acquire a firm grounding in the subject, where before, relativity had been up there with calculus on the terror scale. I was willing to oversimplify to achieve that.

Some scientists dislike simple descriptions – they worked hard to master their subjects, and see no reason to explain them to ordinary people. I take the opposite position – people must learn about science, the discoveries, the way of thinking. If this doesn't happen, science will become the sole property of governments, people will not grasp the public issues of the future, and democracy will become irrelevant.

July 31 – Day 5, Hawaii to Oregon

This is going to be a tricky sail. To sail from Hawaii to the mainland, you try to move clockwise around the East Pacific High, which has a clockwise wind pattern that carries you along. But the high keeps moving and breaking into pieces. I receive weather charts every day by radio, so I know where the wind is blowing, but the high can move a lot faster than my boat can – sometimes it catches me. If it comes to where I am, the wind dies and I turn on the motor. Like today.

On the other hand, it's pretty and the sea is almost flat. Little puffy clouds. I am traveling North – eventually I get to about 40 degrees North latitude, where the wind is more reliable. Then I sail East to Oregon. But it's about 900 miles to the good wind. I have to manage my fuel carefully, and use every bit of wind that comes along.

I hated leaving Kauai. I spent part of the first day watching it get smaller as I sailed away. I wanted my friend to come sail with me, an idea she found charming but impractical. I would have liked to windsurf some more, visit people I got to know, hike to the Hanakapii waterfall.

Finally I turned around and looked forward again. When sailing it's not a good idea to dwell on where you've just been, some even say it's bad luck. So instead I'll look forward.

When I get to Oregon I will have sailed more than 30,000 nautical miles over a period of 4 years. I haven't seen my Oregon friends in over two years, although I stay in touch with telephone and computer messages. I miss my friends, my house.

I don't know what it will be like living in town after so long at sea, but some things are forever changed. My attitude toward water, for example. I get by on about 1/2 gallon of fresh water per day, both at sea and while visiting ports in the Third World, where water is precious even on shore. In Sri Lanka I collected rain water on tarps and sails, because the shore water was unsafe. But I had it easy – for an African villager, finding unpolluted water is a matter of life and death.

When I want to wash myself I put some sea water in a special plastic bag that heats it up with sunlight. Then I wash. For soap I use Joy, the dish washing liquid, which works even in cold salt water (I don't normally identify a product like this, but Joy works). I can even wash my hair this way, which the sailing books say is impossible.

I use as much salt water as possible, to conserve the fresh. I have 60 gallons on board at the start of a passage, and I rarely use up even half. Consider this: a person taking a five-minute shower uses twice as much water as it took me to get from Panama to Hawaii (35 days).

According to the World Almanac I carry on board, an average American uses about 160 gallons of fresh water per day. This doesn't count really obscene things like washing cars and watering lawns. The average household uses 107,000 gallons per year. With the water used by one American house I could save an African village – if I could just get it there. Then I would teach family planning. But I wouldn't just teach it there.

I recently read a book called "The Population Explosion" by Paul Erlich. Did you know America has five percent of the world's population, but uses up 25 percent of the world's resources? This means, in terms of resources used, each American born equals five world citizens. This is a different way to think about family size, and I wish more people would try it. But it gets worse: the average American uses 100 times the resources of a person from, say, Kenya in Africa.

Today, when an American decides to have a child, 100 African children are cramped a little tighter against the world's unequally shared resources. Some might even die. But in the future it will be much simpler: Each new American born will kill 100 African kids, period.

This way of thinking is called "Lifeboat Ethics." In a crowded lifeboat, if someone new comes on board, someone else has to be thrown off, otherwise the entire boat sinks. It's an awful vision, but because of our uncontrolled birthrate, the earth is more like a lifeboat every day.

Most parents don't think about these moral issues when planning their next child. But when they *are* cornered into thinking about them, things get interesting. This summer, one young parent-to-be heard my "100 African kids" argument and responded "But smart people should have more kids, to make up for all the dumb people having kids."

She wasn't the first person I've heard this argument from, and she probably won't be the last, but I still wanted to give her the All-Hawaii unlimited-class ethnic insensitivity award. I saw right away she placed herself in the "smart people" category. What she didn't know is that Adolf Hitler had once used the same argument, which (I thought) placed in doubt her high opinion of herself.

Let's assume for a moment that smart people are better people, a view I don't actually hold, and let's further assume that smart people have smart kids (only sometimes). Somebody could decide who gets to have kids (and who doesn't). The problem then becomes: Who decides? The government? The churches? Everybody for themselves (the present system)?

If governments were called upon to decide who the "smart people" are, they wouldn't be able to resist selecting people who are friendly toward the government, or who are politically powerful, or who spend a lot of money – it would be like the present House of Representatives, a total disaster.

And churches would have the same problem, multiplied about ten times. One church had its chance to rule the world and it blew it. It was very dark for a long time. Modern church leaders with an ounce of common sense would politely turn down this chance to play God.

Which puts responsibility in the hands of individuals, where it belongs. People are free to do exactly what they want – I just hope they think more about it than they do now. And I hope they come up with something better than the "smart people" argument. Are smart people necessarily better people? I don't think so. Most mass murderers are above average in intelligence, some are way above. And some smart people do terrible things with their skills.

Take Edward Teller, for example. He was a physicist on the Manhattan Project, the World War II project led by Robert Oppenheimer to build the first atomic bomb. Teller realized the atom bomb could be used to trigger a much more powerful device called the hydrogen bomb (then known as the "super"). He wanted to build the "super," he was tired of working on the atom bomb, and he was especially tired of Oppenheimer's restrictions on his activities.

A few years after the end of the war, in the time of Joe McCarthy and the Un-American Activities Committee, in testimony Teller cast doubt on Oppenheimer's loyalty. As a result Oppenheimer was barred from government work for the rest of his life, and Teller was free to pursue his superbomb project. Teller then claimed the Russians were working on a superbomb, so we had better catch up. The superbomb was designed and tested. Then the Russians had no choice – they built one too. Later we discovered the Russians didn't intend to build a "super," but when we forced them to, they saved some time by stealing secrets from the West. This is a story most Americans haven't heard – I call it "smart people making policy."

But for those who can't be dissuaded from the idea that smart people are better people, I have to ask "how much better?" Is one smart American kid better than 100 African kids, who might turn out to be just as smart if they lived? And to the smart American parents who make the choice to bear a child without thinking about any of these issues, I have to say "How smart can you be?"

The biggest flaw in the "smart people should have more kids" argument is that *no one* is going to be the one to say "I'm really dumb so I won't have any kids." The only solution is for everyone to have fewer children – the larger questions must be answered by nature, in her own time.

More than a quarter million new people arrive on earth, our space lifeboat, every day. Now get this: each of them is either going to die young or grow up and think about having children. Some will think how smart they are, while they sprinkle their lawn with perfectly good drinking water.

I just sat and watched the sea go by for a while, and another thought came to me: Remember the dinosaurs? There was a time when they dominated the earth. And compared to us, dinosaurs were really stupid – it got cold for a while and they were too dumb to invent mittens and wool socks (and sheep!), so they died out. If they hadn't, we might never have come into being.

Now consider: Why do we think we're the end of the line? We might be the dinosaurs of the future – we may be only a step in the development of some future beings, of great beauty and intelligence, who may someday regard us as we regard dinosaurs. But only if we leave something behind – we're using up the raw material of their future. We're smarter than dinosaurs – but perhaps only smart enough to do something really stupid.

August 6 – Day 11

For the first 10 days the wind blew more or less from the Northeast. I sailed as close to the wind as I could, not very fast, and went North according to the plan. I knew if I sailed North far enough, the wind would eventually switch to Northwest and then West. Yesterday the wind finally switched – dramatically, within about four hours. I had been sailing almost at right angles to Oregon, to get far enough North – now I am bearing directly toward home, for the first time this crossing.

I was concerned that I would sail into the center of the East pacific high, which would have stopped me dead. But nature gave me a break – a storm came in, pushed the high out of the way, and now blows hard from the West.

I am a different sailor. Four years ago I would have avoided stormy weather – this time I hoped for it. It's wet and bumpy, but the boat is moving in the right direction, fast.

When I first sailed, I felt secure tied up to a dock and petrified at the thought of going on the ocean. I have since learned the middle of the ocean is the safest place you can imagine, and approaching land is the big danger – there are more ships there, all those nasty rocks to bang into, even the marinas are risky.

I came to my personal turning point on Ibiza, off the coast of Spain – as I wrote earlier, a storm was brewing, I got blown off my anchor, and I sailed into the marina. That's what normal sailors do when the weather is bad. But within an hour I was tangled in lines, bashing a concrete dock, with my drive shaft pulled off my engine. Without a thought I started fixing things so I could get out on the sea as soon as possible, storm or no, because I knew my boat would be safer there.

Later I decided leaving during a storm wasn't even a little reckless, in fact going into the marina was the reckless choice. The open sea was all bumps and gusts of wind, and spray filled the air, but there was all that space to move around on – just birds and water. As I pushed the tiller against the wind, I thought how much better off I was than two hours before – I thought it was safe to make breakfast, but the wind slowly built up outside, my anchor started to drag an old car tire across the bottom, and Selene inched toward a large concrete mass.

August 10 – Day 15

Today is the halfway point, about 1100 miles from both Hawaii and Oregon. It was wet and bumpy for two days – at one point a wave crashed into my boat and a splash of salt water hit one of my navigation receivers. It died right away, without lingering. Now all I have are the satnav and my sextant – but that's more than enough to find Oregon.

There are some things about modern electronic equipment that make it especially vulnerable to salt water. One is plastic integrated circuits (you know – those little black rectangles that can do anything). These plastic packages have metal pins, and when it gets hot the metal and the plastic expand at different rates, so they slip against each other – so the seal isn't perfect. On a boat, salt water eventually works its way inside the package to a very sensitive silicon chip. When the salt gets to the chip, it dies. I think this is why my receivers, radars and computers have had such short lives. I almost never see equipment survive longer than about two years, unless it's located so that it never feels drop of salt water. On a boat, that's harder than it sounds.

Right now the sailing is nice – a beam wind, smooth seas. The boat is moving briskly, and because the wind is even and the sails full, she is rocking less than when anchored.

I have seen two ships since Hawaii – one boat that passed in the night, just a light, and a freighter sailing from San Francisco to Indonesia. The captain, an Australian, called me on the radio and we talked about sailing. He said, "I've done this for a living so long I can't imagine doing it for fun." Naturally I had a snappy comeback – "I've done this for fun so long I can't imagine doing it for a living."

August 12 – Day 17

The wind is still blowing from a nice direction, and the sky is clear until after dark. The Perseid meteor shower is going on now, but the nighttime clouds are hiding it from view. Too bad – but I saw the Hawaii eclipse, so I shouldn't complain.

When the wind blows steadily, my boat goes on automatic – I don't have to change heading or sail plan for days. Then I make journal entries or write computer programs. Today I've been looking through my log, and typing some of the numbers into my computer.

During my sail around the world I averaged 4.5 knots, or 108 miles per day. The highest speed I recorded in a 24-hour period was 7.2 knots, although that might have been the result of a bad satellite fix – I have a hard time believing Selene can go that fast for more than a few seconds. The slowest speed was 1.2 knots, which happened when I tried to move in very light winds without using the motor, or when I was beating up the Red Sea, sometimes sailing away from my destination.

There's an ideal path between any two points at sea – it's called a "Great Circle" route, so named because it's part of a circle that runs completely around the earth. But sometimes I have to sail around a high as I'm doing now, or sail upwind, or ocean currents pull me in a direction I don't expect – anyway, the actual sailing paths aren't always great circles.

At discouraging times I thought I might be sailing, say, 50% farther than the most efficient path, but I have just added up my daily logbook distances and compared them with the ideal paths. It turns out that the least efficient sail (my sail from Oregon to Hawaii) was only 16% longer than the ideal, and the average of all my passages is 6% longer. Some downwind sails, where I could point the boat as accurately as I pleased, were within 1% of the ideal.

The Red Sea sail was probably the least efficient sail of all, but in order to know I would have had to log a position at the end of each tack, so all the zigs and zags would be included in my log. But I didn't – I had enough to do with steering around all the freighters, adjusting the sails, and keeping the boat pointed very close to the wind, but not so close that the sails "backed" and the boat did a graceful but annoying 360 degree circle while I tried to sleep.

It was during that sail that I wished for a boat with a fin keel, a keel that looks like an airplane wing sticking out of the boat's bottom. That kind of boat goes upwind very efficiently – in exchange, if you bang a rock with the keel, it might just fall off the boat, after which the boat turns upside down (and then sinks). My boat's keel is part of the hull, and it doesn't extend down into the water very far, so I can't sail upwind very well. On the other hand, I've banged a lot of rocks and coral and I'm still here – I guess you have to balance *your* plans for your boat against *nature's* plans for your boat.

August 20 – Day 25

Today I should arrive in Brookings – the mainland is starting to peek through the fog in places. There hasn't been very much wind lately, today none at all, so I am motoring.

A few days ago a big oil tanker, enroute from Long Beach, California to Valdez, Alaska, sailed by. The captain called me on the radio, just as his ship was becoming visible in the South. He told me he was changing course to avoid me, and I should keep my present heading. But, since he was a "working boat" and I was not, I offered to change course so he wouldn't have to – after all, his vessel was a quarter-mile long, a lot more trouble to steer than mine! He diplomatically let me know that he was moving so fast (and I so slow) that no course change I could make would matter very much.

As it approached, I saw his ship really was moving fast, but it still took forever to pass by.

In a way, the oil tanker was the start of my arrival on the mainland. I knew the tankers stayed within a few hundred miles of the coast on their way to Alaska – I had been especially watchful as I came into their zone. Since then I have been seeing a lot of smaller freighters and fishing boats.

I have naturally been thinking about the ways a modern sailor figures out that land is nearby. In the middle of a long passage, the bow of the boat is not special. The ocean looks just the same in all directions, always pretty, and one's attention isn't drawn forward as it might be in a car or an airplane. In fact, it isn't at all odd to pass long spells looking at the boat's wake, perhaps thinking about the place and people just visited, or noticing an entourage of fish that (at least with my boat) have no trouble keeping up.

But as land approaches, things change. The short-range VHF radio comes to life. I always monitor the VHF calling channel, day and night, for the entire crossing. Because I don't have a working radar any more, the VHF radio is cheap insurance – someone might see me and call on the radio instead of running me down. But I rarely hear anything until I am within, say, 300 miles of land. Then I start hearing boats, mostly talking to each other, and I know I have to watch more and sleep less.

Sometimes I listen for AM and FM broadcasts. I begin to hear AM stations from towns on the coast, and I can spin the radio around to be sure I am on course (AM stations fade out when the radio's long axis is pointed at them).

I receive FM stations at a surprising distance, 200 miles or better.

Normally you expect the high-frequency FM radio waves to travel in straight lines (like light beams), but apparently they bend a little. Also some American FM stations are so powerful and well located that if there is a theoretical chance to hear them, you *will* hear them.

Then I have the direct evidence of my senses. I remember as I came within 200 miles of Sri Lanka, big flying cockroaches came out to meet me. But, in fairness to Sri Lanka, I want to say the last evening of that crossing was beautiful in an unexpected way. As darkness fell, hundreds of tiny fishing boats near the coast ignited orange lamps. As I came nearer and passed between them, I could see people lifting nets from the ocean. I could hear voices across the water. It was the most moving arrival of the entire sail – it was as if people took the time to bear candles into a big field in gratitude for the evening, except these were fishermen, and the lights attracted fish to their nets. So the sight of hundreds of orange lights on the sea was a side effect of something practical – but the side effect was no less beautiful for that.

The sound of small, local airplanes has told me I was coming to land. And the color of the ocean changes from a deep blue (signifying purity and great depth) to a slate gray, finally a bright green in the shallowest waters. Floating things, wood, grass, close in. Reflected waves are a sure indication of land nearby – in the Caribbean they didn't just rock my boat a little extra, they came aboard, into the cockpit, into my cabin.

Actually seeing the land is usually anticlimactic – and often you don't see the land very well. When you approach small islands in the tropics, you may only see a palm tree, which is why it's so risky there, especially at night. When I came to Hawaii this March I barely saw it through the awful weather – I saw individual trees and buildings before I made out the mass of the island.

All of these land clues have an effect – you become aware of land, of people. You find yourself looking toward the bow of your boat, as if there is something special lying in that direction.

By the time you tie up to the dock, you'll be able to form sentences, describe the ocean clearly, sit down with other people. The land takes hold of you – but the sea never really gives you up.

Epilogue

W hen I started sailing, I thought I only had to learn about my boat, so it would take me safely across the sea. But as I sailed, I realized I had to know the sea herself. My boat was a walnut shell in the hand of the sea, and I was even less.

A seasoned sailor

I learned to love the sea – but no, that doesn't say it. Before I sailed I thought I was afraid of death. Then I learned something, somewhere among the islands – I had actually been afraid of injustice, of being cheated out of life, say, by someone who couldn't point his car very well.

On the sea I kept my boat in order and wore my safety harness – so if I was swept away, it was the sea, the sea did it. As a result, as the days went by and I faced the risks of sailing, I cared less about death. I only had to avoid outright stupidity – if the sea took me in spite of that, I was hers.

Then, one day as I watched the waves, I realized I had surrendered to the sea – in exchange for my knowing her, she could take me if she wished. I could have stayed on shore, but that would have been merely waiting for death. I had to sail.

Before that day, I believed I could outwit nature, plea-bargain my way out of mortality. But I knew there was something I wasn't getting – I could see it in the eyes of animals. When I looked into their eyes I realized they knew about death, but they didn't believe they could give it directions. I saw a resignation and a fondness for experience that I thought proved how stupid they were.

I no longer believe I can save life up – it has to be spent to have any value. And that in order to live, to have adventure, you have to be willing to die. The sea taught me this, and turned me inside out – among her swells and islands I became an animal, an inhabitant of nature. You can see it in my eyes.

Glossary of Nautical Terms

abeam	*Directly to one side of the boat, 90 degrees to the right or left of the bow.*
aft	*Behind the boat, also, the area at the rear of the boat.*
alternator	*A device attached to the engine that generates electricity.*
anchor	*A metal contrivance designed to hold the boat at rest by grabbing the bottom of an anchorage.*
autopilot	*A device for automatically keeping a boat on course.*
back	*(1) Make the boat stop by reversing the wind across the sails. (2) (Concerning wind) Rotate in a counterclockwise direction (Northern hemisphere). Also see veer.*
backstay	*The wire between the mast and the aft end of the boat.*
ballast	*A weight in the keel, usually lead, that holds the boat upright.*
bar	*A collection of debris at the entrance to a bay fed by a river, often shallow and dangerous.*
barometer	*A device for measuring atmospheric pressure, usually calibrated in millibars.*
berth	*A small bed.*
boathook	*An implement with which to grab things or push them away.*
boom	*A horizontal bar that supports the bottom of a sail and determines its shape.*
bosun's chair	*A seat, usually canvas, used to raise a sailor up a mast.*
bow	*The forward part of a boat.*
bowline	*A useful knot.*
bungee cord	*An elastic cord, usually with hooks on the ends.*
cast off	*To leave a dock, in particular to release and gather dock lines.*
close reach	*A point of sail close to the wind. See pinch.*

cockpit	*An area at the aft end from which one controls the boat.*
CQR	*A popular kind of anchor, meant to sound like "secure."*
Danforth	*A type of anchor that sometimes has a holding power greater than its size. And sometimes less.*
deck	*The top outside surface of the boat.*
degree	*1/360th of a full circle. Ninety degrees is a complete turn to the right or left. One hundred eighty degrees is a reversal of course.*
depth sounder	*An electronic device resembling sonar that gauges the depth of the water.*
diesel	*(1) A type of engine popular on boats. (2) The fuel that powers diesel engines.*
dinghy	*A small boat used to travel in depths too shallow for a sailboat. Some are inflatable, some are wood or molded plastic.*
double-ender	*A sailboat that has the shape of a canoe, pointed at the front and back.*
downwind	*A point of sail in which the wind blows from aft, an easy sail.*
drive shaft	*A rod that connects the engine to the propeller. See prop.*
fax	*(1) A method for transmitting pictures by radio or telephone. (2) A picture received by means of fax.*
fix	*A position obtained by sextant or navigation receiver. See sextant, satnav, gps.*
galley	*A boat's kitchen.*
genoa	*A large jib. See jib.*
GMT	*Greenwich Mean Time, the time in Greenwich, England. The standard time used on a boat for navigation and other purposes.*
GPS	*Global Positioning System. A relatively new navigation system using satellites – not to be confused with satnav.*
halyard	*A line used to raise sails up the mast.*
ham radio	*(1) A radio transceiver used in the Amateur Radio Service. (2) A licensing and frequency allocation scheme by which non-professional radio operators ("hams") can transmit and receive radio messages.*
hank, unhank	*(noun) A fastener by which a sail can be attached to a wire. (verb) To connect or disconnect a sail from a wire.*

harness	*A safety system consisting of a body harness and lines on deck to allow movement around the boat without great risk of falling overboard.*
hatch	*A usually watertight cover or doorway.*
head	*A boat's bathroom.*
headsail	*The forward-most sail on a boat. See jib.*
headstay	*The wire between the mast and the bow of the boat.*
headway	*Progress, usually against contrary winds.*
headwind	*An adverse wind, usually from the desired direction of travel.*
heave to	*Arrange the boat and sails to ride comfortably and move as little as possible.*
HF	*High Frequency, the range of radio frequencies between 3 and 30 megahertz, used in long-distance marine communications.*
high	*(weather) a high-pressure system, characterized by a clockwise wind pattern (in the Northern Hemisphere) and generally clear and pleasant weather. See low.*
hull	*The basic watertight structure of the boat, in particular that part below the waterline.*
inverter	*An electronic device that converts battery power to AC house current.*
jib	*Usually the sail closest to the bow of a boat, usually an efficient sail.*
jibe	*To change course while sailing downwind so that the wind changes sides. Somewhat dangerous in high wind, and hard on the boom and sails. See preventer.*
keel	*A fin at the bottom of the hull that prevents the boat from moving sideways in the water. The keel also converts the sideways pressure of the wind into forward boat movement.*
knot	*(1) Any of the useful tangles of line that keeps things attached. (2) A measure of speed on a boat, calibrated in nautical miles.*
knotmeter	*A usually electronic device to measure speed through the water.*

leeway	*(1) The amount of sideways motion through the water allowed by the keel, usually undesirable. (2) The open space between the boat and land in the downwind direction, a safety margin.*
lie ahull	*Take down all sails and let the boat drift where it will.*
life raft	*A small emergency boat, usually inflatable.*
line	*What a rope is called while on a boat. See rope.*
LORAN	*LOng RAnge Navigation. Ironically, if compared to satellite navigation, LORAN is a short-range system for navigation that uses shore transmitters.*
low	*(weather) a low-pressure system, characterized by a counterclockwise wind pattern (in the Northern Hemisphere), generally cloudy, rainy weather, and rough seas. See high.*
magnetron	*A vacuum tube surrounded by a magnet that generates microwave energy. Used in radar sets and microwave ovens.*
mainsail	*The sail that is hanked onto the mast and the boom. On my boat, the aftmost sail.*
mast	*The principal support member, held up by the rigging, that holds the sails aloft.*
meltemi	*A strong wind in the Mediterranean.*
millibar	*A measure of atmospheric pressure. See barometer.*
nautical mile	*Exactly one minute (1/60 of a degree) of angle on the earth, a size chosen so that angles measured with a sextant can be easily converted into distances. Equal to 6076 feet and change. 1 nautical mile = 1.15 statute mile.*
Pacific high	*A high-pressure system in the Eastern Pacific that provides reasonably reliable winds between the West Coast of the U.S. and Hawaii.*
painter	*A line that secures a dinghy.*
pinch	*A point of sail very near the wind, not usually fast or efficient.*
port	*(1) (direction) Left. (2) An opening in the side of the boat (also porthole).*
porthole	*An opening for light and ventilation, usually watertight when closed.*

preventer   *A line rigged to hold something in place, usually used to keep the boom from changing sides unexpectedly. See jibe.*

prop   *The propeller that is attached to the engine by way of the drive shaft. See drive shaft.*

receiver   *Any of several kinds of radio receiver used for communication or navigation. See satnav, LORAN, gps, ham radio.*

REM   *Rapid Eye Movement, a kind of sleep accompanied by dreams. Indicates lengthy uninterrupted sleep.*

rigging   *A system of wires that supports the mast.*

rode   *A chain, rope or both that attaches an anchor to the boat.*

rope   *What a line is called before it is taken onto a boat. See line.*

rudder   *A paddle in the water, attached to a wheel or tiller in the cockpit, that controls the boat's direction.*

sail   *A piece of cloth, attached to the boat by means of a halyard and one or more sheets and sometimes a boom, that moves the boat by way of wind power.*

satnav   *A method of satellite navigation, also a receiver used for this purpose. Nearly obsolete. See gps.*

sextant   *An optical sighting device that determines the angle between a celestial body and the horizon. Used for navigation. See also satnav, gps.*

sheet   *(noun) A line that controls the position of a sail. (verb) To adjust a sail.*

solar panel   *A large, rectangular device that converts sunlight directly into electricity with no moving parts. See wind generator.*

spreader   *A horizontal metal bar on the mast that holds some of the supporting wires and increases the stiffness of the mast. See rigging.*

starboard   *(direction) Right.*

staysail   *A small third sail (on my boat) between the foresail or jib and the mainsail.*

tack   *(verb) Change directions so that the wind comes from the opposite side of the boat. (noun) Port tack, wind from left – starboard tack, wind from right.*

throttle   *A lever in the cockpit that adjusts the engine's speed.*

trade wind   *A reliable wind in the tropics that blows from the East.*

transceiver	*A radio transmitter-receiver, usually equipped with a microphone.*
upwind	*A usually difficult sail against the wind.*
veer	*(in reference to wind) Rotate in a clockwise direction (Northern hemisphere). Also see back.*
VHF	*Very High Frequency, the range of radio frequencies between 30 and 300 megahertz, used in short-range marine communications. Also a radio transceiver that uses these frequencies.*
VMG	*Velocity Made Good, the boat's true velocity after factors such as leeway and ocean currents are taken into account.*
waterline	*(1) The place on the hull the water just reaches when the boat is at rest. (2) (slang) The length of the hull at the waterline.*
waypoint	*An arbitrary position used in navigation.*
weathervane	*(noun) A mechanical wind direction indicator. (verb) To turn into the wind, usually while out of control.*
whisker pole	*A rigid pole used to spread the jib out on a downwind sail.*
winch	*A mechanical drum used to apply or maintain high forces on halyards and sheets.*
windsurf	*(verb) Ride a small fiberglass board with an attached mast and sail. A lot of fun.*
wind vane	*A mechanical device that holds the boat on a fixed course relative to the wind.*
windmill	*A propeller mounted on a pole that converts wind power into electricity.*
wing-and-wing	*A downwind sailing arrangement in which the mainsail is deployed on one side and the jib on the other.*

12051102R00132

Made in the USA
Lexington, KY
19 November 2011